T0357651

WOLF ACT

LIVING OUT

Gay and Lesbian Autobiographies

DAVID BERGMAN, JOAN LARKIN, and
RAPHAEL KADUSHIN, *Founding Editors*

WOLF ACT

AJ Romriell

THE UNIVERSITY OF WISCONSIN PRESS

The University of Wisconsin Press
728 State Street, Suite 443
Madison, Wisconsin 53706
uwpress.wisc.edu

Copyright © 2025 by AJ Romriell
All rights reserved. Except in the case of brief quotations embedded in
critical articles and reviews, no part of this publication may be reproduced,
stored in a retrieval system, transmitted in any format or by any means—
digital, electronic, mechanical, photocopying, recording, or otherwise—or
conveyed via the Internet or a website without written permission of the
University of Wisconsin Press. Rights inquiries should be directed to
rights@uwpress.wisc.edu.

Printed in the United States of America
This book may be available in a digital edition.

Library of Congress Cataloging-in-Publication Data
Names: Romriell, AJ, author.
Title: Wolf act / AJ Romriell.
Other titles: Living out.
Description: Madison, Wisconsin : The University of Wisconsin Press,
2025. | Series: Living out: gay and lesbian autobiographies
Identifiers: LCCN 2024014079 | ISBN 9780299349943 (paperback)
Subjects: LCSH: Romriell, AJ. | Gay men—United States—Biography. |
Latter Day Saint gay people—United States—Biography.
Classification: LCC HQ75.8.R655 A3 2025 | DDC 306.76/62092 [B]—dc23/
eng/20240918
LC record available at https://lccn.loc.gov/2024014079

for my parents

&

for you, little lost boy—
you found your way through

Their textures—delicate as sloughed sheaths of faith—were enough to convince me that books were once bodies, that the bestial and the divine can reside in the same place.

—MELISSA FEBOS, *Abandon Me*

Contents

Act III

WOLF ACT

The Wolf Boy Overture

IN TENTH GRADE, I was cast in a high school production of *Into the Woods*. I had no name, no lines, only dirt-painted makeup and tattered clothes. On opening night, the boy who played Little Red Riding Hood's Wolf barged into the dressing room wearing nothing but tight leather pants, dark makeup, and a ratted, black wolf-wig. He howled and turned, shaking his ass so the attached tail swung in circles. Though I laughed with everyone else, fear rose up in the way I watched his body move, lingered on his exposed chest, marked the way his tongue licked his own bright red lips. I felt it—a wanting, ravaging, screaming creature I refused to accept could be living at the crest of my throat.

In twelfth grade, I was cast in *The King and I*. Again, I had no name and no lines, cast for the ensemble, a soldier of the King. Strangely, I did earn an extra part in "The Small House of Uncle Thomas" ballet—strange to me because I was cast as the wolf this time—one of two "science dogs," "blood hounds," villainous beasts. Each night, during intermission, I'd remove my soldier costume and slip into the wolf—a look so unlike the wolf from *Into the Woods*. I'd drape myself in shining yellow and black, cover each slice of pale skin, shroud my mouth and eyes in a golden mask. I'd look into the mirror, smile, and bare my teeth because I felt powerful and free.

When the ballet started, I sneaked into the aisles, crouched low, crept in the dark. When Tuptim's voice rang at my entrance, I howled; I sprinted; I leapt onto the stage and rolled. Facing the audience, I swiped my claws and snarled. I don't think anyone could hear me, but I didn't need them to. I snarled and gnashed because I was a wolf, and I needed everyone to believe it. Sinister music smashed against dim lights, and I started to dance.

～

I always wanted to act, to stand on stage and sing. I think I just wanted people to listen. To see.

The function of a musical is to tell a story. The function of a story is to tell the truth. I'm just trying to tell you the truth. But I have never been good at this. So much of my life has been spent lying and hiding and acting and playing games of make-believe. The plot's gone hazy. The details, unsure. There's an existentialism here that could go on and on and on.

So, instead, here's a structure that's simple, parts to play and rules to follow. I'll give you an overture to tell you the theme. A first act to set up the stakes. Here, in the beginning, you'll witness the narrator's life as normal before it's destroyed—and it has to be destroyed. The narrator has to fail in preservation. This is the hero's journey. We must set out and leave our childhood behind.

～

I once heard an old Norse tale about two wolves who race through the heavens: Skoll who chases the sun, and Hati who chases the moon. Around and around the earth, they hunt these chariots of light, creating our days and nights. I learned that during Ragnarök, at the end of the world, they will succeed; they'll swallow the sun and moon and finally stop chasing.

I've heard these old Gaelic stories of Faoilleach, the Wolf Month, and Lleuad Blaidd, when the starving wolf calls out, pleading for change. In the dead of winter, when nights lingered and stomachs growled, wolves crept outside a village and howled: a hungry cry, a deadly desire, simple truths beneath a winter moon. From the depths of their bodies, an aching rumble roared from between their teeth.

When I was young and alone, I acted out Grimm's *Little Red Riding Hood* in the backyard of my childhood home. I played each role, began as Little Red, a girl who meets a wolf in the forest. Beneath the tall branches of an apricot tree, I'd persuade myself to stray from the path, muddle beneath the summer sun, pick dandelions from the earth. Then, I became the wolf, entered the backyard playhouse, gnashed my teeth, and swallowed the grandmother whole. I would take her place, waiting for myself to wander in with the dandelion bouquet, waiting to leap from the bed and swallow him whole too. Stomach ready to burst, I'd curl into my body on the floor of the playhouse pretending to snore.

Everything has a moral, and these tales could teach me how to survive. Once, when I asked my teacher why the hunter must slay the wolf at the end of the story, she told me he had to save the innocents inside his belly. When I asked how the hunter knew Little Red and her grandmother were alive enough to be saved, my teacher said he could hear them screaming from far behind the wolf's teeth.

I've been searching for myself in stories for as long as I can remember. I want them to be about me: starving and chasing and straying and becoming someone new. I once believed if I could find my place in the metaphor, in the universe and its stars and the galaxies above, it would mean I belonged in its marrow.

∽

I grew up Mormon, and I also grew up gay. I'd been howling for God to pillage my savage, salivating desire for another man's flesh since I was eleven. I would race through every bookstore, scream for my mom to buy me another story. I filled myself with narratives so I'd never have to tell my own. My dad wove nightly bedtime tales of my siblings and me traversing the wilds of an enchanted forest. He told us that in this other life, we'd leap from our bedroom window onto the backs of giant eagles who'd carry us into a world of magic and adventure. I'd wall myself behind Cheerios boxes in the morning so I could fill my bowl with sugar. I slipped spoonfuls of crystals between my teeth, grinding it down my throat, filling my belly. After, I washed the Cheerios down the sink, watching their soggy circles swirl into the disposal.

∽

I used to believe in magic, in portals and worlds outside my own. I was pulled into stories like Harry Potter and the Lord of the Rings and the Chronicles of Narnia—heroic tales of escape and traveling somewhere new. I wanted to pry open my closet door. Find a hidden place. Lock myself beyond the world. I imagined a train pulling into a station, a wizard knocking on my door.

But my closet was only ever my closet. I crawled in and flattened my back on the carpet, pressed my fingers against the soft floor, curled into a ball and wept. I howled and punched and screamed against the world that could only ever be real. I closed the door and shut myself off, staying in the dark for as long as I could.

~

Don't throw me out, said Aesop's wolf. *I'm one of your sheep.*

You're only pretending, said the shepherd.

How do you know? I look like a sheep.

You say you are a sheep, said the shepherd, *but you act like a wolf.* Then he broke a branch from a nearby tree and beat the wolf into admitting his true nature. The wolf ran up a nearby hill, never to come down again.

When I asked why this wolf didn't have to die, why a hunter needn't carve him out too, I was told it was because the wolf stopped trying to be something he wasn't. The wolf had learned his lesson. He could be free.

~

I came out with a whimper, but I eventually learned to howl. At twenty-one, I marched in a Pride parade. With rainbows painted on my cheeks and a flag protruding from my pocket, I released the truth from my throat.

Later that summer, I visited a wolf sanctuary in Indiana. Through a wire fence, I watched three wolves play together. Rolling around in the dirt and grass, they yipped beneath a golden July sun. The sanctuary workers stood in matching khaki button-ups and shorts on the wolf-side of the fence. Envy tingled beneath my skin when a wolf leapt up to hug one of the sanctuary workers. *They're best friends,* I was told.

I asked the workers if I could pet and play with the wolves too. *No,* they said. *These wolves are too habituated, too used to being around humans. We can't promise they won't hurt you.*

It feels like savagery created by a cage. Wild wolves pose little danger; unless threatened or starved, they would likely never hurt me. But these wolves are no longer afraid—a simple calm that can make them dangerous, make them hungry, make them tear a human's skin and blood and guts.

And yet, as it is with many things, to embrace either beast risks being devoured.

~

When I'm on a date with a man, I want to remain authentic, but then how do I tell the tattooed boy across the coffee table that I want to tear his skin, devour his lips, gobble up his body? By this I mean we leave the condoms in the dresser drawer. I am a desperate creature—I don't know yet that this will come back to bite me: HIV, infected blood, a cellular infestation, the years of my life dashing by in exchange for a moment of release. I simply crave the taste of flesh, the pressure of another man's body, to never see him again. I've been the wolf on the hill incapable of hiding; the wolf howling hungry beneath a winter moon; one who swallowed a cloak and was shocked to be pried open. I've come to the stage, born with teeth and tongue and tricks. I yearn for healing, for some brittle place of the earth, to place myself in the story, to find that vast eternal something that could make me stop chasing.

ACT I

For me, the fairytale is to be seen for exactly who I am, and
to still be loved.

   —HEATHER GAY, *Real Housewives of Salt Lake City*

Follow the path
to where no one's
ever been.
Don't turn around
until you reach
the end.

   —IMAscore, "Andrew's Song"

Names & Other Prophecies

IN SIXTH GRADE, Lexi brought a baby name book to recess. She claimed she could tell us what our names meant, and we gathered around her on the grass behind the playground, shoulders bumping shoulders, feet stepping on feet, each of us eager to learn. Lexi sat cross-legged at the center of our circle, the rips in her grass-stained jeans opening wide at her knees. She pulled her dark hair back into a ponytail and popped open the book on her lap, flipping to the A's so she could tell us about her own name first: Alexandra. Origin: Greek. Meaning: *The Defender of Humankind.*

We oo'd around her, mouths in tight circles while she smiled proudly, showing us her bleach-white teeth. Her best friend Ashley was next. Old English origin. Combination of Æsc and Leah. Meaning: *Ash Tree Meadow.*

"Like a fairy or something!" Ashley cried, raising her hands to the sky as if in triumph.

Many of us laughed, and Lexi asked, "Who's next?"

We each raised our hands and shouted, "Me!" "Me!" "Me!" and one by one, she flipped through the pages of her book and told us our meanings—like some kind of personality test—and we took on our names like badges. At twelve years old, we played many games like this: folded cootie-catchers and M.A.S.H., little games on paper that could tell us our future—who we'd marry, where we'd live, our careers and our cars—games to give us a small glimpse into who we might become. And around the circle we went.

Derek. German. *Power of the Tribe.*

Nathan. Hebrew. *Bountiful* or *Given.*

Gina. Latin. *Queen.*

My best friend Josh from church: Hebrew for *God is Salvation*—which seemed to track.

My childhood best friend, Taryn: American origin meaning *Terran*, or *Of the Earth.*

Then, we arrived at mine. Lexi flipped the pages, the circle quiet as we waited. "Andrew," Lexi said on repeat. "Andrew. Andrew. Andrew. Ah, here we go." She took a breath. "So, Andrew is Greek, a variant of Andreas, derived from *aner*, which translates to *a male animal.* Most notably associated with Jesus's first Apostle, Andrew. It's a masculine name meaning *strong* or *manly.*"

There were oo's around me, like those that rose around Lexi. Someone whistled. Someone giggled. Josh patted my shoulder and said, "Nice, man. That's a cool one." But something deep inside me quivered. Something shrank. *Manly* felt so superficial. To me, it meant cold. Emotionless. Distant. Strong. Muscly. Sporty. Someone who is obsessed with cars and beer and sex and football. Someone who's aggressive. Even violent. It meant being the kind of person I had never wanted to be.

The naming went on, but I quietly left the circle. I trudged through the half-dead grass of the field behind the playground. It was early October in Utah, and a chill wind swept across my body. I tensed up. I sat back down on the ground, crossed my legs, and pulled at the green-brown grass in front of me, yanking blades out by their roots. I tore them into tiny pieces. And when the wind picked up again, I lifted them to be carried away by the air.

&

In 2021, NPR's Diana Opong did an interview with baby name expert Laura Wattenberg and professional baby naming consultant Sherri Suzanne. In the interview, they discuss why giving names to children can be such an overwhelming prospect for parents, and they give advice to ease the burden. I don't know this stress myself; I do not have children. I am curious, though, as to how one person chooses the name of another. What goes into that decision? How do you reach a conclusion? How do you grapple with the knowledge that your child will have to live with whatever choice you make?

Utah is known for strange names. There are TikTok feeds and Instagram stories rife with the ways Utahn parents spell popular names in unique ways—or make up new ones altogether. One Utah man even made a website, utahbabynamer.com: just pick a gender, set a creativity level, and click the button. You'll find names like Kony Harfito. Scoet Sharker. Jarehd Rax. Beggary Rytit. Hannaugh Leyn. Beigh-Leigh Avalin.

Maybe a generator is easier, though it seems much more like a joke than a real way to choose a name. In the interview, Sherri tells us, "Names are like art and not like science." So, there is no right answer. There's only what you feel. Laura adds that there's been a revolution in naming. It used to be about fitting in. Now, it's about standing out. Individuality. Like a contest to see who can be the most creative. It's a label, and like many labels, it's one we're given—maybe the first one we're given. For most, we hold it for the rest of our lives.

I had a friend in my undergrad years. She and her husband didn't care for their own last names and the family history that came with them, so they chose their own when they got married: Hawke.

My father's cousin was once named Ski Earl Kingdon. The other kids bullied him. They called him *Squirrel Kingdom*. He's changed his name since then, but I can never remember what he changed it to.

There's something important in the stories of the names we choose, and in those chosen for us. I'm searching for meaning, a sense of belonging, some purpose to hold onto.

&

I was named after a hurricane—or at least this is the joke my family tells around the dinner table. I was born on August 21, 1992, and when my parents entered the hospital in Salt Lake City, 3,000 miles away from Miami, Hurricane Andrew was just a tropical storm. By the time they left the hospital, the storm had become a Category 5 hurricane— the most destructive to hit the United States at the time. But my parents hadn't heard the news yet. They couldn't know what they'd named me after.

Ironically enough, the joke that I was named after a hurricane stuck because of how well it seemed to define me. I was a chaotic child: energetic, eager, and thrill-seeking. In the summer before I turned five, I climbed to the top of a silver maple tree in the front yard of our home. I was the youngest of five siblings: three older brothers and one sister in the middle of us all. Still, only my eldest brother, Matthew, fourteen at the time, could climb to the top to help me down.

Later, when I was twelve, I was shot out of a tree with an airsoft gun. I cracked my ribs and bruised my intestine and spent two nights in a hospital where I watched *Twister* with my dad.

My earliest accident came just a few months before I turned three, where I tipped myself off the heavy kitchen bench. The bench smashed my big toe, carving the toenail through the skin. I limped through the kitchen, blood pouring from the wound, my heel thumping on the tile, screaming for my mom who was doing laundry downstairs. She sprinted into the kitchen, rushed me to the hospital, left the house so fast that she forgot to close the front door.

Now, my parents tell the tale of stitches to guests when they meet me, a kind of ice breaker, the same one I once used to trick my peers and teachers when we played two-truths-and-a-lie: "I had stitches six times by the time I turned seven." After the game, I would point to each scar in sequence, a nursery rhyme of my body: *my toe, my chin, the bone below my eye; the center of my head, the left of my head, and another on the right.*

Six times before I turned seven—it always got a laugh.

My family calls me a hurricane as a term of endearment, and I feel their love when they do—as if nothing the world throws at me can stop me from moving forward. Back then, I was happy to believe I wasn't afraid of risk.

&

Growing up in the Mormon religion required a variety of ceremonies, rituals, tests, and covenants: a blessing once born to give you a name; baptism at eight years old; weekly Sacrament to renew promises made at baptism (to avoid sin); other, more complicated things.

One of the most sacred ceremonies was the Endowment, a ritual in a Mormon temple designed to help members prepare for the afterlife. The ceremony is a complex one, comprised of a scripted reenactment of the Bible's creation story and the fall of Adam and Eve in the Garden of Eden, a symbolic washing and anointing of the body, and the gift of the temple garment which we promised to wear at nearly all times— within the temple and out. Members are also taught hand gestures and passwords along the way, secret codes needed to enter through Heaven's gates. One such codeword was a new name, a Heavenly name, the one you'd need to speak at the veil in order to pass on.

To qualify for the Endowment ceremony, a member had to either be preparing for marriage or be called on a two-year proselytizing mission away from home. In 2011, just after I turned nineteen, I completed my endowments as a part of the latter. I was given my special garments and was taught the special words and handshakes I would need to get into Heaven, on to a better afterlife.

Ishmael. That was the new name they gave me. They told me I must hold it close. Keep it a secret. Tell no one. It was my password, and I whispered it to myself as I drove back home from the ceremony.

Ishmael.
Ishmael.
Ishmael.

It felt like a prophecy, some destiny to live up to. I knew the secret names came from *The Book of Mormon.* I would search for its place when I got home. Until then, I kept chanting because this was God's name for me, the one he'd given to me in Heaven, the one I'd whisper back like a key.

&

Alison Stine once wrote that, when naming characters in fiction, "the music of a name—or lack of—makes you feel a certain way. Names can radiate warmth or coolness, familiarity of fussiness, trust or suspicion." She talks about the characters in her novel *Trashlands* and how they're all named after the natural world, a contrast to the apocalyptic landscape littered with plastic. "What's another way to remember a place that washed away? An animal that has become extinct?" she asks.

"Pass it down as a name."

&

Mormon missionaries don't get first names. Men go by Elder, women by Sister. I was nineteen when I entered the Missionary Training Center (the MTC) in Provo, Utah and lost my name. They handed me a black tag upon my entrance, something to wear like a badge of honor over my heart: *Elder Romriell* carved in white letters. Elder is supposed to signify the respect given to our holy calling. And it is holy, right? This was supposed to be the way to salvation.

On the wall of my MTC classroom, there was a painting of the Army of Helaman, the two thousand stripling warriors described in the Book of Mormon. They were young men whose fathers converted to Christ's church and vowed to never fight again. When the enemy came to destroy them, it was their sons who picked up their weapons, crossed into the battlefield, and fought to defend their homes. As the story goes, because of their faith in God, not a single soldier was killed.

It was a metaphor, you see, for the work we'd be doing on our missions, and we sang their story in a hymn every Sunday, "We'll Bring the World His Truth." Thousands of missionaries raising voices, belting lyrics, a promise that we'd be like those kid soldiers. Righteous Warriors. An army of Elders. Names blazing from the tags on our chests. I stood with my class and sang out words I so desperately wanted to believe. That I could go out and change the world. That I could make it home alive.

&

My parents picked the name Andrew because they liked it. They chose my middle name, James, because it carried the legacy of both my dad's father and my mom's grandfather who both shared it.

And while my first name means warrior, James means supplanter: someone who seizes, who circumvents, who usurps.

Someone who might rebel.

And look: I don't know why I'm so interested in names, but I do know they feel important in the ways I understand my own story. It seems so arbitrary—like the ways in which I'd use a mood ring to navigate my own emotions. I use names to navigate my future, but I don't think it's working.

&

The account of Ishmael in the Book of Mormon goes like this:

The story begins with Nephi—the hero of the Book of Mormon. He and his family leave Jerusalem around 600 BC to seek the Promised Land, which turns out to be the Americas. Ishmael is the righteous friend of Nephi's father, Lehi, and he journeys alongside them with his family. He never makes it to the Promised Land, though. He dies in the wilderness, in the desert, in a place called Nahom. He's buried there. His children continue on. His sons become villains in the story. His daughters become heroes. Ishmael is remembered through their actions.

I remember sitting at my desk in my basement bedroom, reading this story, scavenging the index of my Book of Mormon, trying to find other places the name might be mentioned. I found nothing. That was it. He died in the wilderness. He never made it to paradise.

I had wanted the story to mean something, to tell me something about myself. In the secret depth of my body, I had hoped for a message, some private note I could interpret, a story to live up to. I wanted God to have answered something in the name. I wanted him to tell me the kind of person I could be if I just kept the faith. But if this was it, the map he sent for me to follow, what was he trying to tell me?

I laid my head down on my scriptures and gripped tight the fabric of my slacks. Beneath them, I felt the leg of my garments stretched down to my knee. Like my new name, the garments were sacred, a white undershirt and white knee-length briefs with specific spiritual symbols stitched into the fabric. They were to be worn at all times underneath my clothing, a reminder of the covenants I'd made with God during my endowment ceremony: to be obedient, chaste, and dedicated in sacrificing my life and spirit to God and the religion. The only appropriate times to remove them was during sex, bathing, swimming, and exercise. Otherwise, sleeping or awake, they were to be worn like armor—protecting the body and soul from spiritual harm.

There were so many secrets I had to keep. Secret name. Secret clothing. Secret covenants made in the temple. They were just additives to the ones I was already keeping: pornography and sexuality and how much I craved to be held in the arms of another man; how I had to persuade my high school cooking teacher to pass me so I could graduate, even though I had only shown up to three classes; how I used to go hide behind the seminary building beside the school when I skipped those classes; that I had attempted suicide only six months before the day I learned my secret name in preparation for my mission; that I wasn't sure whether I actually believed in God or if I was just too afraid to figure out what life might look like outside of what I knew.

I lifted my head and closed the book. This was just another secret, and I packed it tight in a little box, took it to the basement cellar of my mind where all other secrets were kept. Placed it on the pile. Walked back upstairs. Closed the door. Locked it tight.

&

Growing up, I didn't learn about the canonized saints of the Catholic Church. I didn't hear about them, didn't petition them, didn't even know their names. This is because the Mormon Church regards anybody that has ever belonged to the Church of Jesus Christ, past or present, as a saint. I learned about Christ's twelve apostles, sure—but only based on what was transcribed in the Bible. It wasn't until I took a Medieval Literature course at twenty-eight that I read other stories of the saints, and of course, I gravitated toward Andrew first—my own namesake—and I found out he was titled Saint Andrew, Protector of Wolves, First Called to be an apostle of the Lord. I learned he is the patron saint of Scotland, and the white x-shaped cross on the flag is representative of his crucifixion on the same.

I learned that, in Romania, Saint Andrew's Day is a national holiday—something similar to Halloween, where evil spirits enter our world and wolves come out at night. Basil is placed beneath pillows and garlic is spread around doors to protect from the wolves' bites. Legends tell if you get bitten, you'll turn into a wolf as well. And you must not listen too closely, for it is also said the wolves can speak human language—dark and terrifying things through the cracks beneath your windows. Stuff garlic into your ears if you must. They might just persuade you to follow them into the dark.

&

I met my ex-husband, Jed, when I was twenty-one, about a year after coming out, about two years after returning home from my mission. Seven months into our relationship, on New Years' Eve, I asked him to marry me. Two months into the engagement, we went to Chili's for dinner. As we waited for our entrées—a BBQ burger for him, lemon chicken for me—I gorged myself on baskets of chips and salsa.

"So, when we get married," Jed said as I tossed another chip between my teeth, "do you want to take my last name? Or would you rather I take yours?"

The chip, half-eaten, sliced down my throat. I coughed and sputtered, and Jed laughed, patting me on the back. "Sorry," he said. "I didn't mean to make you choke."

I laughed with him, my eyes burning. "I just didn't expect it." After I hacked a few more fragments loose, I swallowed and said, "I don't know. I guess I haven't thought about it much."

But I thought about it then, sitting in that booth, on a red leather bench scuffed with years of people sliding in and out, in and out. I thought about how I'd never felt fully connected to my last name. I thought about how it was difficult to spell and difficult for teachers and telemarketers to say correctly. I thought about how I'd made up a pseudonym for my future author name when I was sixteen: Alexander Leon. I remembered feeling so excited about how cool that name would look on the cover of a book.

I thought about how there's no direct meaning attached to Romriell, but the internet says it may have once meant *Of Rome*, so maybe my ancestors came from there. I thought about how my family has only ever been able to trace it back to the Channel Islands, and that it was originally spelled Romeril. I thought about the story my dad told us kids— that sometime after the Romerils came to the United States, there was a disagreement on how the name was spelled, so each family changed it to their own preference. Romerill. Romrel. Romrell. Romriell. All similar. All different. I remembered the moment I joined a new Singles Ward right after my mission—Singles Wards being specific Wards of unmarried members 18–30, and they were used to help you find a spouse. In the weeks just after I'd realized I was gay but hadn't yet come out, I met a girl, Kayla Romrell, a Romriell with a different spelling. And when I told her my last name, she laughed. "Oh! So we're related."

"Yeah, that's what my dad says," I told her. "Romriells . . . insert any other version of it here . . . are all related somehow."

It only took a few minutes to discover our dads were distant cousins. "Guess we can't date now," she joked.

I laughed too. "Guess not."

We didn't talk much after that.

I thought about all these things and thought about how, surprising to me—and only after Jed confronted me with the idea of abandoning it—I might actually feel some attachment to Romriell.

All I could stutter out was a guttural "Uh . . .": a non-answer because I was suddenly afraid he would want me to take his last name, Smith, and I was even more afraid of confronting him with the fact that I may not want to. "Well—I just—I think I may actually like Romriell—but I dunno—I haven't loved it too much in the past—I'd think about taking Smith obviously—I mean—if that's what you wanted—is that what you want? What do you think?"

Jed paused, his ice blue eyes staring back into mine. But he broke into a smile and started laughing again. "I'm just joking with you," he said.

"What do you mean?" I snapped back.

"I just wanted to hear what you'd say." He held my hand from across the table. "I don't really like Smith. I don't care what last name we have; I just don't want to keep mine."

"You jerk," I said, shaking my head and laughing too. As our server brought out our plates, I felt just a bit of weight lift from my body.

When we got married years later, he changed his name to Romriell.

After the divorce, Jed went back to Smith. This makes sense. Still, I wonder how it must have felt—leaving a name associated with pain and loss for a name he never wanted to keep.

At some point, I wanted to change my name. Andrew felt so unoriginal. So normal. Hero names are more unusual than that. Aragorn. Arya. Aslan. Even Apollo, the Sun God. God of Light. God of poetry. God of healing and music and knowledge, order and beauty and archery. These people were the kind I wanted to be—someone with a name that meant I could escape or shape the world I lived in. I was so desperately, excruciatingly tired of being locked up.

I tested positive for HIV in the autumn of 2020. I had been talking with this new guy, Terrence, for about three months. We met on Tinder, and he was living in Pennsylvania at the time. I was in Utah. He was coming to visit me for the first time, so I went to Planned Parenthood to get tested for STIs.

After an hour of waiting, the nurse returned to tell me that the antibody test had come back as positive for HIV, but, unfortunately, before I could get an official diagnosis, they would need to send off a full blood sample to test. She placed a needle in my arm and filled small vials with red, and I asked her if this meant it could be a false positive.

She unclipped the blood-filled vial from the needle before delicately pulling the needle from my vein. In her eyes, I saw a kind of sadness, a kind of pity. "It's possible," she said, her voice kind and steady, "but it's very unlikely. Our tests are over 99 percent effective. So, it's possible. Just don't get your hopes up."

I nodded and told her I wouldn't.

On the computer that night, I looked up everything I could on false-positive HIV tests, and I found this guy from Scotland who tested positive for HIV three times in 2002. Then, fourteen months later, he tested negative. He was so baffled by the results, he sued the hospital, but then two more tests came back negative.

His case is famous. He was the first person to be medically tested and documented as one who'd successfully fought off the virus. He worked with specialists, immunologists, and virologists around the world, but no one could explain how it happened. All they knew was that, somehow, during those fourteen months between 2002 and 2003, he'd gone from being HIV positive to HIV negative. And he has remained negative.

His name: Andrew.

Andrew Stimpson.

And I couldn't help but obsess on his name—my name—this tale rolling through my mind that I was so desperate to be true:

Andrew went from positive to negative.

Andrew went from positive to negative.

Andrew doesn't have HIV anymore.

It was a story I so desperately wanted to claim as my own.

&

In the summer of 2021, I went to dinner with a group of queer post-Mormons. My partner, Terrence, came with me, and when the matter of our secret names came up, he laughed at the absurdity. We all did. It felt so strange now. Secret handshakes and codenames and rituals. They just seemed like ways we could try to control the narrative of our afterlives.

"What was your name?" Terrence asked me.

"You know, I can't actually remember," I said. "Funny. It was so important to me at the time."

"You can look it up," Henry, one of our hosts for the evening, said.

"Seriously? How?" I pulled out my phone, eager to search.

Henry laughed. "Well, it's pretty easy. Your new name is chosen based on what day of the month you got your endowments out."

I looked at him with a scowl, mouth hanging open, making some kind of *whaaaa* noise in the back of my throat. Henry just laughed again. "Yeah, so whether you get them out on January first, February first, March first and so on, your name will be the same."

Aghast, I pulled up a website called *Temple Name Oracle*. It charted days of the month and their associated not-so-secret names. I searched through them, reading each name closely until I landed on the sixteenth: Ishmael.

Ishmael.

The name clicked into my memory. I knew it was the one I was given. But whatever enchantment I felt back when I first learned it had gone. It was just a name now. Not mine. Not from Heaven. Not a passcode. Not chosen by God but by my own choice to complete my endowments on the sixteenth of that month. Named by random chance.

I almost felt betrayed. I just laughed instead.

&

I looked up my first name again in the later years of my twenties—after my divorce and relocation back to Utah—and I found another meaning attached to it, one that I'd never seen before.

To be brave.

&

Once upon a time, when I was twenty-five, I moved to Orlando to work at Walt Disney World. And like when I entered the Missionary Training Center in Provo, Utah, I got a nametag upon arrival. This one was white and gold, my name and hometown etched in blue. I was to wear it over my heart at all times—something to show I belonged, that I had some kind of authority. It felt similar to the mission. But different too. Whereas missionaries don't get first names, Disney workers don't get last names. This is purposeful, implemented by Walt himself. He wanted everyone working there to be on a first-name basis with one another. It was his way of creating a place where people could feel like a family, so we could feel special and seen and safe.

At a store in the backlot of the parks, one that only Disney workers could enter, they sold specific frames to showcase these name tags—this trademark symbol of belonging. I always wanted to buy one, and I meant to before I left, but I didn't have enough money to spare. Now, my nametags sit in a tin in my closet. Protected. Hidden.

Maybe, one day, I'll find the time to frame them.

Stain

I WAS EIGHT WHEN I LEARNED my body could make me sin. I was eight when I learned that God created my body imperfect so I could learn how to be perfect and make it back to Heaven. At eight, I'd be taking the first step toward my own salvation: Baptism.

At eight, I was enthralled by the idea of my baptism because it was supposed to do two things: First, it would wash all past sins off my body and spirit, leaving me completely unstained. Second, and even more important, I'd be given the Gift of the Holy Ghost. I believed, like most Mormons did, in the Trinity: Heavenly Father, Jesus Christ, and the Holy Ghost as three distinct beings. God and Christ stayed in Heaven, but the Holy Ghost had the capability to exist on Earth, guiding me through life, speaking messages from God. It would stay with me as long as I stayed pure, as long as I didn't sin. It would help me stay good, and if I was good, I wouldn't go to Outer Darkness—the Mormon version of Hell—taught to be worse than the fiery underworld depths because I would instead be adrift in eternal nothingness, my family and loved ones living in the light of God without me.

As a part of church every Sunday, Mormon kids under twelve attended Primary. Its purpose was to prepare us for our futures within the church, and it's where I learned about baptism and Heaven and the Holy Ghost and the worse-Hell. I also received my CTR ring, the kind we all got, silver bands with green shields. Their translation: Choose the Right. It was a physical reminder of the plan outlined for me since birth. Guidelines for how to make it into Heaven, the ones we all knew:

1. Baptism at eight years old.
2. Church every Sunday.
3. Scripture study every morning and night.
4. Pray every morning and night, at every meal, whenever I needed guidance.
5. Give a 10 percent tithing every month.
6. Don't drink coffee.
7. Don't drink caffeinated tea.
8. Herbal tea is okay.
9. Diet Coke is okay too.
10. Don't drink alcohol.
11. Don't take drugs.
12. Don't listen to inappropriate music.
13. Don't wear inappropriate clothes.
14. Don't watch R-rated movies.
15. Don't date before turning sixteen.
16. Don't get a tattoo or piercings.
17. Go on a full, two-year proselytizing mission at nineteen years old.
18. Do not have sex before marriage.
19. Get married. Preferably while I'm in my early twenties so I can have lots of children.
20. Have children.
21. Have some more children.
22. Make enough money that I can be the sole provider for my family.
23. Meet death with as little sin as possible.
24. Don't be gay.
    Don't be gay.
    Don't be gay.

The list was longer. I had memorized it early. It included no gambling and monthly fasting and attending church activities on Wednesday nights. It could teach me to be perfect. All I had to do was follow the rules. Doing so meant I had a chance to be saved. At the end of things, when I died and stood at the gates of Heaven, I could mathematically, almost scientifically, prove that I deserved to be with God and Jesus and my family. I could hold up my checklist and tell the great judge: *Hey! See? I did my life right. Open up your gates and let me in. I don't deserve to be alone anymore.*

On the Sunday before my baptism, I asked my best friend Josh what it felt like to do it. "They make the water warm," Josh answered thoughtfully, plucking grass from the front yard of my family's house. "At least we don't have to be dunked in a river like Jesus."

We laughed. I was grateful for it too. Cold water. The rapids. Rocks rolling beneath my feet. It was how Joseph Smith and all the early Mormons were baptized. It was easier now, and I was happy for it to be easier, especially because I knew I had to make sure I was submerged completely in order for the baptism to work. If even one toe popped out, I'd have to be dunked again. It was a symbol of our spirits being completely washed clean. Kids made fun of you if you had to be thrown underwater more than once. I couldn't stand that kind of embarrassment.

"You do feel really clean after," Josh said. "You just feel light."

"So that's what the Holy Ghost feels like?" I asked him. I was eager. I yearned to understand.

Josh paused as he pulled up more grass, piling it on the pavement beside us, pondering his words. He had only recently moved into my Ward—the Mormon name for church congregations—but he seemed like the most spiritual kid I knew, by which I mean: when our teacher asked what we thought about in the silence of sacrament every Sunday, he said he thought of Jesus's sacrifice for our sins. I didn't say that I imagined the big, tall chandeliers falling from the ceiling and smashing against the church floor.

"The Holy Ghost just feels like peace," he told me. "It washes over you, and you feel all calm."

I took in a breath. I let it out. Nodded some kind of assent. I figured if anyone could keep the Holy Ghost with them, it would be him.

⁓

Three years later, when I was eleven, I found the word *fag* carved into the thick green paint of a bathroom stall at my school. At lunch, I asked my friends if *fag* was the *F* word everyone talked about. One friend, Mark, who happened to be one of the only non-Mormons of our group, laughed and said the *F* word was a different bad word, but we weren't supposed to say *fag* either. When I asked what the real *F* word was, he pulled me into the bathroom and whispered "fuck" into my ear.

I didn't know much about homosexuality or sex when I was eleven. We didn't talk about it at school, and when it was discussed in church, I was told it was something to never be discussed. It wasn't that we were supposed to get rid of our sexual feelings; God just wanted us to learn to manage them so they wouldn't bring us misery. "Bridle your passions," my teachers said, but bridling sexual thoughts and feelings was hard to do when I didn't know what sex was. I was ten before I browsed one of my older siblings' Human Biology textbooks and learned that penises weren't the only genitals.

Look, I've always been a curious being, which is a dangerous trait in the plan of righteous salvation—what Eve learned in the Garden of Eden—craving knowledge is enough to make all humanity fall to ruin.

I tried not to think about how that consequence seemed rather extreme. As if she was to blame. As if she could have chosen differently.

Quiet and alone in the night, just hours after my friend whispered "fuck" into my ear and I had seen *fag* written on a bathroom stall, I searched online for these new words I'd learned—some investigative search for answers. And I found them: videos and pictures of naked men and women on the screen.

I glanced away at first. Pressed my eyelids together as if I could forget what I'd seen. It was the bad thing. The wrong thing. I had been taught to look away. But I felt heat behind my eyes, some slow stitch of my eyelids loosening, bringing me back to the glowing monitor. My hand moved the mouse, then the sounding click of a trigger. A video played. I crouched in my seat, ducked down and peered around the room as if someone might see my transgression. All was still. I turned back. I watched the video burn. Thirty seconds of heart-racing, skin-searing awe. When it finished, I clicked on another. And another. And another. Film after film, late into the night.

On the day of my baptism, three years before my discovery of pornography, I held onto Josh's remarks about the Holy Ghost and the peace it might bring. It wasn't the first time I'd heard a description like that, a script we'd all been taught. Peace was how the Holy Ghost communicated. Calm. Relaxed. Light. Pure. Still, Josh's confirmation was the proof I had needed, and it exhilarated me. I'd actually be able to feel this abstract thing adults had been telling me I'd feel. I'd finally feel God's presence within me.

On the day of my baptism, I entered the chapel, heart thrumming against my throat. I clenched my fists in some kind of resolution: I would do it right; I wouldn't make the mistake of having a toe pop up; I wouldn't become that story—the one to be told to laughter around the dinner table.

The entrance to the baptismal font was through the men's bathroom. My father entered with me as he would be the one to baptize me. Together, in silence, we walked to the back stall, and he pushed the door open for me. Behind it, on the opposite corner from a pristine, polished toilet, stood a big wooden door. Before I knew it was the entrance to the baptismal font, I had tried to get in. I had imagined secret tunnels and magical adventures, places like Narnia or Platform 9¾, entire worlds locked behind doorways that could lead into an adventure. But while the barrier had never opened for me, when my father turned the handle, the door creaked on its hinges. I hurried through, but my excitement dissolved as I passed over the threshold. It was just a small room, lit by a shallow yellow light above us. Quietly, I studied the shower in one corner, a second door at the end of the chamber, a few hooks and shelves beside me—not a magical world—just another room behind a locked door.

"Do you want to get dressed in here or in the stall?" my dad asked me, gesturing to the bathroom.

I glanced around the shadowed room. "Out there," I said.

I stepped out into the restroom's fluorescent lights and closed the door behind me. I pulled down the tan baby-changing table and placed the black bag containing my baptism clothes on it. It was a simple, front-zip jumpsuit and socks with circular grip spots on the bottom. All pure white. A one-size-fits-most rental from the church.

Piece by piece, I peeled back each layer of clothing, unclipped my favorite clip-on tie, kicked off my black shoes, unbuttoned my white shirt, pulled off my khaki pants, removed everything but my white underwear. I replaced it all with the baptism jumpsuit, sliding it over my skin, zipping it up to my neck. I turned to the mirror and paused. I looked closer. Scowled. The suit looked too big, drowning my body, falling loosely across my thin arms. It looked like it was meant for a bigger boy. A different boy. Like something I was supposed to grow into but hadn't yet. A costume for a part I was trying to play.

I shook my head and took in a breath to pull my thoughts away from ill-fitting clothes. That didn't matter in the end. I knocked back on the wooden door. My dad answered and I walked again into the small, yellow-lit, in-between room. He smiled at me. "Are you ready?"

My stomach twisted. "I think so."

He wrapped his arm around my shoulder like he always did when he knew I needed just a little extra support, and together, we walked out the second door.

~

I was eleven, and pornography turned out to be far easier to access than I initially thought it would be, especially considering I'd been taught it was such a terrible sin. And I was fascinated by what I found. A little hesitant. A little confused. It was straight porn at the time, but still, I eagerly watched the bodies move, engrossed in the way two people could press against each other, the way one could literally be inside another. It was a closeness I suddenly craved.

This was the beginning of my sexual curiosity, my enthralled sense of wonder. I would continue to sneak downstairs to see more—always at night because it had to stay a secret. Because I knew it was wrong. But I wanted to learn. I wanted to know more about this thing no one would talk about. And though I could only do my research at night, it didn't bother me. It seemed the best time to come alive was when the rest of the world slept. When no one else could see me.

On one particular night, a few months after I first sneaked into my father's study, I found myself sitting in front of the computer again, eyes seared by the screen. Following my pattern, I dropped my pajama bottoms to the floor and scooted closer to the desk. As a website loaded, I glanced at the stairs outside the office, stairs that led to my parents' room. Another pattern: I needed to know I'd been quiet enough, invisible enough. I didn't want to think about what would happen if anyone found out what I was doing. They'd never see me the same way if they found out.

But something different happened that night, something outside the pattern, when I watched bodies move on the screen and I felt something shift. The video had seemed normal. Man and woman. They took each other's clothes off. Ravenously. Carelessly. They pressed against each other and kissed. And then, without warning, another man entered the scene, large and muscly and wild. The couple glanced at this new man and smiled. They waved him over. He dropped his clothes. The woman dropped to her knees. The men kissed. And kissed again. The wild man wrapped his fingers into the hair of the other and pulled him closer and kissed him harder, and my stomach coiled beneath my skin. My heart beat faster. Faster. Faster.

I knew so little about homosexuality—or any kind of sexuality—back then, but I knew what it could look like. I knew my oldest brother was gay and that he'd stopped going to church years ago; I knew he had recently started bringing a boyfriend around; I knew Mormonism taught homosexuality was sinful and gay people couldn't make it into the highest kingdom of Heaven; I knew that my brother hugged me whenever he came around; I knew he wanted me to sing with him when he played the piano; I knew that he loved me, and I knew that I loved him; and I knew I was afraid to become him.

But I couldn't stop myself from wondering. I couldn't stop my fingers as they typed new words into the internet search field: *gay porn*.

When my father and I exited the changing room, we walked through a slim, white, curved hallway and came upon the baptismal font. It immediately made me think of a tiny swimming pool. I had always loved swimming, at the pool near our house, or at Seven Peaks Waterpark where my family all had season passes. We had gone nearly every weekend that past summer. While my siblings loved riding the big slides and swimming in the wave pool, I liked to float down the lazy river with my cousin Karli. We loved to swim against the wall until we found a pump of rushing water. When we found one, we'd shout out to each other, reach for each other, pretend we were being helplessly dragged beneath the current, fighting for our lives.

I loved the sweeping feeling, the way the water pushed my body. When I sank down below the surface, I'd stay under for as long as I could—holding my breath—swimming beneath strangers' feet—completely free. I had felt completely free.

I shook my head, trying to rid myself of the memories, as my father and I took our first steps into the font. It was bathed in white light, polished tile and iridescent walls glimmering around it. I wasn't supposed to be thinking about Seven Peaks. I was supposed to be thinking about Christ and Heavenly Father and all the blessings I was about to be given. I was supposed to concentrate on how I felt without the Holy Ghost so

I could make sure I knew what it was like when I felt its presence. Then I could more easily determine when I did the bad things that made it leave me.

I glanced to where a large window framed my family and friends. My mom. My siblings. Josh and my other friends from the Ward. Each sat on the other side of the glass, looking down at me. Watching. I imagined myself in a movie, and all these people had come to see me. On display. Utterly visible. I took a deep breath.

I wanted to make them all proud. I refused to fail.

In the night, naked bodies popped onto the screen. Men's bodies. Gay men. My gut clenched. I shuddered a breath. I clicked the first film. I leaned in closer, mouth dry, eyes alight. There was a humming in my chest, a vibrating, maybe something more like growling—some sweet carnality rising up through my lungs—vocal cords buzzing, teeth and claws thrumming, a beast opening its jaws. I was utterly terrified. Utterly awake. I was ready to be set free.

My stomach boiled, my heart pounded, my mind reeled, my skin shivered, my eyes strained. The videos breathed something deep into my body, an expansion I couldn't understand. I felt myself elevate. These men—their connection—it looked wonderful, so beautiful and open. I knew I should feel shame, that aching darkness I'd been taught that sin was supposed to bring me. But I didn't feel anything like that. I only felt brilliant. And light. Bigger than I had ever been, and my body began to shake.

I was relieved to find the water was warm, just as Josh had said it would be. I continued down, slid my feet across tiled steps until I reached the bottom. The water came up to my chest, and my dad held my wrist, guiding me to the center. When he stopped, he gave a slight pull to his right side, and I turned his direction, following his lead. I looked up to him, and he gave me another reassuring smile, lightly squeezing my wrist so I could know he wouldn't let go. I took a breath and nodded.

I looked up again, into the large window above. I smiled at my friends, and they all smiled back. I met eyes with each of my siblings. Matthew. Christopher. Melissa. Marcus. I found my mom, her smile big and bright, and she nodded to me, as if telling me she was there with me. Our Bishop stood in front of the crowd and gave a small speech. He was the leader of our Ward. I tried to hold onto his words as they passed through the speaker beside me, but they slipped from my mind like my feet wanted to slip on the tiled floor. By the end, I could hardly remember a word. *Spirit. God. Christ. Love. Pure. Washed. Peace. Light. Courage.* They were qualities expected of me, the pressure of living up to them made my knees nearly collapse. I was glad for the strength of my father, holding up my body as water lapped around my chest.

When the Bishop finished, my father gripped my wrist tight in his left hand, and I gripped his in the way I'd been taught, a technique developed so that the person would feel stable as they were dipped backward into the water. It also helped the baptizer pull them back up without dropping them back in. I'd practiced the technique fervently so I could do it perfectly, so I could remain stable when my father's right hand lifted into the air, so when he dipped me down, I could submerge myself completely. Not a toe out of line.

My dad started the baptismal prayer: a short one, a rehearsed one, the one all baptizers said: "Andrew James Romriell, having been commissioned of Jesus Christ, I baptize you in the name of the Father, and of the Son, and of the Holy Ghost. Amen."

As instructed, I lifted my hand to squeeze my nostrils closed. I tried to think about my toes. I tried to think about my eyes and how I needed to shut them tight. I tried to think about Christ and God and the feeling of being without the Holy Ghost so I could always know what it felt like to be changed. I tried to think about becoming pure. I remembered playing in the lazy river at Seven Peaks Water Park with my cousin Karli, diving and swimming and bobbing to the surface. We laid ourselves out on towels, slurping up Dippin Dots and letting the ice cream drip off our chins. We ran to the wave pool and sat along the shoreline and let small waves curve and crash against our bodies so we'd tumble and twirl and laugh. I remember laughing—laughing and laughing until our bellies ached. I remember walking out of the water at sunset, and I remember turning to find bloody footsteps behind me. I remember sitting on a bench with Karli as we cried and showed our moms our bleeding toes, torn against grainy ground beneath the water.

I was submerged. Warmth spread across my entire body, touching every single inch of skin. It felt so freeing, floating weightless in the warm water, held up by the strength of my father's hands. And then I was pulled up. My dad helped me stand. Water fell from my clothes, drops echoing loudly as they struck the rippling surface. A chill air crept goose-bumps across my body. I started to shiver.

∼

Bodies twisted as they entered one another. I was panting, running out of air. My heart burned. I leaned in closer and tried to close the distance. I could almost imagine the breath of men on my neck, telling me to let go, telling me it was alright, telling me I could be free. My body convulsed. My vision blurred. I gasped out, and something white and wet covered my stomach. I looked down, my mouth open and heaving air. I had never done it before, this thing I'd seen the men in the videos do. And now I had. It was like a switch had been turned on. I felt elated and big and new. I nearly laughed.

But my joy evaporated as my breathing leveled, as my body slammed back against the earth with such ferocity I felt dazed.

It was the bad thing. I had done the bad thing.

I shut down the computer, tears in my eyes. I tried to wipe the evidence from my stomach, but it stuck to my hands like honey. Whimpering, I pulled up my pants and ran to the bathroom. I yanked off my shirt and wiped off all I could. I tried to wash my skin clean and then hurried back to my room. I held my blankets tight around my body, and I wept, eventually falling asleep to the sound of my own trembling cries.

∼

I'd done it right. Submerged completely. In silence, my father helped me out of the font. The tile was slick, but I didn't slip like I was so afraid of doing. Before we turned the corner, I looked back into the font. The water wasn't calm anymore, little waves were lapping up against the tiled walls. I yearned to go back, to float in that clear, warm water, to feel the embracing freedom, but my father stepped up behind me, and I walked back into the small dimly lit in-between room.

I crossed the small space to my clothing bag. I wondered if it was bad, how much I wanted to go back and swim in the font. I also wondered if I'd done something wrong by thinking of the water park instead of Jesus while in the font. It felt worse than having a toe pop out of the water. I wanted to ask my dad for a do-over. I felt like I needed a do-over. But he had already started showering.

My clothes felt heavy. They stuck to my body like paint. I unzipped the jumpsuit, trying not to think about how naked I was about to be. When I dropped the cloth, I felt lighter, but cold crept up my skin. I quickly dried and dressed myself before hanging my jumpsuit on a hook beside the door, water dripping onto the tile. Dad said he'd come back for them later.

I decided to wait in the bathroom while my dad showered. I locked the stall door and sat on the edge of the toilet seat, folding myself forward until I could wrap my arms beneath my knees. I rocked back and forth, trying to quiet my thoughts. People had said the Holy Ghost was supposed to be able to do this for me, bring peace to my mind and soul. Josh had said it too. But the thoughts didn't quiet, and I wondered if, because I had allowed the intrusive thoughts of the water park to enter my mind while being baptized, the Holy Ghost hadn't latched onto my spirit. I wondered if it had come and gone. I didn't know whether a wandering mind could be sinful like that.

I didn't have an answer, but I knew the weekly Sacrament of bread and water at church on Sundays was a type of renewal for my sins—a repentance process. I would apologize to God and Jesus and hope they'd take pity on me. I would promise to try harder. To work harder. To control my thoughts. In order for the Holy Ghost to be with me, for God to be able to be near me, I knew I had to do better. I would be better.

The morning after my first ejaculation, I woke to find the white had dried, had stained my shirt overnight. I threw it in the trash. I couldn't let my parents find it in the laundry. I couldn't face their disappointment that I believed would come if they knew. And when I wore a plain, white T-shirt to bed the next night, my mom asked where my pajama top went, and I told her I couldn't find it, and my heart pulsed against the lie.

I didn't do it so often back then. Lie, I mean. That fib would just be one of the first. One of many. I would build a wall with them.

I'm straight.
Of course I went to class today.
I'm in love with her.
I got an A on my math test.
I don't want to dye my hair.

I don't really like that shirt either.

I'm not gay.

I don't want a tattoo.

I don't want a piercing.

I don't watch pornography.

I want to go on a mission.

Seriously, I promise I'm not gay.

I'm not hurting.

I know I'm worthy.

I'm fine.

I love myself.

I'm happy.

You don't need to worry.

I promise I'm fine.

I don't want to die.

I don't want to die.

I don't want to die.

Lies that piled atop each other, and I hid behind them. Locked the other Andrew within them—the one who might be gay. I refused to let him out. Each morning, I told myself, *never again. I will never watch gay porn again.* But the stains on my shirt had been the proof, this reality I could never wash away. There was a beast I felt inside me. Monstrous. Hungry.

Each Sunday, at Sacrament with my family, I would ingest bread and water as symbols of Christ's body and blood—these things he sacrificed for my sins. Tears would line my eyes as my tiny, emptied cups clattered on metal trays. I tried to imagine how with every sin, Christ had to suffer just a little more in the Garden of Gethsemane. I pressed the idea into my mind like a nail. If I could make myself hurt enough, maybe I'd finally stop sinning. Maybe I could be pure again.

Mormon Lessons on Modesty

LESSON I

Modesty is an attitude of propriety and decency in dress, grooming, language, and behavior. If we are modest, we do not draw undue attention to ourselves. Instead, we seek to glorify God in body and spirit.

Outside the second-story window of my childhood bedroom, there was a slanted patch of roof I once came to inhabit as if it were my own, as if I could claim it by simply existing in the space more often than anyone else in my family. It was a private place. Somewhere no one would see me. And in the summer before my senior year of high school, I started laying a towel out on the burning slats of the roof to tan. I just wanted to feel more attractive—something that seemed so important back then. I was a lifeguard. I was surrounded by these popular guys, my coworkers, most of them muscular, consistently shirtless, always lying out on towels against the steaming cement at the poolside. I couldn't help but see the way girls would notice them. I couldn't help but notice them too.

In those days, because I couldn't admit that I was attracted to those muscular, shirtless boys beside the water, I instead told myself that I wanted to *be* like them. To look like them. I disguised lust with envy, though that wasn't much better when it came to my Mormon beliefs. My body was a gift from God, after all. I shouldn't want to change it. To care so much about how I looked felt like a sin.

But I did care. I wanted to change myself, so I started doing all I could to shape my body in the same ways the other boys did. I became a lifeguard. I signed up for a weightlifting class as my high school PE course. I went out on the roof to tan—the slanted patch of hidden roof outside my window because I was still too skinny to be seen by others. I knew muscular men were considered sexier, and all the popular boys had that triangle figure. All the hotshot actors were toned and tall and masculine. Jensen Ackles. Ryan Reynolds. Channing Tatum. Will Smith. Gerard Butler. In the 2000s, they were the guys I always heard people talk about, so I wanted to be like them. I wanted to be attractive. I wanted admiration. I wanted to be noticed and seen and praised and I hated myself for wanting any of it.

It was a murky narrative to be drowning in.

But on one rainy day in summer, I felt a separate—though not entirely different—desire wash over me. I had just watched an episode of *Smallville* with my sister, Melissa. The television series was based on Clark Kent's high school years, long before he ever became Superman, this adolescent superhero played by the tall, broad, muscular actor Tom Welling, whom I'd had a crush on since I first saw him on the screen. In the episode, he'd been fixing a pipe for Lana Lang, his high school crush. As they both crouched down below the sink, Clark turned the wrench, and the pipe exploded. They were both drenched in water. When they stood up, dripping wet and laughing, the camera focused on Clark's chest so the audience could see his sopping white shirt and the skin that could now be seen beneath it. Lana raised her eyebrows, staring alongside the rest of us. It was obvious she wanted him.

After the episode, I went to my room across the hall, the image of Clark's dripping hair and shirt and chest stuck in my head. I shut my bedroom door. I wondered what I might look like with a wet, white shirt like him. In an all too rare instance when I could push away the shame I felt, I threw a white undershirt over my head and stepped out of my bedroom and onto the dark, wet slats of the slanted rooftop.

Water struck the crown of my head; hair plastered against my ears in seconds. I crawled carefully up to the peak of the roof where the two slanted sides met. I placed a foot on each side to better balance myself and lifted my arms to the sky. I looked up and let the rain splash against my face, twitching each time a drop bounced off my eyelids. I opened my mouth and drank droplets down past the crest of my throat. I felt something like exaltation, a serene departure from whoever I had to be within the walls of my own life. Here, I didn't have to wonder if my body looked good enough under a rain-soaked white T-shirt. I didn't have to wonder if I needed to feel bad about wanting a better body. I didn't have to be afraid of what others would say. Here, I could simply be. Here, I was free, and I howled against the storming sky.

At some point later, I crawled back through my window. Tiptoed to the bathroom. Stared into the mirror and considered how the shirt clung to my skin, how I could see the slightest shade of peach beneath it, how my nipples poked through the fabric. And something unfamiliar rose up in my gut—an unsure kind of something—that maybe, just maybe, I could see my body, my own skin, as something to be desired. And the mirror reflected something like confidence—this boy I didn't know. I watched him. I studied him. I bared my teeth and smiled.

LESSON 2

Wearing revealing or sexually suggestive clothing, which includes short shorts and skirts, tight clothing, and shirts that don't cover the stomach and chest and shoulders, can stimulate desires and actions that violate the Lord's law of chastity (e.g. have premarital sex).

I hadn't ventured far out of my comfortable hometown in Utah very often. A week in Seattle for choir tour. A few days in Disneyland with my family when I was eleven. A few days in San Francisco, though I was too young to remember. A week in Idaho with my cousins each year—a place even more rural and small-town than where I currently lived. So, when Ms. Sauve, my theater teacher, offered to take a group of us to New York City for a week and a half that same summer between my junior and senior years, I knew I needed to go. I would find a way to get there.

I got another job as an ice cream scooper at the nearby Coldstone Creamery to get the money I needed. My family didn't have a lot of money back then, but my parents gave what little they had to help me fund the trip. They were even able to assist my eldest brother, Matthew, in financing his own way when he offered to be a chaperone. He was ten years older than me and was working his way toward a degree in musical theater at the University of Utah. Our love for theater and singing were just one of the many traits he and I shared. I couldn't think of anyone better to take the trip with.

We stayed in a small hotel room on the edge of Times Square, went to those big Broadway shows: *Wicked, The Lion King, The Phantom of the Opera, Next to Normal,* toured the Metropolitan Museum of Art, the Natural History Museum, the Statue of Liberty, and Ellis Island. I danced on the Big Piano in FAO Schwarz. I stood atop the Empire State Building, spread my arms wide, let wind slip against my fingers, my body electrified by the pulse of the city. I sprinted through Central Park, scouring paths for the unmapped Balto statue, erected to recognize the bravery of the sled dogs who carried antitoxins 674 miles in 1925, featured in my favorite childhood movie of his same name, the one I watched on repeat until the tape got too worn down to play anymore—the one where Balto is outcast and beaten for being half-wolf, where he fights a bear and nearly drowns in a lake and falls down a cliff so he can save those same people who hate him, where he pushes broken, colored bottles together against fractured light to create an aurora borealis on the walls of a dark and dingy basement because he knows things don't have to be perfect to be beautiful.

And when I found his statue, shining bronze in the afternoon sun, I climbed atop his plinth and placed my hand on his overburnished back. I turned and smiled for the picture my brother would take. And I felt this cliché something, deep inside me, that craved more than my little, small-town life in Utah. In that enormous city, where I feared overstimulation from giant skyscrapers and cracked streets packed with blaring taxi horns and thousands of people passing me, bumping me, crashing against me—I found inspiration, or some kind of peace.

And as we neared the end of our trip, a group of us ventured to an H&M in the heart of the city, years before a store would open in Utah. With little money left to spend, I bought a discounted button-down blue shirt with styled seams and chest pockets and buttoned loops on the shoulders. I bought it because I yearned to be the boy who would wear that shirt, who could walk these New York City streets, who could come alive in a world of art and electricity and culture.

When I got back home, I hung that blue shirt in my closet full of plain white ones because plain white collared shirts and black or khaki slacks were the uniforms men wore to church on Sunday. I wouldn't be able to wear the blue shirt to church, but that was okay. I hadn't planned to. I had school. Parties. Rehearsals for the upcoming fall musical I hoped I'd get into. Any number of outside spaces could suffice.

On one Saturday morning, months after I stood on a rooftop soaking in the summer rain, weeks after my trip to New York City, I stood still, staring into my bedroom mirror. My blue shirt hung from my shoulders, half unbuttoned and draped over a black tank top I'd once stolen from Matthew's dresser drawers. I'd never worn an outfit like it—tank tops were known to be too revealing, and therefore overtly sexual, which is why I'd never owned one before. But I was intrigued by the way the blue shirt trimmed my waist, held tight to my hips, created a triangle; how the new, tapered, black, pre-torn jeans made me look just a little taller; how the exposed skin of my chest made me feel just a little sexier. And though I knew the look to be an immodest one—too much skin—I liked him, that boy in the mirror, the stirring of something that felt like waking up.

I took a deep breath and walked upstairs. In my parents' bedroom, I stood in front of my mom and dad. I had planned on talking to them about my first few weeks of school coming up, how I wanted to audition for the fall musical, The King and I; how I wanted to go to a party thrown by our theater group that evening; how I had so many ideas about how to be the editor-in-chief of the school's literary magazine; how excited I was to be a part of it all. I clung to the pillar of their canopy bed, gripping it tight, holding myself up. My mom glanced up from grading her fourth-grade students' homework, smiling at me. Then her smile faltered. Her eyebrows scrunched inward. She asked, "What are you wearing?"

I looked down at my pale chest, my shirt buttons undone, my skin beneath the rips in my jeans. My cheeks flushed. I said, "Oh—well—I don't . . ." I unclenched my fingers from the pillar of their bed, dropped back down, felt the burden weight of my body strike the ground.

She shook her head, nose scrunched, almost laughing. "No. No. I don't like that. You should button it up."

"Yeah," I said. "Yeah, you're right. Sorry, I didn't realize it showed so much." I buttoned up the buttons, hid the tank top—the one that exposed me. "I'm sorry."

"Oh honey, don't be sorry," my mom said quickly. Sincerely. Like she could tell her words had some unexpected weight. "I just don't think that's you, is all."

I nodded, and she asked what I came upstairs to talk about, and I asked what was for dinner. My dad hadn't determined yet. He asked if I had any preference, and I said no. I walked down the stairs. I knew if they knew I was hurting, they would do all in their power to fix it. They would ask me what was wrong, but I couldn't tell them what was wrong. I couldn't chance it to be true—that I might want something more than this Mormon life could give me.

And I thought about Matthew. How this tank top had been his. How he'd been with me when I'd bought the blue shirt. How, just a year or so before, though he didn't attend church anymore, he'd gone as a gift for my mom on Mother's Day. How he wore his own blue shirt that day.

I thought about how it had been almost ten years since he'd come out as gay—just a year older than I was then. How he'd gone to college at Brigham Young University, the Mormon-run private university in Provo, Utah, and after his first semester, dropped out and moved to Salt Lake City. How he was invited to a party there, how he was offered meth from a friend. How he'd accepted. How he's lived nearly half of his life struggling with substance abuse.

And I thought about how much my family told me I looked like him. How we both loved to sing and write and dance. How I loved him and how afraid I was of becoming him, of living out his story. Maybe my mom had seen some remnant of Matthew. Maybe I just felt my own fear— of the homosexuality inside of me—of the parts I couldn't let out. And I cried quietly in my new basement bedroom, the one I'd moved down to just last week, where it was so much easier to remain unseen and unheard and hidden.

I stripped the blue shirt from my shoulders and held it gingerly in my hands. I felt the soft cloth swim through my fingers, considered the blue color and how it had reminded me of that endless ocean I'd seen in New York—when I boarded a tour boat to the Statue of Liberty just weeks before. I remembered picking the blue shirt off the clearance rack in that big, bustling, electric city. I remember seeing a boy I'd always wanted to be.

I walked to my bathroom and threw it in the trash.

To be absolutely respectful to our bodies as God's gift to us, we must
avoid extremes in clothing, appearance, and hairstyle. We must always
be neat and clean. Our clothing expresses who we are, sends messages
about us, and influences the way we and others act.

Snow drifted lazily outside glass doors in Dhane's basement. I lay
behind the coffee table, hidden from my friends who sat together on the
couches—Dhane, Parker, Dallin, and Jake. There wasn't enough room
up there, so I opted to remain on the floor. I was the only senior there,
the four of them being juniors who had known each other since middle
school. Though they had easily accepted me into their group after being
in the ensemble of *Oklahoma!* and *The King and I*, some part of me still
felt a little like an outsider. Separated and different. Maybe it's why I
stayed on the floor. Or maybe the flat ground just felt good on my back,
like it was lengthening my spine, like I didn't mind the table between us
all. I didn't want to think about it. I distracted myself. I watched the early
winter snow fall against the nearby window, watched how it melted so
quickly, how it dripped jagged down the warm glass.

Dhane's house stood in the rich neighborhood on the side of the
Wasatch Mountains. It was large enough that Dhane, the eldest of his
siblings, had the basement to himself. With its own kitchen, huge flat
screen, and isolation from intruding parents, it was the perfect place for
the five of us to gather. Dhane was also the only other Mormon in our
group. Perhaps this is why he and I connected so easily. After throwing
that blue shirt away, I told myself I needed to strive harder to be righteous. I needed to control myself better. So, I started sticking closer to
Dhane, and together, we felt like the standouts among the others. We
were the righteous ones. I could tell myself Dallin, Jake, and Parker lived
in all the sinful ways I'd been taught caused an unhappy life. Even though
they seemed joyful, ecstatic, and prosperous, I told myself they would
end up unhappy, that somewhere along the road, their lives would fall
apart. I comforted myself in believing the pain of others came from their
refusal to join my religion. I mean—their lives had to fall apart. They had
to. Otherwise, why was I doing all this? Why was I destroying myself to
stay righteous? There had to be a reason. A reward. Something better
on the other side.

That night, we had just finished watching the movie *Sunshine,* one of Dhane's favorites. It depicted a future with a cold earth, one dying in the dimming light of a waning sun. Eight crew members journeyed on a ship strapped to a Manhattan-sized nuclear bomb, hoping to fire it into the sun and restart its life. They succeeded in the end. It only cost them their lives.

I wondered what it meant to create life from destruction. It felt similar to all I'd been taught about the earth being crystallized in the end days of biblical Armageddon. When the world burns and is replaced by a perfected planet. A perfected people. Where there'd be no more pain. No more sin. No more temptation. If this life was simply a test I had to take to get into Heaven, it was one I was determined to pass. I knew sin was necessary for God to test our faith, and yet I wondered if the necessity of sin to become perfected might just be another excuse to sin. Wouldn't it be better to simply be perfect from the beginning?

Too existential a question, really—I wasn't supposed to ask. *Have faith,* leaders spoke into church microphones, that the next world was somewhere out there waiting for us. There, we'd all be reborn into perfection.

My mind snapping back and forth in these thoughts, I watched snow melt against the windows of Dhane's basement. Parker's voice pulled me back when he said to Dhane, "So you and Alyssa have gotten pretty close, I see."

I rolled onto my back and dug my fingernails into the carpet.

Dhane laughed. "Who told you that?"

"Alex said she saw you holding hands in the hall after rehearsal."

"Well," Dhane said, the leather couch squeaking beneath him as he adjusted his seat, "I think we're just seeing where things are going."

"Still," Dallin said in a giddy kind of way, "you two look pretty good together."

Dhane laughed again. "Well, thanks."

"Wait," Jake said. "I thought *you* were interested in her, Andrew."

I reddened in the silence that followed. I took a breath. "Well, I took her to the dance," I said, eyes fixed on the ceiling, "but nothing really happened after that."

"I thought you were going out with Mindy," Parker said.

"I thought you had a thing going with Amber," Dallin added.

I plastered myself to the ground, trying to laugh cheekily, trying to say something that might make sense, as if anything made sense when it came to how I felt toward anyone. I shrugged and mumbled that I didn't know—a rehearsed response when others asked about my dating life. When they asked why I didn't pursue anyone, why I hadn't kissed a girl yet or why I rarely went on dates, I simply mumbled that I didn't know what was going on or how I felt about anyone. Or I'd say that God wanted me to remain untainted; I used my own piety and self-righteous attitude to protect myself from their questions.

But Mindy. Amber. Alyssa. They were my friends. Macey. Rachel. Angela. Kelsey too. The list goes on: all the people I played in my own game of hiding. I led them on. Dropped them quickly. Hurt them. All in an attempt to force myself into a heterosexual narrative that was supposed to be what I wanted. I was supposed to be tempted to hold them. To kiss them. To have sex with them. It was supposed to be hard to hold myself back. But it never was. Not with them.

Dhane, Dallin, Jake, and Parker turned their conversation away from me. They continued talking about girls and dating and motorcycles, but I didn't say anything. Quietly, I peeked around the leg of the coffee table and found Dhane's red socks poking out from beneath his tight blue jeans. I rolled away, closed my eyes, listened to the lead pulse of my heartbeat on my stomach. I choked back my feelings, buried them deep in the gutter of my body as I did everything. I couldn't want him. To hold him or kiss him or feel his skin press hard against my own. I curled into myself, wrapped my arms around my knees, tried to hold myself a little closer.

Homosexuality: I knew what it looked like. I had seen it on TV. In movies. In books. I saw it in my religion, in all the ways they defined it. Sad. Dark. Hell-bound. Disrespectful to God and Jesus and the bodies they gave to us. I saw it in the two-day sex-ed class of my sophomore year—the one where I learned about HIV as the gay disease, an epidemic that had killed so many. And when someone raised their hand to say they heard HIV started when a man had sex with a monkey in Africa, I saw it in the snorting laughter of the class around me.

I saw it in the word *fag* written on the stall of my elementary school bathroom. In the way I asked what it meant, when my friend said he didn't know, when I looked it up on the computer that night.

I saw it in Matthew, in his pierced ears, dyed hair, and joyous laughter; I saw it in all the ways he and I looked alike, acted alike, laughed alike; and I saw it in his addictions. I saw it in the way I feared my journey might be the same if I wasn't careful. If I couldn't control myself.

I knew what gay looked like. I could make sure it never looked like me.

Lesson 4

Like our dress and grooming, our behavior is an expression of our character. Our actions can have a profound influence on us and on others. We should express ourselves through clean, positive, uplifting actions that bring happiness to those around us. Our efforts to be modest in word and deed lead to increased guidance and comfort from the Holy Ghost.

A game of pretend, if you will:

Imagine you're seventeen, a senior in high school, and you just auditioned for the spring play. The actual play doesn't matter. Mine was *The Crucible*, but if this is too dark and dismal, you may pick any other you'd like. Imagine you memorized a Shakespearean monologue for your audition because you hoped speaking in perfect iambic pentameter might allow you to play some act of confidence you rarely feel at seventeen.

Imagine you're at a party on the night Ms. Sauve will release her final list of those who made it into the play. The party is at your best friend's house, and you're surrounded by all the people who auditioned alongside you. The night is fire. Exciting. Ecstatic. Full of dancing and laughing and all the other motions you practice in order to stave off your own erratic fear of failure. You look around at those who auditioned with you and wonder whether they feel the same anxiety, if they want it as much as you do, if you want it as much as you think you do. And, in the midst of all this fear and staving off fear, from somewhere in the house, someone cries, "It's up! The list is up!"

And you pull up the list on your phone. Ms. Sauve has placed it on a website rather than on a piece of paper on the bulletin board of the high school. You wonder why she's done this. You wonder if it's because she wants to allow people to see loss in privacy—to not be bombarded by the celebration of their peers. If she had wanted this, it didn't work.

Your eyes move down each part, each character, and each name placed beside it. At first glance, you don't see yourself, and a small, hollow pit forms in your stomach. But maybe you just missed yourself. You look again. You linger a little longer on each person's name that is not your own. Again, you can't find yourself, and the hollow pit swells.

When you look a third time, you search the list backward. And when you still can't find yourself, you're engulfed by this swelling hole, the pit in your gut whispering: You predicted this. You're not surprised. You don't get to exist in the spaces here, don't get to celebrate with your friends, accepted and praised. This is not your story.

In a silent room with pale green wallpaper, beside a window full of dark winter sky, holding a plastic cup of sparkling juice, you sit. The room's not empty, just silent. Friends around you also peer through the list, and most find themselves. They find each other there. You glance around the pale green room and find they're all glancing too. They meet each other's eyes but shift away from yours. They don't say much. They leave, and you stay. They congratulate each other in the kitchen, and you stay silent beside the window full of dark winter sky, abandoning your sparkling juice on the coffee table.

Now, imagine it's two weeks later. You're standing in your high school hallway after school, outside the door of the theater classroom, beside the bulletin board where a cast list has also been stapled crooked on the corkboard. Try not to look at the list again. You know it by heart now. Just keep your eyes on the tiny window of the theater room door where you can see your friends sitting in a circle, scripts in hand, reading through their newly appointed parts. Through that little window, you can see your best friend—the one born nine days before you, the one whose house has the pale green wallpaper. You can see Dhane, the boy you love but don't know you love. He smiles as he reads his lines, and your best friend laughs beside him.

Stop. Don't imagine what's so funny because you'll just think it's about you. That sort of thinking is illogical anyway. You know it's illogical. Of course it is. You know this. Stop.

Then, the door with the little window that frames your best friend laughing with the boy you love but don't know you love, opens quietly. Ms. Sauve steps out. You turn to walk away as if you can pretend you weren't watching, but she tells you to stop. And you do. And you apologize, though you're not entirely certain what you're apologizing for. Someday, far from now, you'll understand the apology to be a reaction, just muscle memory on your tongue where the word stretches the expansive void in your gut.

"You can't be here," Ms. Sauve says, stern and solid and angry. "You aren't a part of this."

This is another thing you know. Something you've always known. The very thing you've told yourself all along.

You apologize again. You can't look at her anymore, so you look at the ground instead.

"I don't want to see you here again," she says.

The door closes. The lock clicks. You look up, but Ms. Sauve is blocked by the wall again. Through the window, you catch the eye of your best friend. She tilts her head, her eyebrows wrinkling in a sad kind of way. You smile to mask everything else. You wave and walk away.

Imagine when you turn the corner, you run. You run and stumble down the hall, and when you reach the bathroom, you lock yourself inside a green-painted stall. You cry. You scream and sob and cry and choke and punch the painted metal walls of a bathroom stall covered in graffitied words, scratched into green paint so silver metal shines through: *FAG. BITCH. FAIL. HOMO. FUCK. HELL. SEX. ASS. GOD. DAMN. I. WISH. I. WAS. DEAD.*

You line up against the words, spine cracking against a scratched-up wall. You slide to the floor. Tears drip from your soft chin to the hard tiles below: this is the weight you feel—the pressure of your feet against your socks against your shoes against the ground, where you beg God or Jesus or whatever power exists out in the wide expanse of the universe to help you rise, but all you find is silence and you're just pleading and pleading and pleading for someone, anyone, to walk in, to find you there on the ground, to take your open hands and pull you to your feet and finally—finally—see you because all you've ever wanted is to be seen, to be held, to be found—you just want to be found.

But you're alone. And maybe you've always been. Maybe this has only ever been a game of make believe.

You drop your chest to your curled knees and punch the cold hard tiles beneath you, beneath the harsh light of fluorescent bulbs above. And you weep.

LESSON 5

Withstand any temptation to participate in extreme behavior. You should not disfigure yourself. Avoid revealing yourself. Look—

do you see where the story is going?

—this may hurt just a little.

It was the end of my senior year, and Katie, another theater friend, held a yearbook signing party at her house. On the island countertop of her parents' kitchen, our friends met together and passed yearbooks around in a circle, wrote the same caring notes we all hoped to find on our own pages at the end of the night. I held each book tight, tried to hold onto the feeling of the cool, red binding, the eagle imprinted on its faux-leather cover.

I held a little longer to Dhane's when it came. I flipped the pages slowly, passing quickly over the cast of the spring play—the one that did not include me—but paused on the cast photo of *The King and I*, the picture where Dhane and I both stood as shirtless soldiers on the stage. I moved on quickly. I found a blank page and pressed my pen down into the white.

I wrote that I hoped he knew what it meant to me—his friendship, his support, all the joy he'd brought me. I told him I'd never forget about our hike up the Wasatch Mountain, how we climbed past the waterfall, strayed from the path, sidled up the side of a cliff, when I jumped down onto a muddy slope and slipped down the entire hill.

I explained how I admired his dedication to his films and thanked him for letting me be a part of them. I told him that his choice to include me had made me feel accepted and brave and worthwhile. I told him I was grateful for his life in mine. I told him I loved him. *Like a friend,* I added carefully. *My best friend.*

"Dang, Andrew," he said when he flipped the pages of my writing, "you wrote so much." He paused. He laughed. "You are an amazing writer though, so I guess I shouldn't be surprised." I laughed with him—careful to not laugh too long—careful not to look at him too deeply. "I'll miss you, buddy," he told me.

"I'll miss you too," I said.

A week later, he stopped responding to my texts.

Then, Dallin, Jake, and Parker stopped too.

Confused and scared, I called them all. No answer. I gripped my phone tighter. Called again. No answer. Deep in the confines of my basement bedroom, I cried. Fear pressed against my gut, seared my tongue, cracked my ribs. The silent weeks piled up, and on a warm summer night late into June, I left home. Drove in the dark. Found myself parked a few blocks away from Dhane. A broken kind of logic disrupted my rationale, as often happened when I did the things I knew to be wrong. Some mindless state of being, a numb body—disassociated from the Andrew I knew. It was as if someone else had taken control, as if some other boy had snatched up my car keys, moved my feet forward, driven the car, parked it down the street, moved my body to the dark porch, to the glowing, shuttered window of Dhane's father's study there—the same room where he'd once taught me how to edit the films we had created together.

They were there. All of them. Dhane. Dallin. Jake. Parker. My friends. Together. Crowded around the computer. Smiling. Laughing. Snickering at something on the computer screen, some kind of joy seeping between their teeth, while a sharp pain shot across my chest. Pressure built between my temples, fingers clenched, chewed nails dug into my palms.

Shaking, I lifted my phone to my ear. It rang once. Twice. I watched as Dhane picked up his phone, glanced down, shook his head and tossed it onto the table behind him.

A cheerful voice in my ear: You've reached Dhane! Sorry I can't come to the phone right now but leave me a message and I'll get back to you as soon as I can.

I hung up, more tears, throat shaking.

I typed a new number. Called. Dallin pulled his phone from his pocket. He looked at it for a moment. Paused. Pushed a button. The answering machine picked up in my ear, and I hung up. His fingers swept across his phone's keyboard, and my phone flashed with his words: *Sorry. With family tonight.*

My stomach clenched. My body shook. I glanced back through the shuttered window and found Dhane peering at me from his chair.

The night crashed in on me, my heart trumpeting. Dhane looked confused, like he couldn't quite figure out what he was seeing behind the glass. And he stood. And I turned. And I sprinted across the porch, threw myself over the fence, sunk into the prickly bushes on the other side. I crawled a few feet and froze, the sting of cold dirt and pebbles pressing up from beneath my clothes.

I heard the front door open and multiple feet cross over the threshold onto the porch. No one spoke. No one called out. No one looked over the edge of the porch, into the bushes, into the dirt beneath them. No one found me. I heard the door close. I twisted my face into the dry earth.

I don't know how long I stayed beneath those bushes. I don't know for how long the small rocks pressed against my body. What I remember, what I do know: how cold the air felt as it dripped down my throat and pulsed between my ribs; how much I didn't recognize myself—that boy residing within my skin, holding me beneath the bushes, covered in dirt and thorns and stones, under a sea of stars swimming somewhere far far away; how I so desperately wanted to reach up and grasp one shimmering celestial light in my hand, let it pull me far away from that place, that life, that body; how ready I was to be dismantled.

Gracious Ruin

I SAT IN THE BACKSEAT OF MY PARENTS' CAR, traveling down the freeway at seventy—far too quickly. I wanted to take my time, move slower, stop, but cars out the window passed in a blur of dull colors— black, gray, white, red, tan. Every now and again I would see something different, a spark of bright blue or green, and I would rise a little higher in my seat to watch it soar by. But then it was gone, and my eyes would unfocus; I'd fall back into a state of emotional sobriety. It was as if with every mile we moved, I could feel myself crack. My older sister, Melissa, rested her hand on mine, but I couldn't look at her. She squeezed my fingers, and I watched the world outside pass me by.

We were on our way to the Missionary Training Center in Provo, Utah—my parents, Melissa, and I. This was my rite of passage as a nineteen-year-old Mormon boy, to leave home for two years and preach the lessons of my religion. When I was young, I had wanted to serve in order to help other people, to bring them into the religion I loved so much. But on that day, as we barreled down the freeway in the brisk winds of mid-September, I wondered if that was still true. Maybe I believed in redemption, hoping, deep down, this could set me straight. If I gave everything over to God, maybe he could change me—shape me into the person I was supposed to be. Fix me.

Maybe I was just too afraid to believe anything else.

"You're going to be great, you know," Melissa said, smiling at me. She squeezed my hand again.

I held tight to her, trying to hold back my tears. "I hope so," I said.

I'd done well in fulfilling this part of my religious duty so far. I'd completed all the steps I was supposed to. As my nineteenth birthday neared, I'd interviewed with my bishop to discuss whether I was spiritually worthy enough to go on a mission—*Do you have faith in and a testimony of God the Eternal Father; His Son, Jesus Christ; and the Holy Ghost? Share your testimony with me. What does it mean to you to repent? Do you feel that you have fully repented of past transgressions? Have you always lived in accordance with the law of chastity? The law of tithing? The Word of Wisdom? Keeping the Sabbath day holy? Have you been honest in all you have said and done? If not, how long ago did these transgressions occur? What have you done to repent?*—on and on and on. After the interview, I'd filled out my paperwork. I stated that I'd love to learn a foreign language and that I'd love to go abroad.

It took less than two months to hear back—a large envelope addressed from the church's headquarters in Salt Lake City. It was a common thing for family and friends to gather around when someone opened their mission call, for everyone to put in their guess as to where the missionary would be sent, and it's what we did too. We invited all nearby family to come watch me open my letter, and I called my oldest and closest friend, Taryn, to join. And when everyone put in their guesses, it was Taryn who guessed correctly. "Alpine German-Speaking Mission," I read from the letter. "I'll be serving as a missionary in Germany, Switzerland, and Austria for two years, starting September 14."

Everyone cheered. I felt frozen. It was August 9. I had less than a month to get everything ready. Less than a month to get myself ready. September had come too soon.

We pulled off the highway into Provo, and my dad said we still had some time before my designated arrival time, so we parked on an empty road a few blocks from the training center. The MTC was the place designed for missionaries to begin their training. For nine weeks, it's where I would learn how to teach the Word of God, where I'd learn how to teach it in German, where I'd learn how to live my life as a missionary before going to live in Germany, Austria, and Switzerland for the following one year, ten months, and two weeks. It was supposed to feel like a dream to go there, and I wanted so badly for it to feel that way.

On the side of the road, my parents and Melissa took pictures with me. We found another family just down the street saying goodbye to their missionary. We asked them to take a picture of us together, and then we did the same for them. Amid photos, my teary eyes met the other missionary's. His eyes glistened too, and I wondered if he felt the same. Not ready. Afraid. Hurting. Terrified of what would come next.

As I hugged my parents and sister tight, time ticking by in my mind, I tried not to tremble under the weight of their arms. I wanted to collapse, let myself fall on the cement and plead not to go. I smiled instead. I let them know I would be okay. I had to be okay. It was my choice. My choice.

So, we left our little patch of roadside and much too quickly, drove through the iron gates of the MTC. There were two seasoned "host missionaries" waiting for us, and as soon as we got out of the car, they rushed to help me with my bags. The MTC used to allow longer farewells here, but there were too many missionaries going now. The drop-off had become too cramped, too chaotic. Goodbyes must be said beforehand. I thought back to my packet—to the part where I had been told "saying goodbye is like pulling off a bandage: the quicker it's done, the less it hurts." I had to hurry.

The missionaries helped pull my suitcase from the car as I gave a last, quick hug to my parents and sister. As we all cried together, I yearned for each one to not let go. When I separated from my mom, she told me, "Let us know whatever you need. We'll write you as soon as we can."

"Be safe," my dad added, "you're going to have so much fun."

"I'm so proud of you, Andrew," Melissa said.

I nodded and sniffed, wiping my eyes on the sleeve of my brand-new suit jacket, the one my grandfather bought for me. I wouldn't be allowed to call home except on Christmas and Mother's Day. I would only hear their voices four times over the next two years. And I felt scared. Cheated. Bound and dictated by these rules. I wanted someone to tell me not to go, to ask me to stay. But it wouldn't have mattered. Nothing anyone said could have convinced me to stay because to stay would be to fail—to fail God, my religion, everyone. I couldn't go back on it now.

One of the host missionaries told me it was time. The sounds of goodbyes from other dark-suited missionaries surrounding me became tumultuous. I choked on my tongue, and as I followed behind the host missionaries through the bustling crowd I took a final moment to turn back to my family. All three still stood there waving, their eyes puffy, refusing to leave.

Struggling to keep my breath even, I waved back, trying to memorize their features, to hold onto anything I could. My mom's round face and blushed cheeks, so much like mine. Like Melissa too. My dad's black hair, just beginning to streak with gray. He cupped his hands around his mouth and called out words I couldn't hear. I wondered if it was a simple goodbye. I would later forget to ask.

∼

I'm twenty-three and still breathless when the ranger tells us that it's time to start the tour. The hike up to Timpanogos Cave in American Fork Canyon was only 1½ miles, but in that time, we climbed 5,638 feet. It reminds me how poor my cardiovascular endurance is. I make another goal to exercise more that I doubt will actually come to fruition. Maybe it's the trying that counts.

My fiancé, Jed, and I move forward, joining the small group gathering around the ranger, whose name also happens to be Andrew. There are only seven of us in total, which Other Andrew says is good: "I'll be able to show you all the stuff I don't get to show the big groups."

It makes me feel special in a way.

A large wooden door, laden with locks and chains, guards the entrance to the cave. Jagged rocks surround it like teeth, as if the mountain is ready to swallow us down its throat. Airtight and sealed, the door protects the cave from external heat. Other Andrew tells us that four years ago, the cave dried out because of an air leak. "Humidity is important for a cave's survival," he says.

Apparently, air can kill.

He tells us we will pass through three caves: Hansen, Middle, and Timpanogos at the end. Though the caves were originally separated, the National Park Service has since blasted tunnels to connect them. I suppose they did it to make the tour easier, but a piece of me grieves the damage.

Other Andrew unlocks the door and guides us into the first chamber, Hansen Cave. My first impression is that it's just a huge cavern, an empty mouth, a giant natural hole in the mountain. It's only after we settle in and close the door that Other Andrew tells us the cave was once more beautiful than it is now.

"Early settlers ransacked the cave when they found it." His pain is clear, as if the tragedy was worse than anything he could imagine. Maybe it is.

He points out a tiny stalactite forming on the ceiling, dripping water to a stalagmite on the ground. Other Andrew tells us that with enough time, and if it's protected, the two will come together and create a pillar, something that will hold up the cave. That maybe one day there won't be evidence that humans ever touched the place. I look down the path, to the metal bridge connecting to a metal door, and I wonder how that could ever be.

"It makes me sad," I whisper to Jed. He nods. We move on.

The metal door leads us through a blasted tunnel and into Middle Cave. The first thing we see is a small body of water, which Other Andrew says is actually a lake that stretches deep below the rock. There is a pillar beside it, a stalactite and stalagmite that have come together to craft a column from floor to ceiling. At first, it looks as solid as the cave walls, but Other Andrew shines his light behind it. A soft pink glow illuminates the center of the pillar—not rock, but crystal. Minerals built by dripping water over thousands of years. I wonder if this is what had been in Hansen Cave before the desecration. I wonder how much effort it would take to break this pillar too.

How easy it would be to destroy. How easy it is: to cause irreversible damage.

~

After Hurricane Andrew decimated Florida, my parents bought me a book called *Hurricane Andrew: Images from the Killer Storm*. They bought it within just a few years of the tragedy, and growing up, I never read the text, just examined the pictures. Maybe it's what initially created my fascination with hurricanes, their ferocity, their indescribable damage. A regular hurricane can release as much energy as 500,000 atom bombs—nature at its most terrifying, its most destructive. The decimation I saw in those photographs didn't seem real. I couldn't fathom that amount of damage.

Later in life, I was determined to do the research, to understand what it meant to have been born amidst this devastation. And yet, when I placed the book on my desk and flipped the pages, the photos pulled me again. I glossed over the words, page by page, and instead studied the captured trauma—people staring into nothing, a barren wasteland of rubble. They were all that was left. Just them. Just people.

And something stretched inside me. I wanted to place myself beside them—as if I could understand them if I could stand with them. If I could feel the 200-mile-per-hour wind smashing sand against my body, against the walls of my house. If I could see glass windows shatter, hear the sound like a train barreling in through the holes. If I could imagine what it was like to hide in a bathtub, just trying to wait out the storm. Maybe the house would have fallen and crushed me.

I turned to another page and found a photo of a house with boarded-up windows. Spray-painted onto the wood were the words: *ANDREW GO HOME!*

A gut-punch. Somewhat foolishly, I felt hurt, as if they were saying it to me.

As if I had done the damage.

~

A black iron fence stood high above me, spikes protruding from the top like teeth. I peered behind at the maze of orange-brick buildings that made up the MTC. I saw my dormitory window in the distance and wondered if my companion, my partner in the MTC, had discovered my disappearance. He'd gone to a "letter-writing party" in a room down the hall. He'd invited me to join, but I said I wanted to sleep instead. Really, I just had my own plans.

Over the past two weeks, a cramped MTC classroom had become my home. It's where I spent nine hours every day, six days a week, learning gospel doctrines and teaching strategies. Our days were dictated. Wake up at six. Pray. Personal study. Go to the MTC gym. Shower. Go to breakfast. Put on your white shirt, suit, and tie. Go to class. Go to lunch. Go back to class. Go to dinner. Go to the dorms for a few hours of free time before more personal study and a prayer to end the night. On Sundays, we went to the Provo Temple across the street and had major church authorities come in the evening to speak. Our only "day off" was each Monday, Preparation Day, when we could journal, write letters, do our laundry, play sports, meet up with missionaries from other, non-German, zones, and go to the missionary store to buy snacks or pens or notebooks. We also had one hour allocated for us to email home if we wanted.

The MTC itself was split up into zones by the languages we had to learn. While many of the other language groups were large, we, the German-speakers, were tight-knit. We were each split into companionships of two, as had been mandated from the Lord, so we were told. It was for our protection, from outsiders and ourselves—so we could keep each other in check, keep each other holy and worthy. Other than going to the bathroom, we weren't ever supposed to be out of sight of one another: no privacy, no space. There were six of us in my classroom, eight in the classroom down the hall—each in a companionship of two. We studied scripture together there, prayed together, sang hymns, and attempted to understand the principles of our religion.

And it's not like I didn't have fun at times. My teachers, Brüder DaCosta and Brüder Evans, were kind and understanding, having been missionaries themselves not too many years before. Brüder DaCosta told us all about living in the countries we'd be going to—mountainside castles, old forests, amazing cultural traditions, amazing people. The small number of classmates meant that we all became close friends, though my companion and I tended to butt heads.

And yet, the pressure inside me built. Built and built and crushed me under collapsing rocks. And I had no time to discover why I felt that way. I had no time to be alone. My German suffered. Doubts about the religion surfaced. I longed for the solitude of the curtains in the communal showers or the tiny bathroom stalls where I could be alone—if only for a moment. We could only be trusted to go to the bathroom alone.

As I looked back from the border of the MTC, I punched a fist against my head telling myself not to do it, not to leave, but it had only taken a minute to pack my bag. My mind had been warring for weeks. My prayers had become robotic, any hope of a response gone. I think I once believed that if I prayed in just the right way, with just the right words, God would talk to me. A pathway would open. Dust would shift from my faith and it would become something more like knowledge.

"Throw yourself into the work," Brüder Evans said when I told him I had difficulties connecting with God. "These things sort themselves out when you do."

I asked him how.

"Just have faith," he said.

The frosted glass of my tiny bedroom closed in day by day. I walked a dark hallway without support. Faith was something I had once been proud to own. I had stood in church like all the other kids and said that I knew God existed. Even then, in the MTC, at the line between running and fighting, I wanted to believe. I wanted God to tell me I could make it. I wanted him to stop me from leaving, but there was only ever silence. And I ran across the fields unnoticed. My courage to continue dwindled with every step I took—if I could call what I was doing courageous. It felt far more like cowardice, but I'd fallen back into that haze, that other Andrew taking over, the separate one, the one who watched gay porn in the night, the one who was so afraid, the one I had hoped would disappear if I went on this mission. Here he was again. Maybe he would never disappear—a ghost I'd live with forever.

I reached the iron fence surrounding the entire MTC, and, too big to slip through the bars, I persuaded myself to climb.

In Middle Cave, Other Andrew asks us not to touch any of the rocks—even the walls. The oils of our skin can cause damage, can stop mineral buildup from progressing. In certain areas, Other Andrew directs us to remove our backpacks so we can duck underneath the sloped, low ceilings. This is especially hard for Jed because of his 6′ 3″ height and broad shoulders. But we help each other down slippery stairs, through narrow crags, holding hands to keep each other up. And as we slip between the contracting throat of slimming walls, I have to catch myself from reaching out, from making contact with the slick stone around me. I don't know why I feel the urge to touch, to interrupt the process. Maybe it's due to my rebellious spirit, my insatiable curiosity.

I wonder if it's the same curiosity that brought the teenagers, James Gough and Frank Johnson, to Timpanogos Cave in the first place. Their mothers took them to the already-decimated Hansen Cave, and they ran off to do a little exploring of their own. They slid down a nearby incline and found the entrance to Timpanogos. They found it, then they hid it beneath branches and dirt. They didn't want the destruction of Hansen Cave to be repeated. Of course, Timpanogos was eventually found again, years later. This time, though, it was quickly protected by the National Park Service. They examined the cave and all its wonders and professed it a national monument. They declared it something beautiful. Something to be protected.

So why is it that I have an urge to touch these walls—when I know the consequences of my hands against the cave—when the oils on my skin would stop the wall from forming. What if the alteration was invisible at first, but after years, that would change: there would be an imprint of my hand there. The rest of the cave would grow except for this single mark that would forever be damage, and it would be my fault.

What I realize, as I wrap myself between the cave walls, careful not to disturb them, is that by not touching the wall, I'm protecting the cave from myself. Were it not for me, for all people who come here, the cave would not need protecting. It might be better to not come out at all.

~

Hurricanes are born from pressure. They begin as lightning storms over the ocean. They slide across the water, growing bigger as they move through life. Unnoticed in the beginning, they could be harmless. But when the storms grow into clusters, they become tropical disturbances—something to watch, but not yet worry about.

Over time, molecules of water vapor compress and release heat. Pressure rises, releasing hot air like a breath. Clouds compress, release heat, push back. Back and forth, back and forth, intensifying the storm until it becomes a tropical depression. And sometimes, depression is as far as a storm will go. It might cause some damage, but it will be minimal. Depressions usually fizzle out. They fall back to calmer waters.

Sometimes though, the pressure will keep rising. The depression will intensify. The storm will worsen and become a hurricane—this destructive powerful force. By the time a hurricane hits land, it's too late: the heat, the compression, the pressure built up over time becomes too much. The storm comes. On its knees, the world is crushed. Chewed up. Destroyed. Trucks are thrown over bridges. Boats are lifted from the harbor and land on houses. Trees that have stood longer than people are ripped up in ocean waves. The world is gone in six hours. Then the storm fizzles out. There's no one left to blame.

~

After hopping that fence and leaving the MTC, I ran down the street to a hotel and used their phone to call a friend. He picked me up and took me to a nearby Dairy Queen where he bought me a cookies & cream milkshake.

"It's going to be okay," he told me.

"I just don't know what to do."

"I know," he said, "but I think you need to call your parents."

As the sun dipped toward the western mountains, I finally did. Turns out, they already knew. The MTC had called them to see if they knew where I was. "We're just so glad you're okay," my mom said through the phone. "Don't worry. We're coming to get you."

A half-hour later, they were there. They thanked my friend and drove me to the Provo Temple, right across the street from the MTC. The sun was setting. Orange and purple streaked the sky. My dad sat up front while my mom held me close.

"We love you," my mom said.

"No matter what," my dad added. All I could do was nod. "Look," my dad said, "you don't have to go back. You can come home. That is entirely up to you." I just shook my head.

"Is there something else going on?" my mom asked. "Is there something you want to tell us?" I pulled myself up from her embrace and stared into her light brown eyes. Looked into my dad's dark ones. I could see their concern so clearly. And I know now that they suspected the truth of my sexuality. They'd seen the internet history. They'd been waiting for me to come to them. They were opening the door, waiting for me to walk through.

"No," I said. "I'm just overwhelmed." I took a breath. "I want to try again." And I went back. I said goodbye to my parents all over again. Cried again. Walked back through the MTC gates in the dark. The MTC president walked me back to an empty classroom where my class was waiting for me. No one asked why I left or why I came back. They all just told me how happy they were to see me there.

Things got easier for a while. I tried to focus on the joy, determined I could make it day by day. I believed if I could just get to Germany or Austria or Switzerland, I could make it the full two years. At the very least, it would be harder to run back home from there than just hopping a fence. And when it was time to leave the MTC, I couldn't wait to make the journey across the Atlantic. At 5 am, all fourteen of us packed our two suitcases—the maximum allowed—and hopped on a bus to the Salt Lake City Airport.

The journey to Munich, where our mission headquarters was housed, went smoothly enough. After fifteen hours of travel—Salt Lake City to Atlanta to Munich—I thought it would be difficult to appreciate the beauty in anything. And yet, the mist that hung over the small German cottages we walked past felt nothing short of magical. The Alpine German-Speaking Mission leader, President Miles, pointed at buildings as we passed them, giving a tour I'm sure would have been enjoyable to listen to. I could only think of all the Grimm's fairy tales I loved and how they were compiled in this very country, in a city no more than 300 miles away, maybe even in a little cottage not too unlike the ones beside me then. It was as if I might be able to reach back through time and touch that magic. I so badly wanted to.

After our arrival at the mission home, we were granted a two-hour nap—only two hours because too much sleep wouldn't allow us to adjust to the eight-hour time difference. Then, we each had five minutes in the shower before meeting with our trainer missionaries—the ones we'd be companions with for the next three months. We'd also finally learn which specific zone we'd be serving within for that time. After those three months, we'd either stay in that area or we'd be sent somewhere else. We could be paired with a new companion. We might not. It would all be up to President Miles and the inspiration he received from God.

When we met the trainer missionaries, there were many I immediately felt a connection with. Many were outgoing and friendly and talkative. We huddled around a large map of the mission on the wall, searching through the red dots that marked the different mission zones. I fantasized about which I might go to first: I'd heard Zurich was beautiful; Stuttgart too; there were two missionaries there from Vienna, one from Salzburg, another from Innsbruck. The possibilities seemed wondrous.

President Miles eventually called us all to attention, and we started with a prayer, as we did with any meeting. President Miles then gave some words of welcome before the trainer missionaries stood in a line before us. President Miles paired us off one by one. Elder McKee would be going to Zurich with Elder Smith. Elder Nakken to Vienna with Elder Carson. On and on until it came to me—the very last companionship— with Elder Jackson in Bern, Switzerland.

For a moment, I was overjoyed. Elated. Switzerland would be a dream. But then Elder Jackson walked to the wall map and pointed to Bern, which sat at the very edge of the map. White lines crafted borders to represent the different zones, and Bern was the largest. And the farthest away. And while other missions had multiple companionships within the zones, Bern just had one. Elder Jackson and me. Only us. In the outskirts. Alone. No other missionary for miles and miles.

Elder Jackson smiled at me, warm and kind and welcoming.

I couldn't find a way to smile back.

~

Other Andrew pushes a button, and the cavern lights up around us. "Over here," he says, "is The Great Heart of Timpanogos."

A spotlight burns against the giant, thick, rounded stalactite hanging down from the ceiling. Behind it, the cave slopes down into darkness, no end in sight. With The Heart hanging down in an otherwise empty space, I can only imagine a mouth, the gaping maw of a beast, its tongue reaching out to swallow us down. I pause and turn to Jed. "Kinda looks more like a tongue than a heart," I say. He laughs a little and nods.

I also imagine what it would have been like for James Gough and Frank Johnson to see this. For us, it's lit perfectly, each crystal shining under the beams of light. It must have been darker for them—much darker. Smaller too. I wonder if they saw these same pinpricks of light dancing off the crystal. Other Andrew tells us this is as far as the boys went. They turned back here. Climbed back out. Covered up their discovery so no one else could find it.

"They did eventually come back," Other Andrew tells us. "With a few others this time. And with lanterns. They explored around The Heart and found Father Time's Jewel Box. It was after seeing them that the group decided to hide the cave away for good."

When we question what Father Time's Jewel Box is, Other Andrew smiles and leads us through a side path. Stairs run down, carved into the cave floor. They twist in a U-shape down to a dead end. Our small group stops and waits in the silence of a dark room. Other Andrew flips another switch.

The room erupts with light glittering off innumerable crystals. They shine from every wall, hang down from a caramel-colored ceiling. They cascade in colors that don't seem real, colors I can't quite take in, beauty I hadn't expected to find buried so deep. Pale orange dots on light canvas walls. Shimmering blue crystals contort like snowflakes reaching down toward us. Over a ledge, glittering waves of burning sugar rolling over each other across pillars that stick out from the ground.

I reach my hand back and find Jed's. "It's amazing," he says, giving my hand a gentle squeeze.

"I just can't believe it's all down here. That it's always been down here."

In the sparking light, Other Andrew tells us about the crystals, but my concentration can't slide from this astounding beauty. I can understand why James and Frank and all the others turned around when they found it, why they covered up the hole and didn't tell anyone where it was. After seeing the damage to Hansen Cave, how could they not?

So, I agree, and yet they still chose to come down here and see it for themselves—just like I have chosen to enter now. We're all risking the destruction of the cave so we can have this moment of infinite beauty. I wonder if it's worth it.

~

In a short email to be sent to my father, I wrote *I want to come home.*

My mouse hovered over the SEND button.

I'd been in Switzerland for over a week, and I still lived in a haze of spiritual dissonance—this inability to connect to God, to my new companion, to the very religion I was out there to preach. There was something inside me, a pressure in my stomach. I had been throwing up every day, but I couldn't figure out why. This was supposed to all get easier if I jumped into the work. And I had jumped, so what was I doing wrong? I'd only masturbated once since coming to Switzerland. On the fourth morning. In the shower of our tiny one-bedroom apartment. And I'd repented for it afterward. Best I could anyway. I knelt on the ground outside the shower and cried on the bathroom tiles. I'd cried and apologized and resolved to be better. I just needed time to sort through everything. I just didn't have time. And I needed time. I needed a break. But it felt so weak to need it.

My older brother had been serving in Germany for a year at that point, and he seemed to be doing fine. My father had been on a mission when he was my age, and he was sent to Japan. I knew his was harder. Farther away. How was I supposed to tell him I wanted out? He had been strong enough to stay, even after getting appendicitis while there. I felt ashamed for wanting to go home.

But he was my dad. I needed guidance.

So, I sent the email, and it only took a few minutes to receive his response.

What's happening? Why do you feel you need to come home?

I feel sick all the time, I told him. *I can't do this.*

You're wrong, Andrew. I know you can do this. I know it's hard, but it'll get easier, I promise.

I kicked my foot against the ground, my stomach pulsing. I scrunched up my eyes as if I could black out the world and come up with the words to tell him that, no, it wouldn't get easier. That I couldn't just keep try-ing. That I'd reached a dead end in the cavern of my spirit.

I don't know how, I typed. *I just need some time to figure all this out.*

There was a pause, and I imagined my dad carefully picking his words. I wondered if he was in his office, at home in Utah, over 5,000 miles away from me. I could almost see him there, leaning back, his hands clasped across his stomach, poised in the way he always was before he'd say something from deep within.

You can come home, Andrew, his message said. *It won't be easy. And I'd hate for you to look back and regret giving up too soon. But you can come home. It's your choice. We will love you no matter what.*

I stared at his words, slipping the lime green tie he'd sent me my first week in the MTC through my fingers. I imagined light tears sliding down his cheeks and into his beard. I knew he wanted to understand my pain. I knew he wanted what was best for me. I wanted to tell him I didn't know what was best, that I didn't know if I believed in God, that I had drowned my body with pain and self-hatred, buried it deep beneath the mountain of denial I'd spent my whole life building.

Instead, I said, *I love you too. I'll keep trying.*

Cars sped by the sidewalk beside the internet cafe, sending gray slush across Elder Jackson's and my shoes. The busy street rang with German words I didn't understand, and the emptiness inside me grew.

Without meaning to, I wondered how bad it might hurt to step off the curb into traffic. I wondered if it would hurt me enough to send me home. If it could, at least then I could pretend it wasn't my choice to break.

~

On the cover of my childhood book about Hurricane Andrew, there's a bearded man holding a small Chihuahua. He looks over a vast wasteland covered in the broken shards of his life. The trailer park now resembles nothing like a home, and I recall, when I was young, I studied this photo more than any other. I'm not entirely certain as to why. It was as if I could feel his pain. Or maybe I wanted to feel his pain, like I could somehow understand what it was like to be that broken.

Now, all these years later, while I can still see a sadness in his eyes, I can see something more. Something like strength. Maybe more like hope.

I try to imagine what that world must have been like a week earlier. The bustling neighborhoods of Southern Miami. The masses going about their day as if it were any other, unknowing of what power neared them—what insurmountable terror headed their way. They could not know what pain they were about to experience. If it could have been anticipated, maybe they would have avoided the storm.

Though I suppose there's an obvious answer to that question: of course they would have avoided it. When a hurricane reaches Category 5, it creates winds greater than 155 miles per hour. It can raise the height of the ocean by over thirty feet. It can destroy cities, topple landmarks. It can kill. Of course people would avoid such a thing.

And yet, as I flip through pictures of Hurricane Andrew's aftermath, I find several that show survivors helping each other. A girl handing out bags of potato chips. An army doctor holding the hands of an older woman, smiling down at her. Children playing together in ruins that were once their homes. A small girl wrapping her arms around another—perhaps strangers—brought together through strife. United because of the storm.

~

"I'm starting to think about hurting myself," I told President Miles. He sat behind a wide old mahogany desk. Scattered across the surface stood little trinkets: a set of crystal birds, a few picture frames turned away from me, old and worn-out scriptures.

"Hurting yourself, how?" His eyes regarded me softly.

"Stepping in front of a car. Not to die, just to injure myself." I peered down, shifting my feet around the legs of my chair.

"Why would you want to hurt yourself?"

"I just need a second to figure things out," I told him. "I need a break. I need to go home. I don't know why I'm here."

"Things sort themselves out when you dive into the work," he told me as if the answer were simple. As if I should have figured it out for myself. Or maybe he just wanted to help in the only way he knew how. "You'll feel better once you do," he said.

I was three months into my mission—three months out of the two years I would be spending away from home. I wasn't even a quarter of the way through, and I had no idea how to make it through the rest. Things hadn't gotten better. The urge to hurt myself had only grown since that first week. I'd finally summoned enough courage to call President Miles about it.

Now, he sat there, his brow furrowed in concentration. "How about you stay at the mission home for a week," he said. "You can ponder on all of this and see how you feel then. Maybe that will give you the time you need. I really feel like you want to be here."

Not knowing how else to respond, I agreed. After our conversation, I spent days reading scriptures and studying doctrines. I sat for hours in a white-walled study with two other missionaries, silently reaching deep within to find what was wrong with me.

With a yellow highlighter, I marked every word Jesus Christ spoke in the Bible, though I didn't know what I was searching for. Maybe some sort of answer as to why I couldn't just *be happy* or maybe a phrase that would tell me what to do next. Maybe just a shred of proof that could tell me I was doing the right thing. I read through the entire book, and I was left feeling more hopeless than before—doubt caving in on me as I desperately tried to keep my head above the stones. But I was getting buried alive.

A week later, President Miles called me into his office again, and after a vague conversation filled with me stating multiple times, *I don't know, I don't know, I don't know,* President Miles shook his head and said, "What is this really about, Elder?"

I paused. Hesitated. Chewed on my lip because I knew what I needed to say to force his hand. But I was terrified of the manifestation, afraid that if I pried the admission out from deep within my stomach, I'd never be able to swallow it down again.

"I'm having homosexual feelings," I whispered.

He blinked. Swallowed. "What kind of feelings?"

"I'm attracted to men."

"And when did you start having these feelings?"

"Since as long as I can remember."

He stared at me, carved through me. I wonder if, like me, he was trying to recognize a piece still fit for God—a piece that may have been buried deep, a piece I had been struggling to unearth for so long.

"As I said before," he said, though softer this time, "I think you should stay. I think you can work through this."

He paused again.

"But if you really think you need to go home, I will send you back. It's your choice. You get to choose."

⁓

Deep within Mount Timpanogos, we enter a cavern larger than any we've seen so far: "The Big Room," Other Andrew says.

There are steps carved into the stone ground that open up like an amphitheater. Other Andrew points out various colors along the walls, something like Father Time's Jewel Box on a larger scale.

"It's so beautiful," I say to Jed, lifting my camera.

"Let me do that," he says with a smile. "You just look."

I squeeze his hand and walk to the wall. There are orange splatters where rust has grown and yellow aragonite spikes in icy crystals on the right wall. Jed points to more tiny gems sticking out from the ceiling. More crystals. More long processes of creation.

I still want to drink in more when Other Andrew calls us back down the steps to yet another iron door. When our small group stops, Other Andrew announces, "Okay guys, this is my favorite part of the tour." He tells us to turn off all our phones and cameras and anything that makes light because "We're going to do a little experiment called Total Darkness."

My stomach catches. Other Andrew walks over to a small red button. I move a little closer to Jed, and he takes my hand. I don't want Other Andrew to do it. I've always been afraid of the dark. But some secret, strange, surprising piece of me feels excited too.

"Help me count down!" Other Andrew says, though I don't make a sound as I prepare myself for the oncoming darkness, for the emptiness of space.

⁓

After a Category 5 Hurricane passes, there is not much left behind. The storm has stripped the world of everything material, everything recognizable. Houses are gone. Windows are shattered. Trees are broken. There is nothing left for the people who have survived. They're alive. They made it through. The storm did not beat them.

Some stay. Some move away, leaving the remnants of homes they once loved and cherished. They relocate to somewhere less painful, maybe somewhere easier, somewhere that hasn't been destroyed. And for those who stay—they rebuild. They dig into whatever solid ground is left and piece their lives back together. Things will never be the same. What was once their home is now gone, but maybe what they are building can be even better. Those who leave, those who stay—I think they're all just hoping for something better.

In the photographs of an Andrew-decimated Florida, I can't help but wonder how something new could have ever been erected there. In a wasteland of broken wood and trees and lives, I can't imagine how any beauty can be remade—how anything can last. And yet, with every picture of that hopelessness I find, I see another picture showcasing the immortality of human strength.

In an interview, a survivor of Hurricane Andrew, Pat Warren, stated, "It changed me completely. I'm not the same person. There has been a pre-Andrew, and now there is a post-Andrew . . . I never expected anything like that."

~

So I made the choice. I told President Miles to send me back. He booked a flight home, and within a week, I started therapy at the LDS Family Services: Missionary Department. I had a hope that maybe, once I figured out all my issues, I could go back out into the mission field. I wanted it to be true. I hoped, with time, I could find space for God inside me and could return to do his work.

Believe me. I wanted to believe.

I always wanted to believe.

Then, there came a day, three months after returning home from Germany, that my psychiatrist leaned over from his chair beside the desk—a desk placed against the wall so there was nothing between him and me but pure and empty space.

His eyes were soft and steady when he asked, "Andrew, there's something I need to ask you because the answer may give us all the answers we've been searching for." He paused. "Why do you hate yourself?"

"What?" I said. I shook my head. "I—I don't hate myself."

"Yes, you do," he whispered. "Why do you hate yourself?"

I had no answer for him, but over the course of the following week, his question never left me, a quiet voice ringing in my ears. *Why do you hate yourself? Why do you hate yourself? Why do you hate yourself?*

The truth was, I knew I hated myself. I hated myself for coming home early from my mission—for giving up when it seemed like everyone else could do it. I hated that I doubted God, that I didn't believe as strongly as I once did. I hated that I told my mission president I was gay. More than anything else, I hated that I was so goddamned weak and afraid.

At two in the morning, some days after I was asked that question, I sat on my bed, surfing Facebook to distract myself. My eyes lingered over a video titled "It Gets Better at Brigham Young University." Having no idea what it meant, I clicked PLAY.

Stories appeared before me. Students my age at BYU. Students who were gay, who were trans, who were bisexual, who were allies. They told me their stories from the other side of the screen—childhood curiosity, growing up in a religion that wouldn't talk about it, returning home from missions for the same reasons I did. As I watched and listened in the confines of my dark bedroom, I began to cry. My breathing came quick and hard. The screen of my laptop vibrated on my shaking knees. My stomach twisted, and I slammed my computer shut.

I ran to the bathroom and threw the door closed. I collapsed in front of the toilet, my knees cracking against the checkerboard tile. I retched. Tears streamed down my eyes, and I coughed on the foul taste searing my tongue. I shivered so violently that I slipped from the sides of the toilet and fell to the ground. I dry-heaved a few more times before finding enough strength to stand and face the mirror.

The glass, plastered with toothpaste and dried drops of water, showed a boy looking back at me—a foreign, puffy-eyed stranger, lost and scared. I shook my head, attempting to rid my thoughts from poisonous suspicions snaking their way in. It couldn't be. I wouldn't. It wouldn't happen to me. I refused to accept it.

"You're . . ." this other Andrew spoke to me, but his voice faltered from the first word. I begged him to stop. God would not tolerate it. It was not okay.

It was not okay.

I pressed my palms into the counter, felt the surface on my skin as I heaved shallow breaths. My therapist had been right. I hated myself. Of course I hated myself. I'd hated myself from the day I started loving men. A burning built within me, and all the chaos made sense. The storm that had surged through my life had an origin I had chosen not to see.

And quite suddenly, somehow, in a way I would never find the words to explain, the tears didn't feel so painful anymore; they didn't feel so hard. They still dripped from my eyes, but something deep within me had opened. With every sob, my body drained of what had been there before. All the hatred, all the anger, all the knowledge I believed I had about God and Heaven and Hell and myself seeped from my body, creating space. And I found myself smiling. There, in the darkness of the bathroom, a newness opened up within me—a pure emptiness ready to be filled.

I looked back to my reflection, to the boy who stood there—so afraid, so angry, so ready to be freed—and words crept from my throat—the ones I had been trying to bury for so long:

"I'm gay."

~

The darkness in the cave is extraordinary, like nothing I could have ever imagined. Where I thought terror would arise, I find instead comfort, deep inside. Warmth where I had expected cold. Joy in the emptiness surrounding me.

"This is total darkness," Other Andrew tells us, his voice ringing from somewhere I could not see. "And this is one of three places in the world where we can see it. The first is deep inside a cave. Second is the bottom of the ocean. And finally, space."

My eyes can't adjust like I thought they might. Instead, they just feel more relaxed. I want to laugh because I suddenly realize how focusing on the world around me in the light makes my eyes tired. I don't have to try here. In Total Darkness, it's like I'm floating in a sea of shadow, my breath moving even and long.

"Carefully, wave one hand in front of your face," Other Andrew instructs. "Can anyone follow their hand back and forth?"

I try. My eyes move where my hand goes, but it takes me a moment to realize that I don't actually see anything. I can't observe myself here.

The youngest one in our party says he can, but Other Andrew kindly explains, "Actually, we believe we can see ourselves, but we really can't."

I can't help but wonder if I ever had.

⌒

Another survivor of Hurricane Andrew, La Wanda Scott, once said, "I say it hasn't affected me, when in actuality it has devastated me . . . I keep trying to escape, trying to run away. But I can't. It's everywhere. Everyone is trying to hide [their feelings]. But we can only wear a mask for so long. Our true faces will soon be revealed."

⌒

The end of the tour comes far sooner than I hoped. Something about being down in the caves feels eternal. Beautiful. Infinite. And I don't want to leave.

At the end of the tunnel, we find a giant wooden door leading back to the mountainside. As we near it, Other Andrew points up to the right. There's a hole there, big enough to slide through, covered by bars. "That's where James Gough and Frank Johnson originally found the cave. They slid down that hole there."

Jed waits by the door, and I take a picture of the place where it all began. I feel gratitude for the protection of the cave here—that the destruction of Hansen did not befall this one. I capture the moment and move on, and Other Andrew quietly shuts the door behind me.

I think I understand it now: one cave was protected solely because another was destroyed; the beauty and life of one thing is intrinsically tied to the end of another. And maybe a life such as this can be worth the risk, the damage we face. Maybe I can just be happy to have survived, to have been seen, to feel this utterly beautiful, basking in the rich light of a late-morning sun.

If I can open wide my spirit, I might find I can hold it all.

END ACT I

A Wolf Boy Interlude

LET'S IMAGINE WHAT THIS IS—by which I mean, a musical.

The actors have taken their place on stage. You've seen them deliver their stories, embodying sights and sounds and movement and life. I've tried to show you the stakes, what the narrator's life looked like, and more important, how it all came apart. But if the function of a musical is to tell a story, and the function of a story is to tell the truth—I think I'm failing at this. There are so many bits I can't know, and I don't know how to give you the complete story when there's still so much I haven't understood. I'm piecing fragments together in some possibly vain hope that they'll make sense.

Have you seen the pattern yet? The narrative is changing now.

We are coming upon the second act.

Here, you might expect some rising action, some complications in the narrative. I'm supposed to craft a narrator who makes mistakes, and the narrator must make mistakes. This is part of the formula: an obstacle, a twist, a disaster, and a crisis. The narrative gets twisted and warped and complex—I'm supposed to tie myself in knots so by Act III, you won't be sure if I'll be able to make it out alive.

This is what we expect to come next.

⁓

In tenth grade, I was cast in *Into the Woods*. In twelfth grade, I was cast as a wolf in the ballet of *The King and I*. The spring semester before, I was cast in a one-act play put on by the senior theater students, *Criminal Mock Trial of Three Little Pigs versus B.B. Wolf.* They gave me the part of "Second Little Pig," one of three brothers prosecuting the Big Bad Wolf for blowing their houses down. It didn't take long for the audience to learn that the wolf has never eaten a pig. He's the victim. But the Three Little Pigs—they're villains. They eat wolves all the time. My lines as Pig #2 were to admit that if he'd fallen into my boiling pot, I'd have eaten him in a second.

The audience laughed at my confession, and when the wolf's attorney asked me if I believed some wolves could be good, I would determinately say no. I had been warned by my parents that I'd be eaten if I got too close.

∿

I moved to Columbus, Ohio in 2021. It was soon after that Terrence and I started watching *The Real Housewives of Salt Lake City*. The Bravo television program was one of eleven series that documented the personal and professional lives of wealthy women living within a specific region or city. The cast of Salt Lake City's show consisted of six women, including a current-Mormon (Lisa Barlow), a post-Mormon (Whitney Rose), and a sort-of-Mormon (Heather Gay). As you can imagine, the tensions created between these three made for some good TV—but for Terrence and me, it prompted discussions I had never thought to have with him. "Is that true?" became Terrence's most common refrain:

Is it true that Mormons believe in a tiered Heaven?

Yep. Celestial, Terrestrial, Telestial, and Outer Darkness.

And someone who left after making those temple promises—they're placed in Outer Darkness?

Yes.

And that's worse than the Telestial where people like Hitler and Dahmer go?

That's what they say.

And they think Jesus came to the US after he came back to life?

Yeah.

And you can't have coffee?

Yep.

And you get your own planet if you're a good enough Mormon?

Kind of? It's really complicated.

Well, shit.

∿

The first werewolf I remember reading about was in *Harry Potter and the Prisoner of Azkaban*, which might explain why the idea of werewolves has never scared me. In the book, Remus Lupin comes to teach Defense Against the Dark Arts at Hogwarts, all while keeping his werewolf condition a secret from the students. He quickly became my favorite character: a powerful wizard, a smart teacher, a kind mentor. He even taught Harry how to magically defend against dementors—phantom creatures who magically drain happiness from their victims. The fact that he was a werewolf seemed secondary to me. If anything, I felt pity for him. He didn't choose to become a werewolf. And that monster that he turned into—it was one Lupin could not control. It wasn't actually him. He wasn't the monster. The beast came out at night.

～

When I was a kid, I had this recurring nightmare; it would start in a stained-glass church with floor-to-ceiling windows. An angry pig, clothed in blue overalls and standing on two feet like a cartoon character, would break through the doors and chase me out onto a mountain trail. I would sprint up through the woods and up a canyon until I reached a dead end, and a chest at the end of the trail. I climbed in and shut the lid.

But the pig would always find me. He would laugh in a manic way, reach down, and pull me from my hiding place. He would lick his lips and open his mouth and pull me toward his teeth, but before he could take a bite, a giant wolf would appear behind him, grab the pig, lift him up. The pig would squeal and scream for help. His eyes would always meet mine. He would plead for a savior, and I wanted to be one. But I couldn't ever move; my body froze inside the chest.

Grinning wide, the wolf took a bite. The pig became bacon. I screamed. The chest closed. I woke up in the dark.

～

Before my mission to Germany and Switzerland, I attended my first year of college in southern Utah. And after Dhane turned most of my high school friends against me, I couldn't wait to release myself from them all—by which I mean, I moved hours away. But college didn't bring the freedom I expected, the freedom I craved. I was still closeted. Still Mormon. Still with undiagnosed bipolar, depression, anxiety, and ADHD. Still howling for God to purge my soul from those cravings infecting my body. I prayed and still heard nothing. I screamed and still heard nothing. I wept alone at midnight in the lobbies of my dorms.

There's a silence that presses into a moment like this—a quiet kind of suffocation. And when a decade of conformity to my religion couldn't cure me from craving the touch of another man—when my lifetime allotment of sins rose with every persisting gay thought, every desire, every wanting, ravaging, carnal hunger, I crept to an overpass ready to jump. I howled for a savior, wailed against the midnight stillness while racing headlights passed far below.

What could I do when the sin of living outweighed that of taking my own life? What if I was no longer alive enough to be saved? I just wanted to be carved out. I'd only ever been alone.

But there's this version of Little Red Riding Hood I know—the one where she isn't rescued. No axe man or hunter or woodcutter comes. The unnamed girl meets the wolf on the trail and plays a game to race on different paths home. The wolf arrives first, gobbles up the grandmother, then gobbles up Little Red too, of course.

And they die.

They have to die. Death creates the moral of this story: people who make mistakes don't get to be saved. It's the tale told to children so they won't wander. It's told as a warning. As if she deserved it. As if she had any choice. As if she could ignore the inevitability of the tale we wove around her. After all, why should she be saved? It's a better story, isn't it? It's a more chilling tale to tell.

And when I stepped back from the edge of a bridge, I don't think it was courage, but because I was afraid: of disappointing my family, of what might come next, of becoming just another story, another warning, nothing more than another moral that parents tell their children at night so they know not to wander off.

～

When I think about Skoll and Hati, fated to swallow our skies, I also think of their father, Fenrir, most famous of Norse wolves, who will one day gobble up the earth. When he breaks from his chains, when he stops roaring in pain, he will press his lower jaw against the earth, raise his upper teeth to the sky, and then he will run. He will run and chase and devour the world as our sun and moon grow dark. I think of these wolves, and I'm not afraid. I want to know how they grow to be this strong.

I know of another story, the one about the she-wolf who sheltered Romulus and Remus, two human twins. When the children were abandoned by order of the king, she found them, cared for them in her den, let them go when a shepherd found them. The story ends with an overthrown kingdom and the twins' founding of Rome. And though the she-wolf fell into legend, she is remembered as a mother who protects.

I want these stories to be about me, tales that could teach me how to be brave. And when I told my teacher that I felt bad for the wolf who is bound till the end of the world, she told me it made sense; *we are too often cruel to those who are different.*

I close my eyes, listening. I can almost hear his howling: a beast with teeth pried open, pleading, screaming to be set free.

～

Once upon a time, in Pike Place Market, I found a man selling little statues carved from the hardened ash of Mount St. Helens. Hundreds of unique carvings: penguins and lions and trees and children. I decided to buy one to remember my first trip to Seattle, and it didn't take long to decide which one I wanted. I handed the man a twenty and watched him wrap the gray and black carving in bubble wrap and butcher paper: two wolves, muzzles up and bellowing, one younger, one older—as if one might be teaching the other to howl.

Act II

What did it feel like to not have to think about your every
move, to not be scrutinized for everything you did, to not
have to lie every day?

　—*Boy Erased*, Garrard Conley

The last time I conversed
with the Great Sentience,
I asked, *What the hell
are you doing?* and
He gestured at some
cobwebs.

　—Annah Browning, *Witch Doctrine*

Showerhead Reflections

When I was sixteen, I attended a two-day missionary training camp held at the Camp Williams Military Reserve in Bluffdale, Utah. A military base might seem a strange place to hold a religious camp, and it probably is, but it made sense to me. The excursion was called "Camp Helaman," and, if you remember, the Army of Helaman consisted of those two thousand stripling warriors who fought to defend their homes. God protected them because of their righteousness, so they all made it back alive. As missionaries, we were supposed to be like them: warriors and defenders of righteousness.

So, in the blazing summer of 2009, I woke up on a hard military bunk bed, my skin sticky, my sweat-soaked clothes clinging to my body. While most of the other boys had stripped down to their gym shorts or boxers the night before, I had pulled on my sweats instead—thick cotton pants and a T-shirt. I did this while the others laughed with each other, wrestled each other, clasped their arms around each other's necks, ground their knuckles across others' heads, skin touching skin. I made sure to cover up, to shield myself from their eyes.

It felt wrong to be seen so naked. I learned in church to show as little skin as possible, a belief so ingrained, I judged the rest as close to sinners. I thought, or rather, I hoped, somehow, I was closer to God because I hid my body, righteous spirituality contingent on wearing a shirt to bed. And by morning, I was sweating. My blankets lay crumpled on the floor. I must have pushed them off in the night, in an effort, I assume, to let my skin breathe.

As the other boys groaned and yawned, I gathered the blankets from the floor and threw them back over myself, held them up to my chin, turned over and closed my eyes. I figured I'd let the other boys shower first, let them rinse the sweat from their own bodies before clothing themselves for the day. And it didn't take long. As I pretended to sleep, I heard them laugh and joke and complain as they got out of bed and went to the communal showers, joining each other under the taps.

To make sure I didn't look, I tightened my eyelids and thought about how I could never do the same. The gym at school had communal showers too, and I made sure to never go there either. At the swimming pool, I changed in the bathroom stalls, showered with my swimming suit on, averted my eyes and hurried away whenever I heard someone enter. I could never allow myself to be bare with another man. I knew what cravings ached within me. I knew that to want another man was sinful. I was terrified my body would betray me, terrified of what might rise in the moment where my eyes met skin, where the barriers between two bodies suddenly disappeared.

So, I pretended to sleep instead, pretended to wake slowly as they re-entered the room, waved away my friends when they said they'd wait for me before going to breakfast. I told them to go without me. I'd catch up.

When I thought all the boys had left, I walked to the showers and turned off the lights. In the shadowed room, tall spires stuck up from the floor like spears. Each was topped with five small shower heads pointing in different directions. I slipped against the cold, wet tiles as I moved to the nozzle in the darkest corner. That way, just in case anyone came back, I could try to hide behind the thin silver spire. It wouldn't cover much, but maybe enough.

I hung my towel nearby, removed my shirt, dropped my shorts, but paused on my underwear. I knew I needed to remove them, to clean myself. The stench of my own sweat was overpowering. Our first day of missionary training the day before had mostly included traversing the military obstacle courses. Our leaders told us we needed to learn teamwork. We'd be placed in two-person companionships throughout our two years in the mission-field. We would need to work together in order to convert others to the religion, just like we would need to overcome the obstacles in the courses together.

Yet, as much as I was afraid of a two-year mission in some foreign place, I enjoyed the courses. Most stood above deep pools of water in case we fell. We scaled walls, crossed thin beams, crawled through pipeline tunnels, swung from rings and trapezes like monkeys. The summer heat had seared my skin as I stumbled, slipped, and careened into the pools below, laughing with my friends. It felt less like an obstacle, more like a game.

Today wouldn't feel that way. It was supposed to be a more spiritual day. We'd be dressed in our pristine white shirts, ironed slacks, and formal ties. In small groups, we'd bear our testimonies of the gospel and God. We'd read *Preach My Gospel*, the missionary handbook. We'd learn the lessons we'd one day teach to others. This was the more important day, and I needed to be clean.

Beneath the showers, I slipped my thumbs between my hips and the elastic rim of my underwear but hesitated again. Senses perked, I glanced around the room, the quiet space stretching before me. Nothing stirred. Nothing made a sound. Echoing silence. I took a breath and slipped off my underwear, hanging them with the rest of my clothes.

The water came out cool, graveling my skin as I quickly scrubbed shampoo through my hair. The other boys must have used all the hot water, but I didn't plan to stay long anyway. Just enough to cleanse the sweat. I rinsed my head beneath the waterfall, lifting my face into the spray, imagining it was rain because I always loved the rain, loved the way it needled so lightly. I could almost pretend I wasn't at the base anymore. I could almost pretend I wasn't afraid.

Another knob squealed as it turned, followed by the sound of a second showerhead turning on. My eyes shot open, stinging under the spray of water and lingering soap. I gasped and pressed wet fingers against the lids. Blinking through the pain, I saw him, three spires away from me, near the middle of a room, another boy beneath the taps.

It was Eric. Even with his back turned to me, I easily recognized him: a boy in my school, a top athlete, the son of a rich Bishop in a Ward near mine. And though we were in the same English class, I had never talked to him. I had no obvious reason to do so. I was in choir and theater; he played football. I was in the school musical and on the literary magazine staff; he worked on cars in the auto-shop.

But I had noticed him. I noticed he always seemed to have his arm wrapped around different girls in the school hallway. He fell asleep in our English class. I noticed that, though he was on various sports teams, he was often left on the bench. I noticed he was often quiet and composed. It made him mysterious. Cool. Sexy.

It was in our English class that I first caught myself lingering. It would happen without purpose; when my mind drifted and I leaned on my hand and my head twisted toward him, my eyes would linger on the way his head drooped down to his chest or the way he doodled in his notebook. I noticed. I watched. I smiled. My guts would twist, and I'd realize my mistake. I'd shake my head and look away, eyes drying in the effort to lock my gaze on the teacher. It would only work for so long.

Now, in the showers, just like in class, my body frozen, I found myself wavering and watching and tracing every inch: the muscles across his back, the triangle of his body, the way his spine pressed against the confines of his skin, the hard and soft curves of arms, his legs, his back and neck and tailbone, the way water hit those edges and leapt off like waterfalls.

I shook my head and jumped back behind the spire. Eyes wide, I stared at the floor. Ashamed and scared, I whispered a quick prayer to God asking for forgiveness, pleading for his help, begging him to take this temptation away. I knew I should turn off the shower and run from the room, but I couldn't bring myself to reach for the knob. Instead, I tipped to the right, Eric appearing in my line of sight again. His hands were clasped together around the back of his neck now, his spine arched, his face against the cascading water.

I spun. My breath came sharp and fast. Water slapped my back, and I thought about all those videos I'd seen on the internet: moments just like this—when two men met in the communal showers, eyes locking as they stepped toward each other. Their lips would touch, their bare bodies pressing together under the weight of water.

I also thought of how I would cover my body up with blankets every time after I watched such things. I would force myself to think of how Jesus paid in blood for each sin I committed, how I was also damning myself with every second I allowed my eyes to linger on the bodies of two men holding each other, how close this was to murder in the hierarchy of mankind's worst sins. Mormonism taught me to fear the thought of sex as much as the act itself, so the action of two men being naked together, touching each other, bodies pressing, pressurizing, crashing together like that—it was insurmountable in its evil.

But still, I wanted it. I wanted it so badly. I hungered for that touch. I looked at Eric again and found myself transfixed by the way his body moved. It was the first time I'd ever looked so closely at the naked body of a man in real life. I had never allowed myself to pause. So I stared. I studied. My eyes locked on his waist. He turned around.

My body froze.

My mind numbed.

My eyes stared straight into his.

He looked surprised. Maybe a little confused. And I imagined what might come next. Maybe he'd yell. Maybe he'd hit me. Maybe he'd tell everyone I had watched him in the shower. And still, I couldn't move. I couldn't run. I couldn't do anything but stare into the piercing gaze of another naked boy.

Then, his expression softened, as if he knew he'd caught me in a moment of reckoning. The smallest hint of a smile on his creased lips. He tilted his head in a quick nod before closing his eyes and turning back to the water.

I still couldn't move, an animal with eyes burning against headlights. Tears tickled my cheeks. I listened to the cold crashing water and felt goosebumps rising higher and harder on my skin. And I can't know what he meant by that nod, by his smile, but in a life lived in such fear of being discovered, a life so desperate for approval, I think I was desperate for someone to see me. I think I wanted to share it, this growling, aching secret, to have it be okay. I think I wanted his smile to be an act of understanding—bare, naked compassion—as if he might know what it meant that I had watched him, that maybe we were both at a missionary camp, practicing for a religion in which neither of us fit, that maybe he guessed I had never expressed my fear of homosexuality and its place within me to anyone; how I couldn't accept its place within me either. I wanted to believe he was telling me it was okay to look, to be bare with him.

The spell lifted. I swept up my clothes and sped from the room, my feet slipping against the cold tile. I ran from the showers, around the corner, into the bathroom, closed myself within the stall and wept. My naked body shivered against the hard ceramic toilet. Though I believed my body had betrayed me—still, I felt it, this possibility of normalcy I believed he projected onto me, a care more terrifying than anything I had yet experienced. The feeling rumbled beneath my skin, boiled into my veins. I longed for this freedom to be possible. I wanted it, and I hated myself for wanting it.

Though I never spoke to Eric again, though I didn't understand what the feeling meant, a vibration had begun—within me, within that stall, within the bathroom of a military base in the sticky summer of 2009—a vibration like vocal cords shaking and rubbing and thrumming against one another. There was a sound, deep and dark and quiet, rumbling from the gutter of my throat, ready to be released.

Wolf Act

I MET PETER ON THE SET OF MY sophomore year's fall musical, *Into the Woods*. You've heard this story. At fifteen, acting and singing was the closest I'd ever let myself be to the stereotypical gay man I made up in my head: the boy who dressed fashionably, outrageously, brightly; who hung out in coffee shops and bars; who sang and danced and lived his life loud. In theater, for just a moment, for whatever reason, I was able to put those fears of being "too close to gay" aside. The fact that Peter turned out to be in the musical too—well, that was simply a bonus. He was my first real crush: by which I mean Denzel Washington and Ryan Reynolds didn't really count.

I wasn't alone though. Everyone had a crush on Peter. He was outgoing and adventurous, broad-shouldered and handsome, and able to grow a full beard at seventeen. He was always the first to laugh and the first to offer someone a ride home. He could sing and dance, and he loved to make movies. Just the previous summer, he'd made a short action film where he accidentally stabbed himself in the forearm with a sword. We gathered around him in a huddle to watch him flex his fist, the deep pink scar pulsing in and out of his arm.

On day one of rehearsal, the cast read through the script, circled up in hard blue plastic chairs. I had been given a nameless ensemble role, a role that had never existed in the original Broadway production. I would have no lines and little stage time, but I didn't care. I was simply happy to be granted a place in the circle.

Peter, on the other hand, had been cast as the wolf from Little Red Riding Hood's tale, a sexualized role. I listened to him read lines in a faux-graveled tone and clenched my stomach tight. I squirmed in the uncomfortable chair, my blood raced, my mind pulsed through impossible images of him and me together: his arms holding me, his mouth against my ear, his beard scratching against my face, eyes peering deep into me, voice reaching out in the way he read those animalistic lines— hungry, wanting, ravaging. My eyes teared up. My ribs ached. I crossed my legs.

When the first read-through came to a close, I walked out into the street. Cold autumn rain crashed against my head, dripping through my hair, sticking my clothes to my skin. Home wasn't far and, while I had been offered rides by Peter and others, I decided to walk instead. I felt a need to wash myself clean. I knew I'd done the wrong thing again. I'd thought the wrong thought—a gay thought. Not just in porn. Not just my imagination, but in reality. In my body. Just when I thought I couldn't get any worse, I'd gotten worse. I yearned for control. My heart contracted as I peered up and into the sky, the cold October rain biting my skin. I might have been crying. I can't remember. I wouldn't have been able to tell.

I wondered if the dark clouds above might symbolize the wrath of God. I wondered if lightning would strike my body, sear through my veins, send my spirit out to wherever it would go next. I wondered if I could restart there, or if I wanted to. I looked out to the road where cars sped by in the rain, sending waves crashing over the pavement. I imagined one losing control, swerving, striking me down. I wondered if it would hurt less than this.

That fall passed by in blur, the musical a consistent contradiction of joy and pain, every practice just another moment of craving, another crooked shame for how I lingered, for loving the sound of his voice, loving the way he laughed, loving the way he danced across the stage and held Little Red Riding Hood tight in his arms. I imagined donning her cape and dancing beside him. When I had already become someone nameless on this stage so easily, why couldn't I become her instead?

It was another wrong turn, just more animalistic yearning. I had to get control.

On the opening night of *Into the Woods*, fear and anticipation filled the space of our dressing room. We all plastered makeup on our faces, slipped our costumes over our heads, and attempted a collective breath.

I stared into the mirror at my own made-up face. Eye liner made my hazel eyes pop, my hair was made to be ratted and pasted up. I wiped brown lines across my cheeks like dirt and brightened my lips to a more vibrant pink. My heart beat hard against my chest. There it was, my first show, my first time on a stage that large, my first time being seen by so many people. I was relieved to be costumed for it. Though I yearned to be like the main cast—a character with a name and a voice and my own song—in the ensemble, I could still leave my sins and thoughts and urges behind for a moment and become a different person, someone with enough courage to venture out into the wilds and be changed by the experience.

The door to the dressing room flew open, and Peter barged in. You've heard this part before. How he wore nothing but tight leather pants and dark makeup and a ratted wolf-wig. How he howled and turned and spun his tail in circles. How we all laughed, and it shattered the pre-show nerves.

And as he did these things, I wanted him to look my way, to see me, to smile at me, to raise his hand in hello and notice me. For just a moment, I humored myself, feeling what it would feel like to be with him. To have him come sit beside me, hold my hand, kiss my cheek, wish me good luck, and I'd wish the same for him. I'd lay my head on his shoulder and let out stale air from the bottom of my lungs. I'd feel calm. I'd feel collected. I'd feel whole.

And, while sitting in that chair beside a giant mirror, imagining what it might be like to love, tears etched the crevices of my eyes—a wanting, hungry, howling creature living at the crest of my throat because the imagining made me feel so light. So full. It was different from the sexual fantasies I knew so well. I just wanted to be held by him—like he might love me. But that was impossible. I knew it was impossible. It had to be impossible. He could never love me. And I could never love him. God didn't allow men to love each other like that. Satan could manipulate the flesh, the body, our sexualities, but God was supposed to protect my spirit. I had persuaded myself that I might be attracted to men, but I could never love a man. I understood love and sex to be entirely different things. It was my one desperate lifeline to fight this beast inside. But I was losing. I was starving. And they were calling me to the stage. The musical was about to begin.

Bright lights bore down as I leapt onto the stage during our opening song. I looked out into the crowd and found I couldn't see the audience's faces in the darkness. They sat behind a haze of light, a screen of yellow and white. And I felt liberated. Brave. Strong. And perhaps I was. Perhaps I showed some kind of courage by standing there in front of hundreds of people. Just then, it was enough. Enough to be seen—even partially.

Time passed. The musical ended. Peter went to college, and I remained. After his first semester, he left on his own mission to Cambodia. I went off to my own college, and in my first semester, I wrote to him—to ask him how he was doing, to know if he was okay, to ask if a mission was worth all the fear I had about doing it—and his letter arrived quickly. He was so grateful that I'd written to him. He said that the mission was worth it, no matter how hard it seemed to be. And he said it *was* hard. The hardest thing he'd ever had to do. But he loved it. And he knew I could do it. He had faith in me.

I never wrote him back—too afraid of saying the wrong thing—too afraid of the love I still felt for him. But when he arrived home, I went to hear him speak at his church. He'd been gone for two years, and he'd grown up to be even more handsome than I remembered him being. He hugged me when he saw me, told me how much it meant to him that I was there. Months later, he came to my farewell gathering for my own mission. He gave me a tie he'd bought in Cambodia. He said he hoped it would bring me luck.

What happened next: I left for the MTC and then for Germany. I came back home early. And when I finally accepted the fact that I was gay, I came out with a whimper. At last, to some degree at least, I found myself living. Person by person, I told those I loved of my truth.

Peter and I connected more deeply after my return. He understood how hard it was out in the mission field, and he didn't judge me for coming home early. We told each other tales of our struggles to understand mental illness, our hardships with relationships and friends, how we both nearly dropped out of high school, how following artistic passions wasn't always the easiest route to take. And while my crush never left, I resigned myself to his friendship. I told myself it was enough.

Then, about a year after coming home from my mission, on a night hardly different than any other, I found myself standing in Peter's dark kitchen, holding a half-full glass of water, nauseated from the truth caught deep in the back of my throat. I was gay, but I hadn't told him yet. So, I talked about Mormonism instead, how I'd been considering leaving it behind. He talked about how he'd been feeling the same way.

"I think I've just been afraid," he said.

"Oh, they make you *very* afraid," I said, and we both laughed a little.

He looked into my eyes, and there was something like hurt within them. "I don't really know what I believe about God or religion or any of it," he said, "but I also don't really know how to *not* be Mormon."

I nodded. "Yeah, I get that."

"So why are you wanting to leave?"

"Well," I said quietly. I held his gaze. In many ways, we might've looked like siblings these days: blonde-ish brown hair, five-foot-ten, similar build, hazel eyes. And just like those days back in theater practice, looking into his eyes made my stomach pull up against my ribs.

"What is it?" Peter asked, his voice soft. Kind. Open. "You can tell me, Andrew."

One beat. Another. He cocked his head in a concerned kind of way. One more beat. "Well, I've had a lot of mental health issues," I explained. "Most of my life, really. But it's why I came home early from Switzerland. I needed time to sort myself out. And—well—a lot of that has stemmed from the fact that I . . . well . . ."

I paused.

Here it was: the truth, the words lodged behind my teeth for a decade, the desperate yearning to simply be myself, to be gay and for that to be okay.

"I like guys," I said, the words slipping off my tongue before I could swallow them back down. Speaking them still felt like I was speaking a language I didn't know: awkward, tumbling, jagged against my mouth.

A beat of silence. "You like guys?" Peter repeated.

"Yeah."

He paused, watching me, studying me, my words sinking in.

"Well, wow," he said lightly after some time. "Thanks for telling me, Andrew. I know it must be hard."

I smiled. Cool air swam through my open lungs. "It is," I told him, words now tumbling from my body. "I've been trying to figure out a way to stay Mormon while also being me and loving who I love. But I'm not sure if that's possible. So, yeah, I've been thinking about leaving."

I laughed a little, but Peter swallowed. "Wait," he said, "are you saying you're going to date guys?"

"Well, yeah." I chuckled in an awkward kind of way, as if he had told a joke I didn't quite understand.

"And you're wanting to marry a man someday then?"

"Yes," I said, squinting. Tilting my head. Confused.

"Oh."

A break then. A different kind of pause. I set my glass down on the counter behind me.

"Is that confusing or something?" I asked, a thudding beat in my chest.

"No," he said quickly, shaking his head and looking down. "It's—it's just not what I thought you'd say. Because—well—I mean, I've felt that way before too. Back in high school."

Another break, something shattering in the space between us, and I faltered under the weight of what my childhood had meant to me—and wondered whether his might have meant something similar—wondered if he had looked at someone in the same way that I had once looked at him, whether the beast that had gnawed at my stomach for so many years, the one always screaming to be set free—whether Peter had felt it too.

And I saw a glimpse of a life, some shadow life where we might stand together in front of family, holding hands, wearing tuxes, exchanging rings, walking beneath flower petals thrown by our friends. The opening night of *Into the Woods*, beneath that costume, on that stage, had Peter yearned for someone to see him too? To hold him? If I'd asked him then, would he have said yes?

It didn't really matter, I supposed. That shadow life was gone. But maybe it wasn't lost. What if this could be that moment where a happy-ever-after begins? After all the chaos and hardship and villains and trials, the heroes get to be happy. Maybe here, in a dark dorm kitchen, he and I could finally be free and together and light. It felt so close I could almost taste it, and I contemplated leaning in for a kiss. I wondered how he'd react, if he'd push me away. I still wonder what might have happened if I had. When our lips pressed together and our arms wrapped tightly around each other, I wonder whether he could have found a way to shed the costume he'd donned all those years ago. I wonder if he wanted to.

But Peter swallowed again. "But it's something I just have to push away." He shrugged his shoulders and looked down at his feet, bare on the cold tiles. "I'm going to marry a woman someday."

It took a moment for his words to register in my head. So, he planned to marry a woman. I planned to marry a man. A simple understanding passed between us. We saw different paths to liberation, roads that had already diverged.

"Oh. Gotcha," was all I could muster, and another break separated us. "I should go," I told him, turning away, hiding my face from the dim, dying light above.

"Oh," he whispered. "For sure."

"Thanks for having me over," I told him with sincerity. "Honestly, it's just good to know I'm not the only one who feels this way about Mormonism."

He laughed a little, though it felt forced. "Crazy how far we've come."

And, for just a small moment, we met each other's eyes like a mirror: hazel upon hazel. I couldn't help but notice the way his glistened under the dimming light.

I don't know which of us finally broke contact. I just know that when we did and I walked to the front door, he opened it for me.

"Thanks again," I told him.

"Of course." He opened his arms and hugged me goodbye—as if we could find an answer in the embrace, a voice of reason in the way we both held just a little tighter than I expected us to. A little longer.

And I wonder if, like me, he sought understanding, some definition to make sense of this divergence. I was straying from the path. He continued on. There was no way for us to know where either of us were heading.

That would be the last time we'd see each other for many years, though we'd both go on to leave the Mormon religion. He would get married to a great and beautiful woman, and they'd eventually have a kid together, and each time his wife posted a new picture of their adventures through life, ones where they appear so joyous, so full of light, I would try to forget a quietly uttered truth in the shadows of his kitchen in 2012; the way he looked at me with such sorrow; the way I looked at him the same way; the way we broke from the embrace and he closed the door behind me; how I stepped down the stairway, stopped down on the street below, so open and empty and quiet, releasing my breath beneath the bright, full, moonlit sky.

A Dictionary of the Voiceless

PREFACE

If I could define transformation, or rather, what it means to live in this skin, I could figure out my place in the story. I'm trying to find something in the spaces. I am growing desperate. I search for answers in memories: a definition, a choice, an outcome, anything. I've only ever been a lost boy in the woods. I'll pick wildflowers from the path and pickle the petals, let these questions stew and stew and stew.

I'm still searching for what will make me stop chasing.

Allegory

[**al**-*uh*-gohr-ee] *n.*

1. A symbol.
2. An extended metaphor or tale in which characters, places, and objects in a narrative carry figurative meaning.
    a. "Many believe the tale of Christ is history rather than an <u>allegory</u>."
    b. "Christian, Latter-day Saint children were taught to find meaning in the written words of ancient prophets from the Bible. While some believe the stories to be <u>allegorical</u>, the lessons are often delivered like history."

Ballad

[**bal**-*uhd*] *n.*

1. A popular narrative song passed down orally (e.g., words of prophets rang from the Bible, but LDS children are taught to listen to living prophets too—that the prophets would speak for God).

a. "One LDS boy asked his Sunday School teacher if he could be the prophet someday. The boy had hoped that if he worked hard enough, was righteous enough, he could do it. Then, he'd hear God's voice like them: a <u>ballad</u> from a Heavenly Father. Real."

b. "The boy's teacher cocked her head and smiled. She told him that as long as he held true to his faith, nothing was impossible. He found out later, however, that prophets weren't chosen by highest spirituality, but rather seniority. It was an ancient <u>ballad</u> he must adhere to."

Cacophony

[kuh-**kof**-*uh*-nee] *n.*

1. Harsh or discordant sounds.
2. Dissonance.
   a. "In September 2012, when the boy was older, he prayed deep in the woods near his childhood home while a <u>cacophony</u> of sounds from nature surrounded him. He wanted to believe God could tell him it was okay to be gay instead of the punishment he believed it to be" (see *Negative Capability*).
   b. "Three years later, in November 2015, the Church of Jesus Christ of Latter-Day Saints leadership announced a policy change to their handbook, labeling those in same-sex marriages apostates. It meant being removed from God for eternity. Outer Darkness. To them, to God, the gay boy's existence became dissonant, a <u>cacophony</u> of contradictions. He couldn't be both."

Dada

[**dah**-dah] *n.*

1. A movement in art and literature, started in Switzerland in 1916 at the Cabaret Voltaire. Picking up traction after WWI, this movement salvaged relief from the moral and cultural instability that followed the war. They embraced everything and nothing, dissonance, contradiction, intentional irrationality, and the negation of binary artistic values.
2. A childish word for Father (see *Allegory*).
   a. "Heavenly <u>Father</u>? Are you there?"

Elision

[ih-**lizh**-*uh*n] *n.*

1. The omission of unstressed syllables in order to fit a metrical pattern or scheme (e.g., "I don't know" could become "I dunno" and "I am never going to hear him" could become "I'm ne'er gonna 'ear 'im").
    a. "Growing up in his faith, a boy was taught that God preferred proper diction. He was taught to pray without <u>elisions</u> and contractions, to say thee, thou, and thy instead of you, to tell God what he was grateful for and what he needed help with, to start each prayer with 'Dear Heavenly Father,' and end with 'in the name of Jesus Christ, amen.' He believed that if he did these things, followed this pattern, God would be more willing to hear his words. Then, maybe God would answer."
    b. "At nineteen, before admitting to himself that he was gay, the boy thought he could <u>elide</u> the homosexual piece from his spirit. It would be easier to fit that way. He could shift into a scheme of honest spirituality. Perhaps then, he would hear God's voice."

Futurism

[**fyoo**-ch*uh*-riz-*uh*m] *n.*

1. In 1909, this movement arose in Italy and Russia, calling for a rejection of past forms of expression. In his manifesto, F. T. Marinetti advocated for a language unbound by common syntax.
2. A point of view that finds meaning or fulfillment in the future, rather than the past or present.
    a. "The boy wanted to believe in <u>futurism</u> outside of dissonance, a heaven that could include him. But God hadn't spoken to the boy. He'd spoken to the prophet, and the prophet had named the boy an apostate. The boy was to listen to that man or reject, to straighten or break, to conform or unbind. Accept the prophet as the voice for God or find himself in a space of silence."

Ghazal

[**guh**-zehl] *n.*

1. Originally, in Arabic verse, the ghazal dealt with themes of loss and romantic love. In Persian tradition, however, the form took on an intricate rhyme scheme, meter, and length. The subject matter also turned toward erotic longing and religious belief.

    a. "The boy convinced himself he may have an attraction to men, but he could never love a man. Therefore, he wasn't gay. It was his way of separating love and eroticism. He believed, if he tried, he could push the physical attractions down. Then, God could still love him. <u>Ghazal</u>."

    b. "At sixteen, when the boy fell in love with a boy, he asked his Sunday School teacher what it meant when ideas contradicted each other, when the prophet said one thing and his soul said another. She told him to pray again with a more open heart. If the contradiction remains, stay silent. She explained that he wouldn't want to be seen as a false prophet, speaking in opposition to God's word" (see *Cacophony*).

Hymn

[him] *n.*

1. A poem praising God or the divine, often sung (see *Ballad*).

    a. "The boy didn't write poetry growing up. He figured it was wishy-washy, flowery. Over-emotional. He found it odd, then, that his first publication was a poem—a poem cursing God, no less. It had been written in response to a friend's death by suicide eighty-four days after the policy change on November 5, 2015, the one labeling gay marriage 'apostasy.' The friend, Jack, had been gay too. The boy called his anti-hymn 'Funeral Prayer' and published it in a queer-celebrating journal in Provo, Utah."

2. Something that resembles a song of praise.

Irony

[ahy-*ruh*-nee] *n.*

1. As a literary device, irony implies a distance between what is said and what is meant (see *Cacophony*) (see *Ghazal*).

    a. "The boy might find it ironic to pray to God for answers when he was taught God would only speak to the prophet."

    b. "He might find it ironic that he was asked to proselytize his beliefs when he didn't believe them himself."

    c. "He might find it ironic that he'd been actively working to unify the LGBTQ+ community and the LDS religion when the November policy was released and framed him as an apostate."

    d. "He might find it ironic that he wrote to curse God and, in doing so, found himself."

Juxtaposition

[juhk-st*uh*-p*uh*-**zish**-*uh*n] *n.*

1. The act of placing two or more things side by side in order to contrast them or create an interesting effect (see *Cacophony*) (see *Ghazal*) (see *Irony*).

    a "Dark and Light. Good and Bad. Belief and Denial. Truth and Lies. Eternal Life and Homosexuality. Sin and Natural Order. God and Universe. Broken and Less broken."

    b. "Do you—have you—will you—love(d) yourself yet?"

Kenning

[**ken**-ing] *n.*

1. A figurative compound that takes the place of an ordinary noun (e.g., "ocean" becomes a "whale-road" and a wolf becomes a "beast-of-battle").

    a. "In 2012, at nineteen, the boy stood in front of a mirror and finally accepted the truth that he was gay. The person peering at him through the glass was a stranger. Someone he didn't yet know. He called the broken boy 'you're-gay,' and I became just a little less shattered."

Lament

[l*uh*-**ment**] *n.*

1. Any poem expressing deep grief, usually at the death of a loved one or some other loss.

    a. "What it meant to be shattered. What it felt like to put a piece back together. The lament I wrote to heal" (see *Hymn*).

    b. "I received a Facebook message from a previous seminary teacher a few days after proposing to Jed. She lamented on how she had been heartbroken to hear how lost I'd become. She told me I could repent and still be saved. She claimed I didn't have to be lost."

    c. I wrote back that I'd finally been heard.

Metaphor

[**met**-*uh*-fawr] *n.*

1. A figure of speech in which a comparison is made between two objects without the use of "like" or "as."

a. "In 2015, in my first poetry class at Utah State University, we talked
about metaphor, and the idea confounded me: that I could claim
something is what it isn't. That truth could be that malleable. That a
tree could be anything other than itself—beautiful, tall, graceful,
life-giving. How could I say that the tree is the universe? That the bark
is life, the leaves the stars, the trunk something unattainable, the
waterfall beside it the voice of humanity thundering against the earth.
Would they believe me?"

b. "By looking in a mirror, I became something I wasn't, something I
then was. By breaking, I moved past the like, the as. Maybe I am the
universe now."

Negative Capability

[neg-*uh*-tiv kay-p*uh*-**bil**-i-tee] *n.*

1. A theory first articulated by John Keats about artists' access to truth
without pressure and framework of logic or science, "capable of being in
uncertainties, mysteries, or doubts without any irritable reaching after
fact or reason."

a. "When my first boyfriend broke up with me in 2012, he said it was
because he just didn't love me anymore. I remember, afterward,
driving through a Utah canyon to my parents' house. I called my
sister. She told me it would be okay. She told me I would make it
through this. She told me it didn't matter why he didn't love me
anymore because I was good regardless. But I wanted a reason. I
demanded one. I couldn't stand the mysteries attacking my mind
through the mountainside. I couldn't live in negative capability. I
screamed in the car, howled against the wind flowing in through my
open windows, punched the steering wheel, kicked the door. An
answer may have whispered from the mountainside beside me as I
drove. Maybe it fell from the dusty night. I couldn't hear anything
existing out in the void of space. I wouldn't even hear myself."

Onomatopoeia

[on-*uh*-mah-t*uh*-**pee**-*uh*] *n.*

1. A figure of speech in which the sound of a word imitates its sense (e.g.,
hiss, buzz, pow, Dear Heavenly Father, sizzle).

a. "The framework of prayer called out as I trudged through the forest on a bright Sunday afternoon in 2012, only days after my first boyfriend broke up with me. I'd never been good at prayer. I could imitate the steps I'd been taught since birth, but I never heard any voice but my own. I wondered if maybe that's just what prayer was—a one-sided conversation. But on that morning, I needed to hear something. I needed to speak and believe I could be listened to. Answered. That maybe if I stood out in the forest on a bright morning, I'd see God appear in the light and hear his voice. I yearned to know he still loved me. That his mouth existed at all."

b. I wonder if this is all just an imitation.

Pastiche

[pa-**steesh**] *n.*

1. A patchwork of lines or passages from another writer intended as a kind of imitation.

2. An original composition that mimics the style of another author, usually in a spirit of respect rather than mockery or satire.

3. Words fractured against my teeth. I called out to the trees, the forest, the river, the waterfall crashing over pebbled rocks beside me. Enveloped in nature, I called to someone I believed could be greater. I sought a God. A Heavenly Father. For anyone to appear and answer how I could be gay. How I could have found happiness with another man. How that happiness could have been stripped away so easily with the simple words: *I don't love you anymore.* I screamed to the heavens, gnashed my teeth and begged for retaliation. For guidance. For anything. Water broke beside the trees. The universe was utterly awake.

Quatrain

[**kwo**-treyn] *n.*

1. The first week of study for my master's degree, I attended a poetry masterclass at the university. The visiting poet advised all of us listening to write more quatrains, 4-line rhyming stanzas. He claimed that learning to write short pieces could help with brevity, cutting away that which was unnecessary. He advised me to break out of my comfort zone, to lose my voice. He said to never make myself comfortable.

2. In an act of defiance, I wrote three quatrains on how abandoning god
   and finding my voice in writing had been a heroic act of declaration—
   that the poet's claim didn't feel right.
3. Still, I wonder if, to him, losing voice could kindle an act of inspiration.
4. At the same time, I wonder if finding mine ignited this awakening.

Refrain

[ri-**freyn**] *n.*

1. A phrase, word, or line repeated within a poem, usually at the end of a
   stanza.
2. In 2011, when I returned home after only six months into a two-year
   proselytizing mission for the LDS church, I was advised to go to therapy.
   I was immediately diagnosed with Bipolar Disorder, Major Depressive
   Disorder, Generalized Anxiety Disorder, and ADHD, and when I told my
   psychiatrist I'd been having suicidal thoughts, he told me that hearing
   my own voice mattered more than any other. He instructed me to write
   these words over and over again and to never stop believing them:

I survived.

I survived.

I will always survive.

3. To stop oneself from doing something.

Sublime

[s*uh*-**blahym**] *n.*

1. A term identified by the poet Edmund Burke in 1757 as an experience
   of the infinite, something terrifying and thrilling because it threatens to
   overpower the perceived importance of human creation in the universe.
2. Many writers throughout history have believed that to experience something like the Sublime, one must traverse through the wild, mysterious
   expanses of the natural world.
3. I wanted this to be true; that when god slipped away and I listened to the
   universe instead, I could find the answers; that maybe if I disappeared
   into the wild like them, I'd discover truth. I'd find a voice there in the
   confines of the earth.

Transcendentalism

[tran-sen-**den**-tl-iz-*uhm*] *n.*

1. A strain of Romanticism. As described by Ralph Waldo Emerson in his 1836 manifesto, *Nature*, the natural and material world exist together, and we use subjective experiences from these spaces to reveal universal meaning to a person's soul.

2. Five years after coming out as gay, two years after the policy change in 2015, two years after losing belief in the god I understood, I toured the Timpanogos Cave in Utah. In the deepest part of the cave, our tour guide turned off the lights. We were plunged into darkness. And, where I believed fear would strike me in the shadows of the earth, I instead found peace. I found an anti-separation, a soulful place to reside. Somehow, in a place farthest from sky and light and everything else I believed to be the most spiritual, I rose.

Ubi Sunt

[**oo**-bee soont] *n.*

1. Used to begin a number of Medieval European poems, a Latin phrase meaning "Where are they?"

2. The unbridled darkness of Timpanogos Cave held me. In silence, I stood. When everything else dropped away and there was only me, I could hear my heartbeat thudding against my chest, the muscles stretching as my hands contracted into fists. I breathed in. I breathed out. I might have been standing alone. There may have been a thousand people around me. Perhaps, for the first time, it didn't matter. I found a voice inside; I could hear myself living.

3. Where is God now? Where is Jack now? Where did Andrew go? What happened to that unbroken-boy? Perhaps he was never truly unbroken (see *Sublime*) (see *Pastiche*) (see *Hymn*) (hear him).

Volta

[**vohl**-t*uh*] *n.*

1. Italian for "turn."

2. In a sonnet, the volta is the turn of thought or argument.

3. I walked out of Timpanogos Cave, back into the light and air of the mountainside, the experience of darkness and nature drifting away from

me. Pulling a tattered notebook from my bag, I sat on a bench by the cliffside and wrote every feeling, every memory, every breath. And so unlike the years before when I walked into the woods screaming for god, and even unlike a search for an outside voice, I listened to the universe, the sublime, the natural.

And I transcended them all.

Wyrd

[veerd] *n.*

1. An Anglo-Saxon term often translated as "fate" in Old English poetry. But it is different from fate as I previously understood it. Fate implies an inevitability of the future. Wyrd implies an inevitability of the past, and therefore we are pushed into the construction of our own future.
2. A possibility that my future doesn't have to be fixed. The past cannot be altered, but the present is pliant, the future soft. There's a belief that I can step from the mouth of this cavern and remain static, or I can breathe myself in with the universe—something so vastly eternal—and craft my veins into the earth with ink.

Xinshi Pai

[**shin**-shih **p'ai**] *n.*

1. A nineteenth-century poetic movement initiated by Huang Zunxian. Because I loved this form of "New Poetry," I ascended into Huang's words: "I cannot be bound by the ancients."
2. I cannot be bound by the ancients.
3. I cannot be bound by the ancients.
   I refuse to be bound.

You

[yoo] *n.*

Pronoun for second person, plural or singular.
In writing, using "you" causes the reader to become the central character within a story. You becomes one with I. All become you. You become me.
In #46 of Walt Whitman's "Song of Myself," he claims:

no one can travel that road for you.
You must travel it for yourself.
It is not far. It is within reach.

And when I held open my notebook at the top of Timpanogos Mountain, deep in the Utah canyons, I walked to the edge of the cliff and looked down. The earth miles below: rocks, rivers, gravel, insects, grass, trees. Up above, in the bulk of eternity, a sky with wild stars sleeping in sunlight. Within hours, they'd wake with the moon and construct their galaxies on the canvas of the universe. But it was just me there.

So, I smiled, and I screamed. My voice rebounded in echoes across the mountainside, my spirit dancing in the zenith of cosmos and sound and being. I would have asked what road I'm traveling—if I was moving toward the universe. Or god. The sublime. Jack. You. Everything.

Or, for the first time, if all that was left was me.

The Magic Kingdom

PART 1, FORCED PERSPECTIVE

Isn't that what we all desire: to be the heroes and heroines of our own stories; to triumph over adversity; to experience life in all its beauty; and, in the end, live happily ever after?

—DIETER F. UCHTDORF, Second Counselor in the First
Presidency of The Church of Jesus Christ of Latter-day Saints

I'M UNSURE ABOUT SO MANY THINGS, and when it comes to the story of my marriage, I never know where to begin. I want it all to be simple—some equation I can follow—guidelines for how to be a good husband, where I could mathematically, scientifically, input the numbers and have my answers. But stories of love and lust and rebellion are never this simple, and when it comes to my marriage, I'm only ever lost for words.

I came out as gay at nineteen, and I had hoped it would be *that* moment, the movie moment—in *Love, Simon* where Simon and Blue kiss atop a Ferris wheel; in *The Prom* when Emma and Alyssa dance together at a celebration they built for themselves—some moment where I would finally release myself from the gross expectations I'd been burdened with. But that's not how the story goes. I only stepped a toe out of that closet door. I came out just enough to persuade myself I was *living my truth*—the only concession I would make to this part of me while everything else stayed the same. I would still go to church, still refrain from alcohol and coffee, still stay the good Mormon boy I always wanted to be. I used to say I'd still get married in a Mormon temple if they ever decided to allow it.

I remember a meme I once saw: the Salt Lake Temple in the background, standing like a storybook castle, placed beneath bright words in slanted writing: *If this isn't your castle, then you're not my prince.*

This was my dream—the fairytale life I craved.

~

Jed and I first entered the Magic Kingdom in Walt Disney World in 2018, just a few days before I was to begin my new job there. We'd just moved to Florida from Utah and though it was January, it felt like a warm spring day to us. The perfect day, I hoped, to feel some magic.

I'd discovered the opportunity to finish out my undergraduate degree by completing an internship at Walt Disney World just five months before. I had been obsessed with Disney movies since I was a kid, watching my family's cassette tapes on repeat until they were nearly worn out. While all my other friends *grew up*, preoccupied with things like *Kill Bill* and *The Fast and the Furious*, I snacked on sour gummy worms and cheese cubes and watched *The Little Mermaid* and *Beauty and the Beast* and *The Lion King*, singing along in the living room of my childhood home. It was a dream to work at one of the parks, though I'd never told anyone about it until Jed. Finding the internship with the Disney College Program seemed the perfect way to live out that wish. So, we packed up and moved to Florida.

On our first trip to the Magic Kingdom, in the early hours of the morning, we parked in the 150-acre parking lot and took the monorail in. We crammed ourselves inside with all the other guests and gawked out the window at all we could see: the cloudless sky, the green-blue lakes, the Contemporary Resort—through which the monorail passed on its way to the park.

We disembarked with everyone else and waited through the entry line. We walked beneath the Walt Disney Railroad Station and found ourselves on Main Street USA, the park's main thoroughfare. I immediately saw the Town Square Theater where I'd eventually get photos taken with Mickey. I found Tony's Town Square Restaurant, modeled after the romantic Italian diner from *The Lady and The Tramp*. There was a confectionery with all its sugared treats, a barber shop, a jewelry store, an expansive art gallery, and multiple gift shops with all kinds of Disney paraphernalia. I wanted to stop, to see them all, and I would in time. I would have almost two years to pulse through the aisles—rows upon rows of clothes and costumes, stuffed animals and fairy wands, the ever-changing Mickey ears and seasonally themed souvenirs. But it was my first day in the park, and there was something else I had to find first.

Cinderella's Castle stood as a beacon at the end of Main Street. Its stone-walled base surrounded a pale pink tower within, both adorned with purple rooftops and gold lining. In the center, above the open gate, perched a curtained balcony and an intricate white clock. The castle had been built as if on a small hill with stone paths on either side leading from its gate to a stone courtyard below. A platform stretched out between the pathways—the stage where Mickey and friends would perform throughout the day. The castle looked just as glorious as I'd imagined. Just as beautiful and brilliant as what I'd seen in other people's photos. And yet, there was more—some kind of magic pulsing out from the ground. I was so close now. I needed more. I needed to feel its materiality, it's tangibility, some kind of proof that the life I was living could be real.

I picked up my pace, sped past all the shops and restaurants and open courtyards where people would stand to watch the nightly *Happily Ever After* firework show. Past the tranquil moat full of quacking ducks, the perfect green lawns, the multicolored, manicured gardens. I barely paused at the corner Plaza Ice Cream Parlor—the place I'd be working for the next seven months. I took a picture and moved on. I'd come back later. For now, I just needed to reach the castle.

I slipped to the left-side stone ramp and started up the steps, Jed right on my heels. In moments, we stood before the open gate, staring into the passageway through to the other side. I could see a twirling carousel beyond—something I learned was demanded by Walt. He wanted guests to always see life within the castle. A beautiful sentiment, really. Tears ran down my face, and Jed placed his hand on my shoulder.

Slowly, we made our way into the corridor. On our right was the waiting area for Cinderella's Royal Table Restaurant—the one placed in the center of the castle, just one floor up. On our left, five grand mosaic murals covered the wall—over one million pieces of glass placed to chronicle the story of Cinderella. I abruptly stopped at the first panel, a fifteen-foot-tall, ten-foot-wide image of Cinderella sweeping ash from the fireplace while her stepmother and stepsisters left for the prince's ball.

"I had no idea this was here," I told Jed. He said he hadn't known either. Somehow, in all the times I looked up pictures of the castle's facade online, I'd never thought to look up what might be inside, never imagined there could be something even more grand and beautiful there. I reached out and pressed my fingers against the small glass fragments. Each one was smooth, the colors brilliant, pieced so carefully together to create the image. I couldn't imagine how many hours and people it would take to put something like this together, but I could feel a vibrating presence, the spirit of concentrated, careful hands.

I moved onto the next panel: the fairy godmother and Cinderella in her gloriously transformed white gown. In the next, Cinderella fled the castle ball. Then came the scene where she tried on the glass slipper before her kneeling prince. The final panel was an image of her and the prince riding away on a white horse—maybe after their wedding, maybe toward some happily-ever-after ending.

I met Jed in the spring of 2013, on the dating app Jack'd, just a year after coming out as gay. I still felt so inexperienced in the ways of dating. I'd only had the one boyfriend before him, and we'd only lasted three months. I had never really dated anyone in high school and had only started having sex over the past six months. So when Jed showed up on my doorstep to take me on our first date, I had no clue what to expect. I knew the app version of him to be funny and handsome, so I was relieved to see it was actually him when I opened the door. He was just as tall and broad-shouldered as his photos suggested, with bright blue eyes, diamond-stud earrings, and short brown hair swept up into a fauxhawk.

He drove us to Olive Garden in his dad's pickup. We both ordered the chicken parmigiana. We went back to my place afterward, watched *Easy A* and *Pitch Perfect*, and we fell asleep on the couch. When we woke up at 2 a.m., we found out his car had been booted in the parking lot. I tried to pay to get it removed, but my card was declined. He laughed it off and offered to pay instead. I half-expected this to be the end of our time together, figured he'd be too annoyed and upset to want to go out with me again. But he texted me the next morning. He told me he had a wonderful time with me. We went on another date a few nights later.

It only took me a month or so to tell him I loved him. And when I did, he said it back.

He seemed perfect to me. He made me laugh. He was kind and charming. He was supportive of my writing career, and he was just as obsessed about Disney and Harry Potter as I was. What more could I ask for? Even more, when I told him I didn't want to have sex with him until three months in because I was serious about him and I felt like sex had been getting in the way of feelings for previous guys I'd tried to date before him, Jed respectfully agreed.

So, we made a plan for our three-month anniversary. We went to Olive Garden for dinner. Both ordered the chicken parmigiana. We went for a walk in the park. Then, because I'd just moved back in with my parents and he was living with his, he rented a hotel room for us to stay the night together. It had been so long that when he pressed against me, I yelped out in pain. He apologized. I told him to try again. The pain seared. He asked if I was okay. I clenched my teeth and nodded. He picked up his speed. I closed my eyes and tried to steady my breathing. Neither of us noticed a few drops of blood had dripped lightly onto the sheets.

~

Walt Disney World is a park of illusions. It's a production. It's why the workers are called *cast members*, why visitors are called *guests*, why our uniforms are called *costumes*. It's why standing in guest areas is called being *on stage* and back areas are *backstage*. This is their illusion at its most basic. More complex secrets include: the pumped-in popcorn smell on Main Street to make you crave their food; forced perspective in the construction of Cinderella's Castle and other buildings to make them appear far bigger and grander than they actually are; and the Utilidor system beneath the park—a maze of giant, winding utility tunnels that run under the Magic Kingdom, used by cast members to enter and exit the park without being seen. Aptly nicknamed the "underground city," the Utilidor seemed to have everything: a cafeteria that included a Subway restaurant, multiple locker rooms with showers and a gym, many break areas, a hair salon, rehearsal rooms, storage rooms, administrative offices, prep kitchens, character costuming houses, and waste removal services. And though it might seem like the tunnels had been built like a basement beneath the park, the Utilidor sits on ground level. The park stands on top, on an incline so gradual that guests don't realize they're moving in an upward trajectory. It's a trick—something used to keep the magic alive.

On day one of my Disney Traditions Class—the first part of my training to be an official cast member—I was taken on a tour of the Utilidor with some of the other new recruits. From Disney University, we took a bus to the tunnel entrance at the back of the park, right behind the

Be Our Guest Restaurant. When I stepped off, I couldn't help but feel startled by the sight. At the base of a two-story wall stood the concrete entrance, and just above, a blue sign read THE MAGIC BEGINS WITH YOU! Cast members walked in and out of one side of the tunnel while golf cart-like cars sped by on the other. The walls inside were made of concrete, and a series of suction pipes ran along the ceiling—an easy, clean way of removing trash and waste from the park. And though the tunnels weren't dirty, they were surprisingly plain. Simple. Human. I wasn't sure what I imagined I'd find down there, but I knew it wasn't that.

As our small group made our way inside, I wondered if there was a discreet way to take a picture or two for Jed. I knew he would love to see it, and it pained me to think that he wouldn't ever get to, but photography in the tunnels was prohibited. We were told this multiple times. It was in the contracts we signed to work there. No videos. No photos. I could lose my job if anyone caught me doing any of it. *One day*, I thought. We'd find a way for him to see it one day.

The first place we stopped at was the cafeteria (the Mouseketeria) where half-costumed cast members sat together, gossiping about one thing or another. Near the center of the expansive room was a large round table full of performers—prince and princess actors on break. It was a strange sight: Rapunzel eating a meatball sub, Tiana eating an egg and sausage biscuit, Peter Pan guzzling a can of Dr. Pepper—all with hair done up and perfect makeup but wearing gym shorts and loose T-shirts like they were off to some slumber party. They were the coveted working roles of many. I'd auditioned to be a character performer too, but I didn't make it past the first round—unsurprising, really. We had to showcase our dancing abilities, and it's not like I had ever taken the dance lessons, not like I'd ever revealed to anyone that I'd desperately wanted to do so my entire life. I couldn't really expect anything more than my placement at the Plaza Ice Cream Parlor.

Our group left the cafeteria and continued on our tour, reaching a curve in the hall where a purple stripe ran along the wall, emblazoned with the title, "Fantasyland." It led to another tunnel with bright red walls, stretching far longer than the previous ones, where the floor slanted in a small decline before leveling out in a small tunnel running farther than I could see. Our guide led us down to the slope's bottom where she came to a stop.

"Guess where we are now," she said, smiling. We all glanced at each other.

"The main gate?" one boy tried.

"The train station?" another said.

"Nope," our guide said jovially, feeding on our continued suspense. When no one tried again, she laughed. "Well, we are actually standing right beneath Cinderella's Castle."

"Woah," we all said, looking up, glancing from one side to the other as if we could see the castle through the stained and dirty pipes above our heads. A loud rattling echoed from above, an indication of trash being suctioned out of the park. It was an exceptional facade, this gilded tunnel system, and it crafted some kind of cognitive dissonance in me. I just never would have imagined a place this unremarkable and odious could be the foundation of a fairytale dream castle. And I wondered which was more true: the beauty up above or the ugly down below.

It was a pointless question to ask.

~

In general, Jed and I were happy. He cared about me, and I cared about him. And even though so much of my love language was felt through touch and he didn't really like touching anyone, I told myself what we had was good enough because I was loved; at least I was loved. And because I had feared being loved was an impossibility, his love was all that mattered. It was far better than being alone.

The first time I cheated on Jed, I hadn't planned on doing so. Five months into our relationship, I was in Salt Lake City, attending an event held by the Trevor Project. Back then, I was fighting for a bridge between my identities, queer and somewhat still Mormon. I was determined to connect them. I was about to become vice president of USGA, that same unofficial gay-straight alliance where I met my first boyfriend—unofficial because BYU was owned by the Church, and they couldn't be too outwardly supportive of LGBTQ+ rights. But that's exactly what we were fighting for: a bridge, or any amount of acceptance. And that night, our current USGA president was receiving the 2013 Trevor Youth Innovator Award for his attempts.

The event was being held at a luxurious Radisson Hotel in downtown Salt Lake City. I sat with the president and the other three invited USGA members, and we listened to the multitude of speakers telling stories of how everyone in that room was changing the world. I wanted so badly to believe it was true. And when our president stood on the stage and said how grateful he was to the four of us sitting at that table, I tried to cry because everyone else was crying—because I felt I should. But my heart raced. I smiled though I felt the numbness coming, my mind glazing, by which I mean: I knew I needed to disappear, to release and lose control.

I excused myself and hazily walked to the restroom. I locked myself in a stall and pulled out my phone. I clicked through my usual porn sites, but realized I craved something more. Something dangerous. Ravenous. Real. And though I had deleted Grindr, it was like my body took over my mind. I downloaded the app again.

I found him quickly. He was staying in the hotel, just 250 feet away. He said he was *so horny* and just *wanting some ass.* I told him I needed to be used. He said he was ready to destroy me whenever I wanted to come to his room. I told him I'd be there soon.

I rejoined my friends for the afterparty out in the courtyard. Tall heating lamps had been placed around the tables to keep out the early November chill. Beneath long strands of hanging yellow light bulbs, I told my friend I had never tried alcohol before, and he bought me a rum and coke because "You have to start somewhere."

The five of us clinked our glasses, toasting the award and all the work we'd done over the past two years to get there. I took a sip and choked. I hated the taste. Hated the way it seared my throat as it went down. But the haze of my mind thickened, and that was what I wanted. I took another sip. I slowly slipped away.

I told the others that I wanted to head out early and that I'd call my parents to pick me up, and we said our goodbyes. I walked toward the entrance, but after turning the corner, hopped an elevator instead. Exiting on his floor, I walked to the Grindr-man's room. I knocked and he told me to come in. The room inside was low-lit and grand. I found him on the king size bed, fully naked and erect.

"Get to work," he said.

And I did.

~

One night, some months after starting my job at the Plaza Ice Cream Parlor, my coworkers invited me for a round of drinks after our shift. It wasn't the first time they'd invited me, but it was the first time I said yes. And I called Jed to ask if he wanted to come with me, meet my friends and have a fun night out, but he said he was too tired—a common refrain he gave when it came to meeting my friends or having dinner with my family or going to my open-mic poetry readings. Against my better judgment, I asked if it was okay that I went out with them anyway, and he said, "Fine."

My friends took me to a bar across town, a place with bad music and okay drinks and aggressively mediocre food, but it was a goofy kind of fun, and I finally felt a part of the work group. I got home late, but Jed was still awake, watching *Gilmore Girls* in the living room and playing *Pokémon Go* on his phone.

"You're still up?" I said, kicking off my shoes at the door.

Jed didn't turn around, but he said, "You know how it is. I can't sleep when you're gone."

"Oh, right," I said, a familiar, rushing sense of guilt sweeping over me. I made sure to get ready for bed as fast as I could.

The next day, as I slipped back into my work shoes, my green-and-white pinstriped costume under my arm, I told him I'd miss him and that I wished I could just stay home, spend the day with him and our dog and just relax.

Jed smiled. "Well, you could have hung out with us last night, but you decided to go be with your coworkers instead." He paused. Then he laughed.

"Oh," I said, quieting. "You don't have to say it like that." I could feel it—this bubbling, squirming heat in my gut.

"What?" he asked, his laugh turning into a scoff. "It's true."

"I mean, I guess," I said, "but it doesn't mean that I didn't want to hang out with you."

We were both quiet after that, and I finished getting ready. It wasn't the first time he'd said something like this. It was another refrain—one he often used after I'd gone out without him. But for whatever reason, that time hit harder. Deeper. Sharper. In a way that I noticed—maybe because I was already so raw, already feeling so alone without my family or old friends around. Or maybe I was just ready to break.

"I gotta head out," I said, pulling my keys from the door side keyring. I walked to him and leaned in for a kiss, but he turned his head: his way of telling me he was upset. "Look, I'm really sorry about last night," I said. "I didn't mean to make you feel bad."

Jed sighed. "I know. I just missed you is all." He turned and gave me a small peck on the lips.

"I know. I'm sorry," I said again. "I'll see you after work, okay?"

That night, as I changed out of my mint-green pinstriped Ice Cream Scooper costume, my coworker called to me from down the hall, "Yo, Andrew! We're all going to Shake Shack! You coming?"

"I can't," I said. "I gotta go home."

"Lame," he said, jokingly. "Well, maybe some other time." And he left.

I stayed on the bench there for some time, holding my stomach, feeling tears press against my eyes. I felt like it was foolish to cry. I told myself I didn't know why I hurt so much. But I did. I just didn't want to admit it. There was a pain gnawing at my ribs that I didn't want to name—an agony coming back up to bite me.

～

If you were to ask me how many men I've slept with, I wouldn't be able to give you a number. I couldn't even give you an estimate. This is how dissociative I had become—before, during, and even after Jed. I was taught to swallow down every sexual urge I had, and when I couldn't, I made sure that sinful, alternate Andrew only ever emerged in secret. What had begun with pornography and masturbation when I was eleven had transformed into complete sexual deviancy. Into cheating. I'd upped the stakes, but the urge was the same.

After I moved back to Utah from Florida, about six months into Jed's and my separation, I discussed this dissociative feeling with my psychiatrist. I told her it was like my mind switched off, and she told me it was likely a manic blackout—a symptom of my bipolar disorder. I'd be awake, but not in control, unaware of my actions or my surroundings or even my own body.

"I feel like I become another person," I told her. "It's like this overly sexual version of Andrew takes over. It was pornography when I was a kid. Now it's sex."

She explained that many people with bipolar feel this way. "It seems like you might be experiencing hypersexuality too," she added. "Manic episodes that increase compulsive sexual wants. Inhibitions are lowered and you desire forbidden things."

Out the window, I watched a tree in the snow-glazed garden and a squirrel climbing through its dead branches. "Andrew," she said to me, her voice soft and warm, "hypersexuality and manic blackouts pair together in some really difficult ways. But we'll figure this out together."

I always wanted to believe I could find a way past it. Disassociation. Manic blackouts. Hypersexuality. Numbing. Becoming an alternate Andrew, one I could blame for my wrongdoings. These were just labels and names I used to rationalize meeting strangers in the night, when men said they didn't want to use condoms, when I said I didn't care, when I let them use me in whatever ways they saw fit. As the stress and stimulation of the world became too much, I numbed my mind and let my body take over. I craved connection, gratification, for something forbidden, to lose control.

There's a contradiction here. Have you seen it? The pieces were starting to come together, a picture I could finally begin to see. Even if I didn't understand it yet.

I wanted to live some fairytale fantasy—I've said this before. I wanted to live happily ever after with Jed and for that to be enough. But I also wanted to let go. I longed to be free—of expectations, of my life, of Jed, of the monster I believed I had become. I just wanted to start over, but I knew it would cost me everything to do so.

Listen—

I want to tell you I learned my lesson that first night I cheated. I want to tell you the version of this story where I didn't ever repeat the mistake, where the guilt and despair I felt going up to that man's room would be enough to make me never do it again; where I learned my lesson; where I determined my life was worth more than a one full of deceit and danger. And it's not that I want to tell you that Jed and I went on to live happily forever together—I just wish I could tell the version where, when we ended, I didn't bundle it up and make such a mess of things. There would be a clean break. We'd move on knowing we had made our marriage the very best thing it could be, and we'd thank each other for the adventure.

But that's not the story I get to tell.

My story goes like this.

～

It rained on my wedding day, and that was supposed to mean good luck. At least, that's what people had been telling me: my mom, my aunt, Mrs. Collier who lived down the street, our officiant, Robert Kirby, who was a close friend of my father's and wrote for the *Salt Lake Tribune*. But at the edge of Draper Historic Park, in a car with my cousin and best woman, Karli, I squinted up into the dark gray sky. Jed was running late, but he wasn't far behind. He'd be there soon.

In the car, I gripped tight onto Karli's fingers, accidentally pressing my chewed nails into her skin. I felt her twitch, but she didn't pull away—just placed her other hand on top of mine. "This doesn't feel like good luck," I admitted, trying to laugh.

She told me the feeling made sense. After all, I had planned an outdoor wedding in a public park, mostly because the price-point was so much lower than an official $10,000+ wedding venue. And because I knew it would be an outdoor wedding, I had spent hours looking over weather statistics in order to find the historically driest day of Salt Lake Valley summers: June 11.

The irony was frustrating.

And I thought about how, years before this, just a week after my engagement to Jed, I received a message from my high school seminary teacher, Sister Savage. In it, she told me she loved me; she told me she was praying for me; she said she wanted me to find true peace and joy. Then, at the end, she included a link to a video. It was an interview done by the Church, which told the story of a gay man who was a member and decided to marry a woman and have kids in order to remain in the Church.

My stomach thudded against my jaw as I watched, and when I asked Sister Savage why she sent the video to me, she told me she sent it because she cared about me and wanted me to find eternal happiness. *The doctrine of marriage will never change*, she wrote. *And I know that happiness can only be found in living the gospel. I believe in a living prophet and in the scriptures. The Plan of Salvation. Gender is an important part of the plan. It is only between man and a woman that we can procreate. Your spirit does not struggle with the tendency. Your body does. Our bodies have appetites and passions. My intent was never to be hurtful but to give you hope! That the atonement can allow us to overcome the temptations to act.*

Paragraph after paragraph, she went on. Though never mentioning the engagement, she continued calling me to repentance, telling me she loved me, telling me I was sinning, repeating that she loved me, repeating that my love wasn't real.

In my response, I told her my story, and I told her I was perfectly happy. I said it wasn't her job to call me to repent, that I loved Jed and my life couldn't be summed up into some temptation of the body. I told her I appreciated all that she'd taught me in my teen years and that she had always been my favorite teacher. I told her that I'd love to see her at my wedding if she was willing to come.

I'm very sorry! she wrote back. *I follow the doctrine. I'm not going to write anymore. Still love you and appreciate you. I can't go to your wedding because it is breaking God's commandments. I know you'll never be happy breaking what God has commanded. But I will always love you! Love all people!!!!!*

I return to her message every now and again, even still, trying to understand the depth of hate speech coated in love. And while she and I never talked again, as I looked up into that clouded, stormy sky on the day of my wedding, I thought about her message. I wondered if she would have thought of the weather as god's wrath. His disapproval. I wondered if my mom was right instead—that it really could be a message of good luck from the universe. I guess, in the end, it's all just superstition.

"At least the overcast day will make for great photos," Karli said, crouching forward in her seat to see the dark sky clearer.

"At least I love the rain," I responded, trying to slow my breathing. A light whistle swept out with my air.

Jed was running late, but he was on his way. He'd be there soon.

～

I couldn't tell you when I started to notice him. I can only say that I did. I was working at the Plaza Ice Cream Parlor. He was a Coordinator—Disney's version of a supervisor—at the Main Street Bakery next door. We shared a cramped backroom, kitchen, and breakroom—and at first, I only knew him in passing. Bumped against him as I brought dirty dishes to the sink. Brushed his arm while clocking in. Heard his belting laugh from down the hall. I'd meet his eyes from across the breakroom tables, and I'd feel a jump in my gut when he wouldn't look away. He'd raise an eyebrow and give me a smile, and I'd feel a rising blush burn the skin of my cheeks and neck. I'd look away, and by the time I'd glance back, he'd be in conversation with whoever was beside him—as if he'd never looked at me at all.

A few months into my time at the ice cream parlor, there was a day where we found ourselves alone at the breakroom table, and we began to talk—our first time officially meeting. He introduced himself as Chris. He was about to turn twenty-four and he'd been working at Walt Disney World for years. He was born in the South, but he'd always wanted to work for Disney. He'd only recently become a Coordinator, but he had dreams of moving up the management ladder. He loved movies and water parks and being out in nature. He greeted strangers with *Merry Christmas!* all year long because it could get them to laugh. And he loved to make people laugh. He had a kind face and a solid frame, black hair and deep brown eyes that always lingered just a little too long. His gaze made my body flutter in ways I had long forgotten I could feel, foreign shivers through my skin, a deep hunger in my belly.

I could tell he wanted me, and I knew I wanted him, but I knew the danger of cheating with someone from my real life. My in-the-day life. At night, in the dark, on anonymous dating apps, when my mind shut off and the other Andrew came out—that was one thing. For Real Andrew to do it was quite another. It was riskier. Far easier to get caught. Far more difficult to forget and pretend it hadn't happened when I'd inevitably see the guy at work the next day.

At some point, while having a conversation with another worker, the subject of my marriage came up, and I heard Chris say from behind me, "Wait, you're married?"

I turned and found him a mere foot away from me, his sultry face fallen into something more like disappointment. Something more like anger.

"Oh, yeah," I said, knowing my voice shook with the words, "I thought you knew."

"I didn't," he said. He turned sharply and walked away, and something deep inside my throat ached.

His flirtations stopped after that. There were no more lingering eyes. No more raised eyebrows. No more brushes on my arm. And while I had hoped it might bring some relief, I only felt absence. Emptiness. Hunger.

I had forgotten what it felt like to be seen with such animal wanting, and now that I had felt it again, there was no way to trick my mind back into forgetting. What came next had less to do with hunger and more to do with inevitability.

~

In the distance, a huge tent flapped in the wind and rain, and beside it, an even larger gazebo, nicknamed The Whisper Dome because of its echoing effect. Years before my wedding, perhaps a lifetime before, I had stood on opposite sides with a friend while we whispered secrets to one another: *I'm in love with Taryn; I'm in love with Kate; Kimberly said Jamie is gay.* We laughed and ran away, racing each other to the clean-cut, grassy fields.

The Whisper Dome lay hazy in the storm, but I could still make out the barrier of umbrellas guests had used to barricade themselves from the rain. More people had showed up than expected; nearly a hundred by my parents' calculation. A hundred people stuffed into a gazebo—and in the middle of a storm like that, I could only think of the support as heartening. There were even people from my childhood Ward that had shown up, something I never thought would happen. I wanted to make sure the event was worth their time and effort—worth risking their salvation.

I squeezed Karli's hand. "There's no pressure," she told me. "This is your day. You get to move through it in whatever way feels right to you." I couldn't bring myself to answer her, a cold empty feeling deep in my stomach. I stared at our fingers, still intertwined. After another minute, she asked, "Are you okay?"

I peered into her eyes, and in the overcast afternoon, the dark brown blended seamlessly into her irises, contrasting her light hair—so similar to the color of mine. We always tended to look alike—even when I dyed my hair dark brown and showed up to our family's Thanksgiving dinner to find she had done the exact same random thing. We screamed our elation when we saw each other, quickly asking my brother to take a picture.

"I just think, for the first time, I get what people meant by a stomach twisting in knots," I said. I attempted a laugh, but the sound fizzled in my throat. "I think I'm just nervous."

She paused, and my heart thudded against my ribs. "Are you still wanting to go through with it?" she asked me.

"Of course!" I said, releasing my hand from hers. "I want to marry Jed. I'm just stressed about everything."

"Okay, I'm sorry," Karli said, raising her hands in defense. "Is it just the rain then, or what's specifically stressing you out?"

I didn't answer right away. Instead, we listened to the steady, slapping rain on the windows. "Just, all of it," I eventually said, my words picking up speed. "The wedding. Walking down the aisle. The food tasting good. If people will be upset about having to show up in the rain." My voice tumbled quickly, bottled-up fears like a list. "I don't really know, I guess. I just feel all twisted and heavy."

"I think that's how you're supposed to feel," Karli said, steadying the air with a reassuring smile.

"Yeah, probably," I said. "I just wish I knew more people who've gotten married. I feel like I don't even know what a normal marriage looks like, or if what I'm feeling is normal."

Her smile slipped. "Yeah. I guess that makes sense."

I was twenty-three, but I hadn't been to many weddings so far. A cousin on my dad's side who got married by handfasting. A second cousin on my mom's who got married in Vegas. My sister, Melissa. My brother, Christopher. They each got married in the Mormon temple when I was too young to participate. In any case, I knew Mormon weddings to be strange—really just meaning they didn't match those I saw on TV shows and movies.

I remember dressing up in my sister's wedding colors before going to the temple when I was sixteen. Melissa and her husband-to-be, Steve, went upstairs with everyone else who had done their endowments already: some of their friends, my parents, Steve's parents, my grandfather, Christopher and his wife, Jenn. But the rest of us—Karli, my brothers Marcus and Matthew, my grandparents on my mom's side who had never joined the religion, some others I can't remember—we remained on the ground floor, in a waiting room emblazoned with swirling patterns of brown, gold, and white. I was too young to make the temple covenants, so I wasn't allowed to see my sister get married. Just like I couldn't see Christopher get married some years before. It seemed so unfair—and it is, really. But it's what we all believed to be right at the time, no matter how much we'd all come to regret it later on.

So I had very little experience when it came to what a wedding was supposed to look like. And I found myself crying, this aching admission crashing from between my teeth. "I'm doing it all wrong. I know I'm doing it all wrong." I slapped my hands against my face, covering my eyes and cheeks, holding back the tears I didn't want to cry because it was raining on my wedding day and that was supposed to mean good luck and I was afraid at how much all of this didn't feel like good luck.

~

The inevitability of Chris changed everything. After a few weeks of essentially ignoring me, we'd started to talk off and on again. In my first five months working at Disney, we'd gone from glancing to flirting to nothing at all to something like friends. And yet, I still felt the craving to have him look at me again in the ways he once did. I still felt fluttering in my chest when I heard him laugh. Still imagined what it would be like to be held gently in his arms. But we'd found an appropriate distance as friends, and I told myself that was for the best. Even the idea of a workplace affair made me anxious.

Then, at the beginning of June, I learned he would be leaving on an extended trip for his birthday. He'd be gone for two weeks, and a surprising, crashing, despondent sadness bled into me. We said our goodbyes in the shared kitchen, and I hugged him. And he hugged me back. And his arms wrapped tight around my shoulders.

I'd later learn this to be the moment—the one where I held him for just a little too long. It changed everything. He heard that burning, howling creature deep within me.

~

Jed finally arrived and the rain crashed ever harder. A knock on the car window let me know it was time to begin the ceremony. Karli squeezed my hand. I took a breath. I opened the door and found my mom there beside me, her red-brown hair falling in light curls, her jet-black cardigan and white blouse flowing over the intricate flowering print of her monochrome skirt. Holding a giant white and green umbrella above our heads to keep us dry, she took my hand and helped me from my seat. I hugged her, and a familiar warmth flooded through me. Calming me. She squeezed just a little tighter, and in her arms, I suddenly didn't feel so afraid.

"How're you feeling, hon?" she asked as we parted.

"I'm great, Mom."

She kissed my cheek. "I'm so happy for you."

"Thanks."

We steadied ourselves at the end of the waterpooled sidewalk while Karli went ahead. I took the umbrella from my mom's hand and listened to the sound of pattering rain on the canvas. We linked arms, and from the hazy gazebo in the distance, I heard the faintest sound of music begin. As rehearsed, we counted to ten before we began to walk.

～

A few days after Chris returned, I took the bus back to the cast member parking lot with him and a few of our coworkers. As we all parted ways, Chris offered to walk me to my car. I said yes. And look: it's not like I didn't know what this meant. Of course I did. I knew by the way he looked at me when he asked, by the way my lungs smashed against my throat, by the way my chest inflated and my skin tingled. I knew what he wanted. I knew what I wanted too. What I was so afraid to want.

Between my car and another, we hugged goodnight. But we didn't let go. We held onto each other, his arms around my waist, mine around his neck, our heads resting on each other's shoulders. I could feel him breathing and I was breathing with him. Together. In some kind of unison, pulsing beats beneath our veins, the heat of two bodies building and boiling and expanding. I could feel my arousal. I could feel his too. And we pulled our bodies just a little closer together.

One minute. Two minutes. Ten. Then, his lips were on mine, his breath hungry and burning across my tongue. I swept my fingers across his head, squeezing him closer as he dipped his hands beneath my shirt, carving his fingernails into my back. And in a dark parking lot, beneath the night and moon and stars above, we held each other as close as we could.

～

The wedding was beautiful. Jed arrived and we both walked down the sidewalk aisle with our mothers, holding umbrellas above our heads to try and stay dry, an instrumental version of Christina Perri's "A Thousand Years" playing sweet in the background. We held hands before the audience while our little dog Lance whined for our attention nearby. Robert Kirby officiated with beautiful, inspiring words. He told us to look out into the crowd, and we did. He said that there was a reason they'd all come out to support us, that our love was just as real as anybody else's, that we were being held up by so many. And I couldn't stop smiling.

Yes, it was a beautiful wedding. A gorgeous white cake with cascading red, purple, and blue flowers and the words "Happily Ever After" written down the tiers. Tables with laminated Disney quotes and brass lanterns overflowing with those same colored flowers. There was catered ice cream from my old boss at Coldstone and my dad's homemade meatballs. And Karli was right; the rain did make for stunning photos. It was a rainy day. A beautiful day. A beautiful wedding.

And yet, when I remember that day, something dark boils up. A frustration. An angry shame. Because I didn't dance. Not with Jed, not with my mom, not with myself, not with anyone. I did not dance at my wedding. Above all else, this stays with me. It's not like I was consciously avoiding it. I think there was this fragmented part of me that figured Jed wouldn't be into it, so I never asked. He hadn't been interested in writing vows either, though I can't remember his reasons. I think it had something to do with avoiding clichés. I just remember agreeing to it. I remember saying I didn't care about it either.

But I did care. I wanted to say why I loved him and for him to say why he loved me. I wanted to tell all those people sitting under that rain-drenched gazebo, huddling close to their umbrella barrier, why it mattered that they all came out to witness. I wanted to dance with him across the gazebo floor. I wanted to have that moment. I had dreamed about it for so long.

But I told him I didn't care. I lied. It seemed like such a small thing to sacrifice.

～

Chris and I didn't have sex that first night we kissed. That didn't happen until a few weeks later, when our days off finally aligned. Jed was working, and I told him I picked up a shift. I drove to Chris's apartment instead. He opened the door and smiled his big warm smile. He picked me up in his arms and carried me inside. He placed me gently on his bed and kissed me. Slow and steady, he laid himself on top of me. I tied my legs around his waist and savored the weight of his body pressing down on mine.

So, my affair with Chris began. I call it an affair so I can differentiate between that and my previous cheating. The difference: I had actual feelings for Chris; I was falling in love with him—rapid, hard, and intense. And where Jed and I never had sex, Chris and I were a perfect match. He helped me explore my deepest desires. He showed me how sex could be more than an indulgent, self-effacing act, and I wondered if I'd been wrong all these years—that sex and love could somehow coexist—that maybe it was something I could have.

But then there was Jed and all the pieces of me that still loved him—for all he had been and could potentially be. As desperately as I wanted to be with Chris, I desperately didn't want to leave Jed, so I didn't break things off with either of them. It was a manipulative thing. And it was cruel. And it's not like I didn't know better. I felt it in my core. I was more selfish and destructive than I had ever been before. In all the ways that mattered, I had become the villain of their stories. Of my own. And maybe I always had been. I was selfish and sad and sick and scared and self-sacrificing and self-hating and angry.

I'm all too ready to destroy myself.

~

So Jed and I got married. And as time passed, in the moments I felt unsure about my marriage, I'd remember the faces of all those who came to my wedding—my family, my friends, my family's friends, even people from the Ward I grew up in—how they smiled, red-eyed and proud. I would think of Robert Kirby and the article he wrote for the *Salt Lake Tribune* about marrying us—about how uplifting we were, how deep and full our love was. I'd think about another article with Jed's and my engagement photos plastered on the front page of Utah State University's student newspaper—the one titled "USU Married Student Housing Welcomes First Gay Couple." I'd think back on Sister Savage's words, and I felt like I had something to prove. Something to preserve. I felt like it all made me into some poster child for normalizing gay marriage in Utah, like my life could be an example of how gay marriage wasn't doomed to fail like I'd been taught to believe. And it felt like savagery, this cage I created with hopeful words, and I would think on all these things. Hold them too tight. Remember them too often. Press them into my mind like a nail. I'd force myself to stay.

And I stayed.

And we were happy, Jed and I. For a good while, at least. Our relationship had its ups and downs like all do, but it felt like things we could handle. He worked as a supervisor at a plasma donation center. I worked at the campus library while writing my fantasy novel and completing my degree. We took trips to Disneyland when we could save up the money, and when our first dog Lance passed away, we tattooed his pawprints on our bodies. We adopted another dog soon after, a husky named Kira, a wild and loving girl.

And on we lived.

~

The roads to Walt Disney World were winding. I mean this literally. Even after traveling on them for seven months, I still sometimes took a wrong turn. I forget things easily—like keys and backpacks and getting gas before the tank runs out. Consequence of my ADHD, I suppose. What happened might seem inevitable then. I took a wrong turn while trying to reach a gas station before work, and before I could make it back to the correct road, my car sputtered to a stop. Empty. I'd run out. On a road far from any station I could reasonably walk to.

I called my insurance company because I'd gotten the deal with free roadside assistance. They said they'd call someone to bring me gas, but it might take upward of an hour. I was already late for my shift—I had just transferred from the Ice Cream Parlor to work at California Grill, a ritzy restaurant on the top floor of Walt Disney World's Contemporary Resort. Being late when I was so new felt frightening. Like it could be reason enough to let me go. But I knew Jed had just gotten off work and was driving home, so I called him for help. I told him what had happened, and he came to meet me on the side of the road.

I sat in his car, blasting the AC against my sweaty face. He asked how long until the gas would arrive. It had been half an hour already, but the app said the assistance was still an hour away. Hesitantly, I asked if there was any way Jed would be willing to wait for the guy so I could go to work—late, but that was less penalizing than not going at all. At least it would be something.

Jed looked at me when I asked this, and he said no. He said he couldn't. He had just been diagnosed with diabetes two years before; he was worried about going low in the heat.

"Oh yeah, that makes sense," I told him. "I'm sorry." And I meant it. My sister had diabetes too. I knew the implications of what could happen if he stayed there without any AC or food.

"Well, do you think you could maybe go get a gas can and some gas from the station real quick?" I offered.

Jed paused. "It's just, I think I'm already going low," he said. "I need to get some food in my system."

I swallowed. "Gotcha." I felt foolish. "Okay. Well, thanks for coming anyway. It was nice to have AC for a minute."

"Did you call work?" Jed asked. "They should be understanding of all this."

"Yeah, I did. I'll just need to tell them I'll be a little later than planned."

We were silent for a bit, listening to the whoosh of cars speeding by us.

"You should go get some food," I told him, trying to keep my voice steady.

"Yeah," he said. He gave me a quick peck on the lips. "I love you."

"Love you too."

He paused again.

"You know, this is why I told you to not put off getting gas."

"I know."

"Just try to remember to do that from now on, okay?"

"Yeah." I tried to laugh, but the sound got caught in my throat. "I guess I learned my lesson."

"Just keep me updated," Jed said. I told him I would.

I stepped from his car and walked back to my own. And he drove away. And I watched him drive away until he disappeared. And I remained. And I could feel my eyes straining to hold back my emotion, my stomach turning over and over and over.

I texted my boss and told her I was still waiting for the gas guy to come, and she told me to just take the day off; it would be okay. I told her I appreciated her understanding, but I would try to make it as soon as the guy arrived.

But then the hour passed, and the app still said the gas was forty-five minutes away, so I texted Jed to see if he could just come and bring me some gas now that he'd eaten, but he said it didn't make sense to do that because it was a twenty minute drive for him to get to me—and that wasn't even including the time it would take to go buy a gas can—so it would end up taking about the same amount of time, and I just said "Okay."

But I wasn't okay. I didn't feel okay. I sobbed against the steering wheel of my car. I screamed and punched the dash. And I wanted to call someone—anyone—to come help me, but I didn't have anyone to call. I didn't have any real friends there, and my family was all back in Utah or out in the Midwest. I was alone.

At some point, I texted Chris to tell him about what had happened. He texted back immediately: *I'm so sorry, Andrew. I'm at work, but I can leave right now if you need me to come pick you up. We can go get ice cream or see a movie or whatever you'd like.* And as much as I wanted to say yes, I said no because I couldn't ask him to do that for me. I told him I was fine.

Another hour passed. Help still hadn't come. It would take over three hours in total for the man to arrive. He apologized, saying the roads around Walt Disney World were really tricky and he kept getting turned around. I told him that's how I ended up here in the first place, and he laughed. He told me to have a good evening, and he left.

I texted Jed to tell him I'd gotten the gas. He said I should just take the night off and come home, but I told him I still needed to go to work. But I didn't. Instead, I drove an hour east. Out to the ocean. Out to a bank of empty beach.

There was a rage that had built inside me—like I had never felt before. And I thought about all the best relationships in my life: Melissa and her husband, Steve, my brother Christopher and his wife, Jenn, my parents. I thought about how I couldn't imagine any of them leaving each other on the side of the road like this, a refrain coming back and back and back to me: *he left me; he just left me.* And I screamed out into the dark ocean. I screamed and screamed and screamed because it hurt. Everything hurt. I fell on my knees, pressing deep into the sandy earth, wishing the ocean could just wash me away into its depths.

And that burning, howling creature deep within me? The one Chris had heard when I hugged him just a little too long—I think I finally heard it too, rebounding across the water from where I remained. I could have choked on my own words. I listened to the sounds escaping from my throat.

~

Jed and I had been married for just over a year in 2017 when I first saw the Disney College Program listing. And when I told Jed about the possibility of doing it, of finishing out my degree by joining the program, I tried to stay as nonchalant as I could.

"Hey, what if I wanted to apply for The Disney College Program?" I asked. "Their applications just opened."

"Oh," Jed said, surprised. He blinked a few times and laughed. "That'd be cool and all—I just don't think we'd have the money to move right now."

I laughed, saying quickly, "Yeah, you're right." And I moved on.

A week later, I was lying on the couch with Kira, scratching behind her ears as she panted in the summer warmth. Jed walked in, stopped, and paused.

"Yes?" I asked.

He looked at me and grinned. "You should apply for The Disney College Program."

"Huh?"

"I've thought it through, and I think we can make the money work if you still want to apply."

Moving through my whiplash, I jumped up to hug him. I kissed him. Thanked him. Ran off to apply. And I got in. I received the email offer from Disney in October. They told me I was to start my internship at Walt Disney World that coming January. Just three months away. Only three months to figure out how we were going to move ourselves across the country. But Jed and I shrugged off the stress best we could. That didn't matter. This was the dream, and the dream was coming true.

We scavenged up enough money to pay for a U-Haul, and my dad and my brother Marcus offered to help us with the drive—one that ended up taking us three days to complete. We arrived in Orlando and entered our beautiful top-floor apartment just twenty minutes from the Magic Kingdom, an apartment so perfectly placed that we could see the nightly firework show from our back deck. And we started to unpack.

Halfway through, we heard quiet booms sounding in the distance.

"It's starting!" I heard Jed yell, and all of us ran to the back deck to see. Sure enough, there they were: the *Happily Ever After* fireworks. We couldn't hear the music, couldn't see the projections they placed on Cinderella's Castle, but that night, with all the boxes lying half unpacked in our new apartment, those bursting lights were enough. Out in the warm winter air, I began to cry—a swelling magic in my body ready to burst.

~

In early 2019, thirteen months after our move to Florida, Jed I said our goodbyes in the parking lot of our favorite Pizza Hut, just a few miles away from Magic Kingdom. And when we said it, we hadn't meant forever—just for a while. He'd go off to live with his friend in Seattle. I'd stay in Florida until I figured out what I wanted to do next. And on the day he left, I wept into his shoulder. And he hugged me tight beside his small black Malibu packed to the brim with boxes and pillows and all the things we could fit for his 3,000-mile drive. The move meant we'd be living on opposite corners of the country, and in those weeks before, when we had determined that we needed space apart, I didn't realize how literal that would be. And while I knew I had no right to cry into the shoulder of the man I had hurt so deeply, I also knew that I had no right to be held by him. Still, he held me. He held me and told me he'd call me when he got to his first hotel. I couldn't bring myself to respond.

I'd told him about Chris, and we'd spent the past four months in Florida trying to piece our marriage back together only to find that things were getting worse. We decided we both needed some space to figure out what we actually wanted. The truth is, my heart was never in it—though it would take years for me to admit it. I was still in love with Chris. Still too afraid to break things off with Jed. I didn't believe myself deserving of either's devotion.

When I finally let Jed go, we stared at each other for a long while. Two minutes. Five minutes. Thirty minutes. Maybe an hour. I don't know how long we stood there, two feet apart, feeling the space between us, not knowing what might come next—not knowing our path would end in divorce instead of reconciliation—not knowing we still had plenty of time to hurt and heal.

When he disappeared down the road, I fell against my car and sobbed, guttural chokes scraping against my throat. The hot February sun beat down on my neck. I slid to the ground, tiny specks of gravel scraping against the soles of my shoes. I still loved him, and maybe that's what hurt the most; I decimated the life I had always wanted, some fairytale dream where I got to be the hero: meet a man, fall in love, live happily ever after. When I was a kid, I imagined I had a place for myself in the stories I loved. All those years later, I still hadn't changed.

And look, I know fairytale endings have only ever been just that. Fairytale. Make-believe. False. Magical. Uncomplicated. And my life had become anything but uncomplicated. I was the villain, an enemy I was determined to destroy, though I don't know if I ever did. I don't know if I won that battle. I only know that I was lost.

Here: a story

Imagine you're standing at the edge of a forest. It's a forest you've seen but never entered. You've only ever made it to the entrance before turning back, but this time is different. This time, a wolf has crossed onto the path, a wolf clothed like a man, walking on two legs. He leans against a tree beside the entrance, and he tilts his head to you. He tells you there is a choice to make: you may turn back to the road you've traveled before, the one that leads back home; or you can traverse the wild woods, through the trees and the path beyond them, leaf-strewn and terrifying.

You ask the wolf what lies on the other side. His response is simply to grin.

Time is running out, counting down down down.

He says you must make a decision.

So you make the decision.

The Magic Kingdom

PART 2, UNICORNS AND BROKEN THINGS

Happily ever after is not something found only in fairy tales. You can
have it! It is available for you! But you must follow your Heavenly
Father's map . . . The day will come when you turn the final pages of
your own glorious story; there you will read and experience the
fulfillment of those blessed and wonderful words.

    —DIETER F. UCHTDORF, Second Counselor in the First
    Presidency of The Church of Jesus Christ of Latter-day Saints

WE WERE NEARLY BROKE WHEN JED LEFT FLORIDA. Because of
this, and because we didn't know the future of our relationship, instead
of renting a U-Haul truck, we rented a 15′ × 10′ storage unit near our
apartment, across the street from the cast member parking lot for the
Magic Kingdom. Jed packed what little he could fit in his car and left
for Seattle, but I hadn't decided where to go next. I had thought about
returning to Utah. I could stay with my family and figure out what to do.
I had even interviewed and accepted a job as an assistant manager at a
Starbucks in Salt Lake City, only to turn it down.

So I knew I was staying in Orlando for the time being; I just had no
idea where I was staying, and after Jed left, I only had a few days left on
our lease to figure it out. Money was a serious thing to consider—seeing
as I had so little. Even though I'd gotten promoted to a full-time position
in Magic Kingdom Attractions as a part of the *Peter Pan's Flight* and *It's
a Small World* team; even though I was also working part-time at a Starbucks in Universal Studios; even working sixty- to eighty-hour weeks, it
still felt like I was living paycheck to paycheck.

There were times I thought about living out of my car—something I'd
heard many Walt Disney World cast members did. I mean, I had a large
SUV to sleep in; I could put all my furniture and boxes in the storage

unit; Walt Disney World was a 24-hour business, so I had unlimited access to the Utilidor, its showers, food, and gym. Maybe it could work for a while. I could save enough for whatever came next: rent a place, buy a place, stay in Florida, move back to Utah.

Or, maybe I'd go somewhere new and disappear entirely.

I first watched *Unicorn Store* some months after Jed left. I assumed it would be a nice escape—this movie about a thirtyish-year-old girl obsessed with unicorns. It begins with Kit getting kicked out of art school because, when her professors ask her to create a self-portrait, she doesn't do what they expect. She covers her canvas in smudged pastel colors and covers them with golden glitter. She breaks from the borders, and the painting explodes across the wall, up to the ceiling, down to the floor. She's trying to tell them something, but her teachers don't understand—as is often the way of these things. They click their red pens, check their boxes. Likeness: *Poor*. Detail: *Poor*. Technique: *Poor*. Effort. Care. Emotion. Balance. Originality. All rated *Poor*.

They tell her she's failed. They kick her out, and she has to move back home with her parents.

Look, I'd always had a plan for my future. It was laid out for me from birth. Fall in love, get married, work, make money, work some more. I'd have some kids, grow older, retire, and reach the end knowing I'd done the best I could to follow god's will. Just because I left Mormonism didn't mean the plan had changed—it just no longer included the religion part.

But after Jed left, even that blueprint was gone, burned up in the aftermath of my ruined marriage. I'd failed in everything I'd set out to do. My life looked nothing like I imagined, and there wasn't a plan for this.

In the end, when I told Chris about my thoughts of living out of my car, he begged me to come live with him and his roommate instead—even if it was just until I got back on my feet. I agreed. "Until I can find my own place," I told him.

He took my hand and said he was happy to help me look.

Angry at herself for being kicked out of college and frustrated at her own childish unicorn obsession, Kit packs away all of her art and Care Bears and unicorn things. She gets a temp job at a PR agency in an attempt to prove to her parents—and herself—that she's an adult. As she stands at a copier all day, copying documents for reasons she doesn't know, her boss intrudes on her work, questions her about her long-term goals.

"I would like to not be a huge disappointment," Kit says.

They both laugh.

~

Chris and I were walking through Disney Springs—a themed outdoor mall and entertainment complex near the Walt Disney World parks. Since Jed left, it had become one of my favorite places to go. It wasn't packed with such huge crowds as the parks, but it had much of the same magic: a beautiful lake at its center, grand bridges, a dine-in movie theater, restaurants, merchandise shops, and the largest Disney store in the world. I longed to wander the streets and lose myself along the waterfront.

That day, we bought coffee, saw a movie, ate lunch, had a quickie in the bathroom, and were now walking along the lakeside drinking more coffee. It was as perfect a day as I could imagine.

Except—my stomach kept contracting. And my chest kept tightening. And my fingernails pressed deep into my palms. My heartbeat thudded against my throat. Because I couldn't stop thinking about Jed—about what he would think if he knew I had continued my relationship with Chris.

It sometimes felt foolish to care so much. It's not like we'd agreed to stay celibate. But we had agreed to keep trying to work things out, and Chris was the bomb I'd brought into our marriage. I walked a line of both—telling Jed I wanted to make things work with him; telling Chris I wanted to leave Jed but just didn't know how.

I knew both things to be true.

I also knew it was cruel.

I was so afraid of hurting either of them that I avoided a clean break. Instead, I found myself in the murkiest mud pit on the ground of my own created wasteland. So, no—I wouldn't let myself be fully happy with Chris, no matter how much I felt like I wanted to be. It was the punishment I gave myself for my transgressions. Happiness, I thought—true joy—it wasn't meant for someone like me.

At the edge of Disney Springs, Chris and I turned a corner and stopped. A crafted archway stood at the back of a building on the waterfront. I couldn't remember ever seeing it before. But Chris had. He'd purposely led me to it. "Isn't it cool?" he asked, walking closer.

"Yes?" I said with a small laugh. "Kinda cool, kinda really weird."

Chris laughed too and waved me to come look closer. The fifteen-foot structure had been placed on a large brick plinth, crafted from what looked like concrete, clay, rocks, shells, and other materials I couldn't place. It had at least ten carved faces poking out the front like masks, all different, some smiling, some waving, some sticking their tongues out or praying. Chris wrapped his arm around my waist and kissed my cheek as I came to stand beneath it.

~

One day, Kit receives a letter, inviting her to *The Store*—a place that supposedly sells *what she needs*. She reads curly, handwritten words that tell her, *Never be alone again.*

The Salesman at The Store tells Kit that he wants to give her a unicorn. She doesn't even have to pay for it; she just needs to meet the requirements.

1. Build a home worthy of a unicorn.
2. Have financial security.
3. Surround the unicorn with love.

And so Kit begins her journey. She hires Virgil, a hardware store employee, to build a stable in her parents' backyard—though she doesn't tell him it's for a unicorn. She designs a pitch for her PR firm, hoping it will grant her a promotion. She works to heal her relationship with her parents by going on an "Emotion Quest" trip with them.

The journey she's taking: she is trying to change her life.

~

"You two are a cute couple," someone said from behind us. Chris and I turned from the arch to see a middle-aged man grinning from the base of the brick steps. "Would you like a picture?"

"Sure!" Chris said, handing the man his phone. He pulled me close, and we smiled for the photo.

"This almost looks like a wedding announcement," the man told us, returning the phone. "Something to think about?" And he left.

And he wasn't entirely wrong. Other than our choice of comfortable shorts and T-shirts, the pictures could very well work as a save-the-date kind of photo.

And I could almost see it: my life with Chris; walking down an aisle again, meeting him at the end, celebrating, dancing; he'd keep moving up in the Disney company, and I'd keep trying to be a writer; we'd buy a house, live happily till the end. It was a life I could see myself wanting, and yet—and yet—my gut tensed again. And the image folded.

More shadow lives danced around me, leading in vastly different directions, crafted through the choices I didn't know how to make. My marriage fell apart in part because I didn't know who I was or what I wanted. I'd lived my entire life for other people—for my religion, my family, my friends, the men in my life. Now, I just wanted to live for myself, find myself, maybe journey across the Pacific Northwest or *Eat, Pray, Love* my way through Europe. But how could I do that when I was afraid to leave Orlando, afraid to let go of Jed, afraid to leave Chris, afraid of the unknown, afraid of everything?

Chris took my hand in his, and we walked away from the arch. We planned to stop by again at some point, but we never found the time.

⁓

To put it simply, Kit fails. She argues and yells at her parents during the Emotion Quest. She presents her colorful and flamboyant ideas to the PR firm, but they tell her she's childish and she's let go. That night, she goes on a date with Virgil, and she tells him about The Store. She tells him she's getting a unicorn. He doesn't believe her, obviously. How could he? So Kit takes him there to prove it.

But The Store is gone when they get there. The building is empty, and Kit believes it to be her fault—that she failed at making her life good enough for a unicorn so The Salesman left. Angry and hurting and hating herself, she lashes out at Virgil and runs away. When she gets home, she tears from her walls all the art and unicorn paraphernalia she's collected over her lifetime, and she throws it all in the trash.

⁓

A month or two into my separation from Jed, I found my own place to stay in Florida. A friend from my time at California Grill had a roommate who needed someone to take his lease, and I agreed. I told Chris, and when I did, his face shifted. I couldn't quite tell what he felt. Something like sadness. Something like anger. Maybe even fear.

I asked him what was up, and he said, "I guess I just don't see why you have to move out."

"It's not a breakup," I said quickly. "I just need a fresh start. I need space to figure myself out. This was always the plan."

"I just feel like we're moving backward."

"Backward?" I asked. "But we didn't have a normal start, Chris. I don't think there's a backward to go to."

"We've been together almost a year, Andrew."

I shook my head. "I know, I know. But I've told you: I need some time to figure out who I am and what I want. I can't do that living here with you."

He was supportive in the end—or as supportive as he could bring himself to be—and in April, I moved into my new place. I brought in my bed, desk, dresser, and bookshelf from the storage unit. Chris helped and stayed the night that first night while I unpacked and set up. He left for work in the morning, and I stayed home. For what felt like the first time in a long time, I was alone.

∼

Kit's mom sees her throwing out all her things and asks Kit to come sit with her. She asks if Kit's cleaning up. "Growing up," Kit corrects before collapsing onto the bench of their breakfast nook. Her mom offers her a s'more and tells her a story, attempting to brighten the space between them. They talk about Virgil and how Kit doesn't think she'll ever see him again after what she did. Her mom tells her she doubts that, but Kit shakes her head, tears dripping down her face.

"Listen," her mom says, "I just want to tell you one thing." She places her hand on Kit's and meets her eyes. "The most grown-up thing you can do is fail at the things you care about . . . And you're going to be just fine."

I began to cry.

∼

At some point, maybe a week after moving into my new place, I sat on a warm patch of grass in front of Cinderella's Castle. After over a year of not writing anything, I'd gone there to try doing so again. I leaned back against a short iron fence and took a selfie—the first one I'd taken in about five years. I posted it to Instagram, and within an hour, my mom called me.

"How're you doing, sweetheart?" she asked me. It was the same question she'd been asking every day since Jed left—a small caring act I could hold onto.

"I'm actually doing better today," I told her. "I'm writing again, so that's good. I'm feeling good."

"I thought you might be," she said. I could almost hear her smiling from over 2,000 miles away. "I saw the picture you posted, and I just thought something seemed different."

"Really?" I said, almost laughing.

"You just looked different. More confidence. More peace. You just looked more sure of yourself, I think."

"Well, thanks, Mom." I felt some kind of warmth wash through me, a feeling entirely separate from the sharp sun scratching at my neck. "I appreciate that a lot."

As we finished our conversation, she told me she loved me and she missed me, and I said the same to her. After hanging up, I paused. I took a breath. I looked up at the gleaming pink and purple castle, and I smiled. I picked up my pen and began to write.

～

One day, Kit hears hammering from outside. She goes out and finds Virgil has finished her stable, though it's different than she imagined. He's painted the exterior in all the pastel colors she loves. He's filled the inside with all the things Kit tried to throw out. Purple, pink, and gold beaded streamers hang from the ceiling like rain. The walls are covered with her old curtains, her old ribbons, her art from all periods of her life: unicorns and rainbows and fairies and a woman surrounded by golden light.

"It's an art show of my life," she says, tears in her eyes.

I was shaking, though I didn't know why. I felt something bubbling from beneath my skin, some different kind of craving, the vibrations of a life ready to be lived.

～

I'd had a long day at work when I crashed onto my bed and turned on Netflix. I had spent two hours of my shift in the blazing heat, organizing the strollers parents left behind while they took their kids on the rides. I just wanted something to distract me now. The movie looked cute and fun—that's why I chose it. I wasn't that into unicorns, but to watch the story of someone who could embrace magic like Kit could—I wanted to see what that could look like. I hadn't expected it to unlock something. I hadn't expected the folding of my throat, the tears, the pain in my chest, the ache in my limbs. I wanted to jump and run from my room, but I couldn't tear myself away from the TV. I was utterly enthralled. Completely terrified. Unsure and alive.

I watched Kit stand in the stable with Virgil, watched as she got a phone call from The Salesman, as he told her the unicorn was waiting for her at The Store. She asks why he'd disappeared, and he tells her that the store wasn't for Virgil: "He's not going to see it if he doesn't believe it." When she hangs up, Virgil tells her that The Salesman was dangerous. He could be lying to her. It could all be a trick.

"I know!" Kit yells. "I know! I know! I'm stupid, but he says that the unicorn is there. It's ready for me."

In her voice, you can hear the longing for it to be true. She wants it to be. She wants it so badly—and I wanted it for her. Because if this magic could be real for her—maybe it could be real for me too.

Outside of a stable crafted from the joy of Kit's life, Virgil says The Salesman has to be deceiving her. Kit clenches her teeth and scowls. "But . . . I just don't know." She stumbles over her words. "It's just—I'm confused, and . . ." Her shoulders dip. She meets Virgil's eyes. A pained expression crosses over her face, and she sighs.

"I don't want to wonder my whole life."

So, Kit goes back to The Store. The Salesman has returned. He tells her to go to the back; her unicorn is waiting. And she does so—opens the big wooden door, walks into the dark on the other side. She continues onward, coming upon a golden curtain. Hesitantly, she pulls it aside and rainbow light spills out, blinding her. She lets go. Everything falls back into darkness. She pauses as if bracing herself. This is it. She's about to find out whether the unicorn is real, and we're about to find out with her.

Do you want to know what happens next?

We're nearly at the end of the movie; just a few minutes left. And yet, when it comes to the unicorn—whether it's real or imaginary—I'm not sure it matters. That's not what the story's about. The curtain, that's what's important. Because Kit would never be able to move on, to live, without knowing what stood behind it.

So she opened it. She saw. She learned. She understood. I think I did too.

The movie ended, but I remained on my bed for a while, listening to the credit music. Still shaking, still crying, tears still rolling slow and light down my cheeks. My body felt numb. My mind felt numb. I didn't know what to do next.

⁓

I pulled myself up. Stumbled to my bathroom shower because bathrooms and showers have so often been my safe place: where I first accepted I was gay, where Eric saw me, where I felt he accepted me, where I eventually accepted myself.

Inside, I made the water as hot as I could bear, turned my body so the drops crashed across my back. I took my usual stance—all my weight on my left leg, right knee bent, head dipped, hands clasped around the back of my neck. I had turned on music—my song obsession playing on repeat: "Broken and Beautiful" by Kelly Clarkson.

Ever so slowly, I felt my muscles tense. I shook harder. My thoughts moved faster. I clenched my fingers tighter around my neck. The reverberations of noise inside my body matched the sound of music beating across bathroom tiles: elongating, stretching, snapping back against my spine. I wrapped my arms around my stomach and hugged my own body, and a great burning built within me. It was a feeling I had such difficulty recognizing. Not pain. I knew that feeling well. More like regret. Fear. The dull ache of a life half-lived. I had failed in everything I'd set out to do. Failed at marriage, failed at love, failed my writing, failed my family and my friends and myself.

I collapsed onto the tub floor and wept, steam rising from my skin, filling the bathroom, coating my lungs with its vapor. And in a way I hadn't prepared for, my thoughts quieted; words spilled from sobbing throat, slamming against my body: I told myself I forgave myself. That maybe I even loved myself, a thought so inexplicably foreign, words tasting sweet and sour on my tongue.

And I thought back to a day many years before when my therapist asked me why I hated myself. When I told him I didn't. When I realized I did and realized it was because I was gay and trapped and closeted. And almost exactly seven years later, in a bathroom miles and miles away from the one before, I realized I had learned nothing. Nothing had changed. Not really. I was still hiding who I was and who I wanted to be. I was still afraid of ever being fully seen. But I was finally ready to let loose.

And in my mind, I saw that little Andrew, the one who would sneak down to his parents' computer seeking enlightenment, the one so scared of being known and seen and heard, so afraid of being alone that he'd lied and schemed and loved in all the wrong ways. The hurt Andrew. The lost Andrew. The same one standing outside a window watching his friends smile and laugh without him, the one collapsed in a high school bathroom after being told he didn't belong. I saw him. I finally saw him. I reached out, stretching through the twisting bands of time, and I wrapped my arms around him. I embraced him. I told him I understood he was just doing the best he could. This pain—it wasn't all his fault. He was just trying to survive a narrative he would never fit—he could never fit—and I told him it was okay to hurt. I told him it would get better someday. And it would. I had to believe it still could.

And I held myself tighter.

~

I changed direction. I spoke with a professor from my old university and found the program had an opening for their graduate degree. I applied that April. In May, I got in. I would be starting the coming fall. My lease was up in July. I had two months to get everything together and move back to Utah.

When I told Chris of my plans, he was supportive enough, but I could tell it pained him. I could tell he wanted things to be different. He told me he would move to Utah if I asked him to, but I couldn't ask. I know it hurt him for me to say no, but I also know I would have hurt him more if I'd said yes. I wasn't ready to love anyone. I don't think I could if I'd tried. I'd spent my life trying to exist in a body I was taught was impure and unlovable, always desperate for affection—by which I mean I was terrified of being alone—by which I actually mean I knew I needed to learn how to be alone in order to survive. I'd gone from living with my parents to living with my friends to living with Jed to living with Chris. I needed to be on my own—an overwhelming kind of sadness.

And in some circular story, I didn't have enough money to rent a U-Haul, so, like Jed, I packed everything I couldn't fit in my car into our storage unit. My brother Marcus flew out to help me drive back across the country. And on the final night of my time in Florida, Chris, Marcus, and I went to see the Happily Ever After firework show—the same fireworks I saw from afar my first night in Florida, the same one they put on every night. In the grand courtyard of the Magic Kingdom, in front of Cinderella's Castle, I watched the show that had shaped my life for so long—not knowing if I'd ever see it again. And as the castle lit up in grand lights and projections from all the Disney movies I cherished, I cried. Not sadly. Not happily. Simply the sheer amount of emotion spilling over as lyrics reached out to me, burning into my bones: *The story comes alive; a new adventure there in your eyes. It's just the beginning; feel your heart beat faster. Reach out and find your happily ever after.*

And it felt so childish—to cry at a Disney firework show like this, to be so moved by this song, to know I was still chasing some version of happily ever after. But beneath those cascading lights, I wrapped my arms around my own body, felt my ribs, my stomach, my neck and back and wrists. My knuckles whitened as I clenched my fingers together, as I pressed into my skin. I felt warm wind brushing my hair, smelled popcorn and coffee and sweets. I lifted my gaze and found the burning sky opening up, like transcendence, the slight upturn of my lips, a pause and a breath, the rapid beating of my heart.

In the morning, with my life packed in the back seat of my car, I said goodbye to Chris. Like with Jed, I wanted to believe it wasn't forever. I told him we would keep talking, that we'd find a way to make things work. I didn't know then that I was lying. We'd break up that fall.

I found myself standing at a curtain—answers waiting on the other side: something light, something dark, maybe magic or beast or boy come to destroy me. I feared what might change once I pulled it back, but I was so much more afraid of never finding out. There, on the edge of everything, I wanted to believe I wasn't meant to be destroyed, that maybe, just maybe, I could allow myself to heal.

As Marcus and I drove away, I looked back and waved to Chris, an ache lingering deep in my bones. I was leaving him behind. Him and everything else. Disney and fairytales and love. I couldn't know whether it'd be worth it.

Listen: we're standing on the precipice, and there's a moral to the tale I'm telling. I can feel it grinding against my throat, burning my blood and guts and skin. Can you see it?

I'm getting so tired of searching.

END ACT II

A Wolf Boy Interlude

ONCE UPON A TIME, there was a boy lost in the woods. He came upon a wolf, and the wolf asked him to dance. So they danced. They danced and danced and danced away from the path, into a field of wild rainbow flowers. The wolf picked one at its stem and gave it to the boy as a gift. The boy graciously accepted and placed it in his basket full of bread. When he looked back up, the wolf was gone. The boy was alone again. Lost in the woods forever. Or so the story goes.

~

At thirteen, I still went to church every Sunday morning. In Sacrament Meeting, a man stood at the podium in a bright white shirt and red tie, and he told us a parable about a merchant and his perfect pearl and the jewel box he'd crafted to hold it. But when the merchant proudly displayed his treasure to others, he found the people loved the box more than they admired the pearl. And when the man at the podium told us this tale, he also told us it was a metaphor for our bodies. He claimed that we were all so focused on the container, we had forgotten the purpose for which it was built.

As he continued into stories of Peter and Jesus and John the Baptist, my mother's voice rang in a whisper beside me: *Andrew, stop holding your breath.* And I released air from my lips like a gasp because I hadn't realized I'd been holding it. My mom took my hand in hers and smiled. *You have to stop doing that, honey,* she told me.

I nodded because I knew she was right. But how was I supposed to stop a thing I didn't know I'd started?

~

A few weeks after returning home from my mission, I tried to become friends with Dhane again—some taste of a high school crush lingering in the back of my throat. And he seemed to want to be friends too. So, in that attempt, I never asked about the yearbook ghosting. And he didn't bring up the window incident. Perhaps we both wanted to pretend those parts of ourselves weren't real. I should have known by then that things are never that simple.

He left on his mission to New York City just a few months later. I went to his farewell talk. He told me to keep in touch. And I did—for a while at least. I came out soon after he left, and I never told him, too afraid of how he might respond. It just seemed like a conversation better had in person.

Two years later, a year into my relationship with Jed, I messaged Dhane's mom to see when he was coming back. I knew his two years were up, and I hoped there'd be a good time or day to come by to say hi and congratulate him on his return. I got a message from her account a few days later:

Hello Andrew. There is no need to contact me. Please do not try to through my family. Thank you.—Dhane

I never saw him again.

~

There's a wolf sanctuary in Indiana where I watched wolves jump and snarl and play. I was also told I couldn't join them. Years later, in the North Carolina Zoo, I saw red wolves trotting through their enclosure, and there, on the other side of the fence, I felt a familiar yearning, like calling, some desperate wish to touch, to run and jump and hunt alongside them. That night, I emailed the zookeeper; I told him I was writing a book with wolves at the center; I told him I wanted to get closer than I had ever been. To meet them. Maybe, if possible, even touch one.

It felt so strange to me—this desperate wanting to pet a wolf. It seems arbitrary when I think about it logically. What difference would it really make? To be up close. To touch. To feel the vibration of their heartbeats alongside mine. So, after emailing, I told myself it didn't matter that much. I can always go see them. Witness the wildness from afar. It would be good enough. Even when I was so tired of accepting a life that was good enough.

I was so tired.

The next day, he emailed back, and he told me he would love to sit down and chat with me, but it wasn't possible for me to meet the wolves. And though I knew this was the likely answer, and it felt foolish to care so much, I dropped my head to my desk and cried.

~

When it comes to fairy tales, my favorites are those that are rewritten: *Into the Woods, The 10th Kingdom, Wicked, Once Upon a Time*—the latter being a TV show that reinvents Little Red Riding Hood to also be the wolf from the Peter and the Wolf story: a shapeshifter, though she does not know this at first. She learns she is a wolf when she devours her lover, Peter. As the full moon pulses in the sky and Little Red finally wakes, she finds Peter's remains in the red-stained snow, and she screams.

This is different from the Little Red in *Into the Woods* who, after being carved out of a wolf's stomach, sings out into the audience that she knows things now that she didn't know before, that capes can't actually protect you even when they should. And it doesn't come as a surprise that when we see Little Red in the woods during the second act, she's wearing a wolf's skin and bearing a dagger like a fang.

So I suppose she's right to sing her song. After all, wearing sheep's wool didn't save Aesop's wolf; wearing grandmother's clothes didn't save Little Red's. It's a moral I'm so desperate to learn.

~

There are many wolves in Norse mythology, most having some relation to the Trickster God, Loki, most famous for tricking another god into giving him information on how to kill Baldr—beloved son of the All-Father, Odin. And it was the death of Baldr that brought Loki's destruction. After Baldr was killed, the other gods forced Loki to watch as they transformed one of his sons into a wolf and made the wolf tear apart his second son. Then, they used his son's entrails to tie him to a pile of rocks deep in the earth. And since that wasn't enough, they decided to hang a serpent above his head that would drip a venom onto his face for eternity, searing and burning, causing Loki to grind his teeth and scream and tremble. A just punishment, right? And he should be punished. I mean, it makes sense. He's the villain in the story of the gods. But still, it just seemed cruel.

And yet, I felt some kind of sorrow for Loki, for this incredibly cruel fate, and when I held up my hand in a graduate Norse mythology course to question whether his punishment fit his crime, a girl in class interrupted me. "It's what he deserved," she said. "He's the cause of all suffering in the world. He'll bring about the end of everything."

I paused because her words were ones I'd heard before, an all-too-familiar argument. And it wasn't a surprise to hear it; I knew she was a devout Mormon, just like I once was. Her vernacular was that of Sunday School, where I learned of Satan's rebellion, where I learned about Eve's.

"I guess I just understand why he might be angry enough to do that," I said. "Maybe the gods deserve to be destroyed."

~

Eight years ago, when I first began this book, I didn't know it was a book I was writing. I didn't plan for any essay to be a plot point in a larger narrative arc. I simply followed the request of a teacher to list off the top ten things I was too afraid to write about, and then I wrote about them: essays about god and sexuality and my body. I just wanted to tell the story, and over the years, essay by essay, I saw the structure build. The essays: just fragments of self, written by a boy trying to figure out what the memories meant and how he became a wolf. And not a wolf.

Years later, while sitting on the floor of my tiny one-bedroom apartment, I wrote essay titles on sticky notes and laid them on the ground and found a pieced-together narrative in the stories I wrote while living them: stories about Mormonism and sexuality, my family and my friends, how I hated my body and craved the bodies of other men, how I fell in love and out of love and contracted HIV, and how, just a month before, I tattooed I CHOOSE JOY on my forearm.

If you feel tangled in the narrative, fighting to loosen the knots, that's okay. I understand. I'm here at the page, and I'm telling you to keep pushing through. We're entering Act III here, and Act III is supposed to bring resolution, all these pieces crashing toward each other. We're working our way toward the finale. I have to believe an answer is coming.

~

Wolfish terminology is as follows: Swedish and Norwegian, *varg*. Icelandic, *vargr*. Both have double meanings: wolf and wicked person. The Gothic word *vargs* (*warg* in Old High German, *warc* in Middle High German, *verag* in Anglo-Saxon) stands for murderer, stranger, outlaw, evil spirit, and wolf. Those declared as wargs were banished forever from human society, forced to live in the wild.

In J. R. R. Tolkien's Middle Earth, wargs are giant, beastly wolves ridden by orcs and feared by others. In George R. R. Martin's *A Song of Ice and Fire*, wargs are people who can enter into the minds of animals, can see through their eyes, can control their actions. One of the main characters of the series, Bran Stark, gains these abilities and uses them to journey into the ancient northern wildlands. While he can warg into crows and magical weirwood trees throughout the Seven Kingdoms, he most commonly links his mind with his companion direwolf, Summer.

These words and others like them revolve inside my head as I try to navigate their stories. A warg is a wolf, a wicked person, an evil spirit. A warg is to be sent into the wild. Bran is a member of the Stark family—represented by a direwolf in its coat of arms—he is a warg and he is one of the heroes of his story. He is sent into the wild. He is protected by his wolf.

I'm interested in definitions and double meanings, in contradictions and contranyms. How we can weather a storm, or we can weather and wear away. How we temper to soften, or we temper to build; from dust to dust, we sprinkle our particles and then wipe them away.

There's something to understand in this. As the stories go, I am either wicked or good. So, here, flip a coin—place me in a version of the story that makes sense. Hero or villain. Hero or villain. I'm tired of trying to figure out the part I get to play.

Flip. Stop. Open your hand. Look closely. Tell me—

where are we going next?

ACT III

Choices, numberless as grains of sand, had layered
and compressed, coalescing into sediment, then into rock,
until all was set in stone.

   —TARA WESTOVER, *Educated*

I'm no angel. I'm not dead.
I live inside a little nest of words
and I live inside your head,
my story living and living.

   —SHANAN BALLAM, *Inside the Animal*

Howl

IN A RARE MOMENT OF MY TEENAGE YEARS, I found myself howling. Laughing. Sprinting down an empty street at midnight. I was sixteen, a full moon had broken through the clouds, and, as Parker had said: *Wolves just can't help themselves.* He took the lead, jet-black hair scattering in the wind behind him. The rest of us followed—Dallin, Jake, and I—as he raced from Kenzie's Halloween party, nearly tripping over the front threshold as he fled.

I had felt myself loosening up over that summer between my junior and senior years, I had turned from the boy hiding in the corner of every party into the one who danced in the middle of the living room. After all, I was seventeen now. I had been holding myself back since I was eight. Nearly a decade. I was eager to be reckless. Not too much. But somewhat.

If you remember, I met Parker, Dallin, and Jake the previous year when we were all cast in the fall musical, *Oklahoma!* I'd grown close to them quickly, perhaps because they were the first group of non-Mormons I'd consistently associated myself with. It felt as though, with them, even for a moment, I could be just a little freer—and I so desperately yearned to be. We banded together like a pack. Like a family. We even garnered a nickname together: the theater werewolves.

We had arrived at Kenzie's Halloween party together, and we had arrived dressed as werewolves—by which I mean, we came with black hairspray bricking our hair, dried mud smudged in spots over our skin, and torn-up white T-shirts and black shorts. And when the rare Halloween full moon emerged that night, we ran into the street. And we howled.

Other party guests followed out the door, laughing and pointing as we cried out in the cold night air. Parker hopped onto the hood of his car, slipped his fingers into a particularly large hole in his shirt, and pulled. The cloth tore easily in half, and he threw the shredded leftovers on the ground. Girls on the porch whistled and hollered. Parker smiled in a sly kind of way and lifted his chin to howl again.

Dallin and Jake rapidly followed suit, ripping their shirts from their bodies too, but I hesitated. I had never done something like that before—purposely showed so much of my skin to my friends. Except in swimming pools, but only because that seemed a more morally correct way to do so. I wasn't supposed to show off my body. A step closer to sex and all that. A valid worry seeing as I couldn't help but linger for a moment on Parker, on the way the moonlight slid off the lean, muscular frame of his chest, the way his teeth gleamed beneath the stars.

I grabbed the holes of my shirt and pulled, threads tearing like brakes on screeching wheels. Shrapnel cloth scraps fell to the ground. I heard more whistles from the porch as Parker lowered his hand to help lift me onto the hood of his car. The metal bent beneath our weight, but we didn't care. We bared our teeth, lifted our eyes toward the luminous sky, stuck out our bare chests, and released our voices into the night, vocal cords vibrating like song.

In the moment that felt like eternity, I set myself free.

Piercing

It's the autumn of 2019, just a few months after I left Florida, and my heartbeat thrums against my ribcage. The high ceilings, tiled floor, and pale halls of Southcenter Mall in Tacoma, Washington manifest a clinical aura in a space I would typically find the opposite. I always thought malls were somewhat dirty places. Full of cafeteria food smell and horrible restrooms. But that wasn't the case here. I try to relieve a churning stomach by concentrating on getting my ears pierced at a place that looks so clean because, more than anything, I fear the outcome. I fear infection.

Jed guides me through a maze of clothing and game stores toward the place he'd gotten his ears pierced at nineteen. Eight years ago. Roughly the same age as when my brother Matthew pierced his. I suppose I'm just a decade behind both of them. It often seems like my lot in life—to be somewhat culturally stunted. My therapist said this is common for many gay men and women who didn't come out in their teenage years. Instead of searching for self-discovery and identity in middle school, we play this game in our twenties.

When I told her this makes sense, seeing as I'm twenty-seven and just now figuring out that I like to wear brightly colored scarves and tight vests instead of graphic tees and zip-up hoodies, she smiled. She told me there's no shame in my age of exploration, but I still feel like I'm coming late to the world.

"Internalized homophobia is a bitch," she said to me. I laughed because the truth of her words hit me hard. Then, in an effort to explore identity outside of my own homophobia, she told me to do something *fabulous* this week.

"I've wanted to pierce my ears for years," I told her.

The timing seemed perfect. I was about to fly out to Seattle to visit Jed. It had been eight months since we separated. I was coming to visit him anyway—we're still trying to figure out what we mean to each other. So here I am. Trying. Plus, he understands me better than most, and I've missed that.

As we walk the mall's hallway, I glance to his ears. Diamond studs— it's what he's worn as long as I've known him. I wonder what kind might look good in my own ears: studs, hoops, dangles, barbells, ear threads. Honestly, I just hope they end up being even and straight and clean.

Various scenarios run through my head, most circling around how worried I am about the pain of self-mutilation. It's been a mantra for years: I'm more afraid of getting a piercing than I am of getting a tattoo. Logically, I understand the foolishness of the thought. The pain of the tattooed paws on my chest would far outweigh the pain of a pierced ear.

I wonder then if the fear exists because, when piercing, the needle goes all the way through—a chosen wound—a literal hole punched through my skin.

8.

I know the first evidence of pierced bodily alteration came 5,300 years ago from Ötzi the Iceman, who was discovered with pierced ears and sixty-one tattoos covering his body. Five-millennia-old body modification. I can't help but wonder why he wanted to alter his being in such ways. The crisscrossing tattoos lacing his skin are believed to have been crafted by fine incisions followed by pressing charcoal into the wounds. The positionality of the markings tells us that he probably obtained the tattoos as a kind of therapy—like acupuncture—pressed into parts of the body that receive considerable wear and tear throughout a lifetime: ribcage, spine, wrists, knees, calves, and ankles. Scientists believe they were a bid to soothe his pain.

It's hard to know, though, why Ötzi pierced his ears. I wonder if it was spiritually driven. Maybe a fashion choice. Perhaps he too fought to alter himself, to become someone new. I want to ask him why, but he died 5,300 years ago.

I've wanted to ask my brother, Matthew, why he pierced his ears in his late teens, but I never have. I was young at the time—nine or ten. I remember thinking the earrings odd because Mormonism had taught me that only women were supposed to have them. Still, I liked them. I wanted them. I yearned to decorate myself, just like him—hair dyed dark, rings on his fingers, ears pierced with studs. I was jealous of how free he must feel.

The freedom I craved is similar to the way Matthew used to sing in the car. We both loved musical theater, and we both took singing lessons from the same teacher, Doris. She taught us how to open ourselves up, to breathe deeply, to never close ourselves off. Matthew seemed to find this space easier than me. He would belt out songs in the car for my mom while I murmured notes next to him. I didn't like my own voice. At fifteen, it wasn't beautiful like Matthew's. It wasn't full of vibrato and depth and years of training. Once, while "Empty Chairs and Empty Tables" from *Les Misérables* blasted through the car's speakers, my mom called from the front, "I want to hear both of you sing."

I shrunk into my seat, but Matthew nudged me. I met his eyes, so like my own, and he smiled. "Remember what Doris says. We have to open ourselves up." When I shook my head, he placed his arm around my shoulders, pulling me close. "I'll sing with you. Don't worry."

And he did.

And for one of Doris's recitals, Matthew and I performed a duet from the musical *The Mystery of Edwin Drood* called "Both Sides of the Coin." Previously, it had been hard for me to take the recitals seriously. As a teenager, I was so obsessed with trying to fit in with my friends that practicing daily like Matthew seemed nonsensical. He would sit for hours each night, practicing at the piano, his voice filling the house like the scent of his morning coffee. But my apathy changed when I got the chance to sing *with* him; I wanted to do it well for him.

In the family room of our childhood home, we practiced together. He would play the piano and, together, we'd sing out the words:

I am not myself these days—for all I know I might be you.
There's more than room enough for two inside my mind.
I am likewise in a haze of who I am from scene to scene;
What's more, we two (we four, I mean) are in a bind!
For is it I or is it me?

Matthew also choreographed a dance for the song. We twisted around each other, he and I—two brothers, almost exactly ten years apart—dancing together, laughing at the absurdity of the lyrics, tripping over each other's feet. I didn't know at the time that he suggested the song to Doris. Maybe because he wanted to show me how much fun it could be to sing and dance. Maybe he hoped I'd open myself up to the possibilities of freedom this could bring.

It was because of Matthew's strength and positivity I didn't fully comprehend the battle he'd gone through to survive his own narrative. At fifteen, I didn't know Matthew had dropped out of Brigham Young University after his first semester, how he'd fallen into a meth addiction. How he'd been diagnosed with HIV. I didn't understand the depths of the years he'd lived through—years of relapsing and sobering, relapsing again, getting sober again, going to AA, doing everything he could to survive. Because I was the youngest member of my family, Matthew and my parents sought to protect me from the truth. For a long time, I didn't know the version of my brother that struggled and worked so hard to sing and dance there beside me. He made it appear so easy.

7.

Five years before our duet, when I was ten, in the midst of Matthew's hardships, my mom called me into her bedroom. When I neared her bedside, she reached out to me from under the covers. She and I both have bad circulation, so we both pile blankets over ourselves to keep warm. Matthew has this too. Our round faces also reflect my mother's. My family refers to these things as the *Godfrey Gene*—Godfrey being my mother's maiden name. This isn't the only thing we joke about being passed on. Empathy too; forgetfulness; other, less definable things.

My hands were cold as I threaded my fingers into my mother's warm touch. She liked to hold my hands when we talked, as if it was her way of being connected, something I could mimic myself. But I wasn't paying attention to her hands; I looked deep into her eyes. I could see my reflection in the irises.

After asking me how I was doing, she paused, and I sensed her battling with herself. It was as if something was fighting to get out of her, but she didn't know how to release it. She removed one of her hands from mine and placed it atop our pile of fingers, her warmth spread over my skin. "I just wanted to talk to you about something."

I kept staring into her eyes, letting my reflection in them blur. "Okay."

She paused again. She leaned in toward me and smiled. "Well, it's just, you know Matthew's gay, right?"

I couldn't help but roll my eyes and smile too. "Well, I kind of figured." Matthew had been bringing his boyfriend around for a few months at that point.

She laughed. "Yes, well, we thought you knew, we just wanted to make sure."

I laughed beside her. It died out quickly, and we were both silent for a moment. She studied me. Searched me. Tried to close the distance.

"You're not though, are you?" The question rang from her in something just louder than a whisper.

"No. No," I said instantly, shaking my head, as if I'd been trained for the question. I couldn't be gay. I knew what being gay meant: boyfriends and tattoos and cigarettes and drugs and alcohol and piercings. It meant families being broken apart and older brothers disappearing on younger brothers. So, no, I wouldn't be gay.

6.

I wonder if Matthew's earrings inadvertently caused my association with gay men wearing earrings—as if piercings could be a calling card to recognize one another. Maybe it's why I was so afraid that being gay could be synonymous with being Matthew, with following his path— the only path I believed a gay man could take because I didn't know any other gay men to prove differently. And even after I came out at age twenty, I still fought to avoid any further association with the culture of being *flamboyantly gay*. Perhaps it's why I started out as a musical theater major my first semester of college and then switched to English quickly after. English seemed less obviously gay. It was an idea which bled into others. I determined early on that I would never drink alcohol. Or smoke. Or get a tattoo, or take drugs, or pierce my ears. I wanted to be the *good* gay son, the one to be proud of.

Even within this decision, I wanted to understand more about the culture I was suddenly existing within. I researched the history of homosexuality in the library of BYU, the same school that Matthew dropped out of years before. Alongside discoveries of Harvey Milk and the Stonewall Riots, I found an article discussing the fad of piercing ears as a way of identification. The article, published by the *New York Times*, claimed that gay men in the late twentieth century began piercing their right ears, hanging a single article of jewelry as an indication of their sexual identity.

One gay man living in New York at the time explained how, "in a world where you can't dress flamboyantly, that's a very discrete signal."

Still, the idea that a pierced right ear could equate homosexuality has been argued for years. A sound technician in Chicago thought the whole idea was "stupid," and that it seemed as if the rumor was yet another stereotype for gay people so others could "spot the faggot in the room."

Skimming through the article, I subconsciously lifted a hand to my right ear and pulled down the earlobe, stretching the skin. After rubbing the flesh between my thumb and forefinger, I pinched down with chewed fingernails. A shot of pain—I gasped and released.

I felt a duality: I wanted to distinguish myself as a man who loved men, but not destructively—an image branded into my mind of my brother—a gay man with dyed-brown hair, a love for musical theater and writing. And pierced ears. And addicted to meth. I refused to be like him, to reflect his journey. And, for a long while, because we didn't speak of these things, I believed my parents' suffering came from his being gay. I didn't learn till later that his sexuality had never been an issue for my family.

When Matthew moved back into my parents' house, I lived in the basement. Matthew made coffee most mornings, the smell of beans filling the house. After waking to the scent, I walked upstairs to find my father in the kitchen making breakfast. I asked where Matthew was, marking the coffee dripping into the pot on the counter. My dad gestured to the snow-covered backyard. I wanted to go find him and bring him in from the February chill, but my dad told me to stay inside.

"Matthew needs time alone."

I think a small part of me understood his meaning—that the scent of coffee wouldn't be strong enough to cover up the smell of smoke—but I didn't like imagining Matthew sitting alone in the backyard, in the cold, with nothing but his own thoughts to hear.

I didn't see Matthew come back inside. I only heard the shower run before I snuck out to the backyard. I didn't know what I wanted to understand, what I hoped to gain from the knowledge, but I walked out—down the small alley at the side of our house where weeds sprouted from bricked ground, down to where I found a carved tree stump. Cigarette butts littered the snow, ash lying atop scuffled white powder.

I could almost see him there, sitting on that stump, smoking his cigarette, drinking his coffee in his blue plaid pajama bottoms he'd gotten two months before, on Christmas Eve. Alone. And I wondered what hurt worse: the knowledge that he had been out there, or the fact that nobody told me why.

I believe this to be my initial understanding of addictions that dug deeper, stronger, more destructive. My brother's suffering, the battles he faced with methamphetamines, the tension he had with my parents, his partners, with me—it would all be hushed up and hidden away. Most information I would find piece by piece, discovered through the sheer will to understand.

Matthew didn't stay in the house for too long that time—though I don't remember where he went next. I don't know if that leaving was the time he moved in with his partner. I don't know if it was when he went to the recovery house in Boise. I just remember prescription drugs stolen from my parents' bathroom cabinet. Even after he left, they kept their medications in their bedroom closet instead—behind a door that could lock.

5.

Jed and I rise up on the escalator of Southcenter Mall to the second floor. The pungent assorted scents of melted cheese and teriyaki is lessened up here, and I'm grateful. My stomach can't handle more nausea. I can't help but fear how my parents will react to the holes in my ears, to my claim of self-identity. Twenty-seven, and I'm still righteously conscious of how my parents could react to my choices, especially the ones that looked like Matthew's, even though we've all left Mormonism behind now. I imagine it in their eyes—the fear—the unbridled tension of knowing I'm not my brother and realizing how much I look like him. Our off-blonde hair, red beards, round faces, stockier bodies. The way we both love musical theater and writing. The way we laugh. Our homosexuality. I dread seeing a flash of unsettling in their eyes, a fear of how easy it is to disappear.

At some point, Matthew got da Vinci's *Vitruvian Man* tattooed across his back, and I don't recall who didn't want me to see it. At my grandparent's house, my brother took our uncle and my parents into a separate bedroom in order to show them the artistic choice. I stayed in the kitchen with my grandmother. I don't think anyone expected me to be so curious, to wonder where my brother had gone with the other adults. Maybe there was a hope I wouldn't care. But I slipped from the kitchen. With four siblings and many more cousins, I'd learned long ago how to blend in and disappear.

The door was open. I saw multiple bodies surrounding my bare-backed brother. Between his shoulders, I saw it: creasing black lines, the perfectly proportioned man with four legs and four arms stretching to the outside of a circle. I didn't know much about da Vinci back then. I didn't know that when a tattoo needle touches bone, the pain is excruciating. I didn't understand the pain Matthew must have gone through as the needle swept across his spine to craft the *Vitruvian Man* on his back. All I knew was that it was beautiful.

My uncle saw me first. "Andrew!" he shouted in surprise. I jumped, startled. My eyes locked with my parents before landing on my brother, meeting the expression peering over his shoulder.

He slipped his sweater over his back and turned to me, smiling in a guilty kind of way. "We didn't want you to see," he told me.

My mother pulled me aside later that night to talk. "Are you okay?" she asked me.

"I'm fine."

With a hesitant laugh, she joked, "Now, don't you go getting one, okay?"

I met her eyes, sensing the fear, seeing the pain. I couldn't do that to her. I would never do that to her. "I won't. I don't want one. I promise."

At twenty-five, I got my first tattoo: paws imprinted above my heart, made from the pawprints of my first dog, Lance. It was my way of honoring him. He'd died too young, hit by a car on a late January night.

When I called my mother to tell her, I rapidly explained how this tattoo *meant* something—it wasn't just a needle I threw against my body because I wasn't satisfied with myself. She laughed and told me she knew that.

"I don't know why you were so afraid to tell me," she said. "I'm not upset, Andrew. I love you."

I hope she'll believe the same of these earrings, that I'm getting them for a *reason*. That I'm discovering myself. Though I wonder why there should even need to be such a reason. Still, if I can persuade my parents, then maybe I can persuade myself that it's different from Matthew. That I'm different.

4.

The day I left for Seattle, my dad drove me to the airport, and I admitted to him for the first time my fears of becoming like Matthew—of how I'd hidden myself and my identity away because I didn't want to become him.

"You didn't have to do that," he told me.

"I know."

He considered me for a moment before continuing. "I know how that feels though. I felt that with my brother too. I think maybe it's an inevitability of the younger sibling—to want to break free."

I was quiet then, digesting the words, a question I'd wanted to ask for years bubbling up inside me. I had never asked it because any conversation that had to do with Matthew's addictions felt off-limits. As if we might be able to pretend the problems never existed if we just pushed them down. And yet, I knew that was the issue—that closing myself off had caused so much pain.

"Did Matthew ever disappear? Did he ever run away?"

My dad looked perplexed, and so I told him I had this memory of absence, and how it's confusing because I wasn't sure if it actually happened. I felt it was easy to remember the moments he was there, but I didn't know how to remember a hole.

"No, he never really disappeared," my dad said. "Though he did drop out of BYU after a semester when you were nine or ten. He didn't tell us." He explained how maybe through the secrecy and drugs, it may have felt like Matthew wasn't around as much. I told him it made sense, but I knew I was lying. I didn't know how my brother could have been absent enough that I convinced myself he wasn't there at all.

My dad hugged me close when we arrived at the Salt Lake City airport. It felt like he was trying to tell me something in the embrace, and I tried to hold onto it.

3.

Jed describes pierced ears as an immediate but momentary pain. After about a week, I shouldn't feel the metal-filled hole in my earlobe. I'll forget about the absence. I hope it's true. I ask him to remind me of this as we arrive at BJP, the place where I'll be pierced.

He whispers it to me again outside the doorway. "It'll heal, Andrew."

I nod, staring at the floor-to-ceiling windows of the tattoo and piercing shop. The doors are wide open. I can see, even at a distance, that the store is full of glass. Glass cases. Glass cabinets. A hundred different mirrors. I appreciate the transparency.

Still, I stop for a moment when we move into the store. Fear bubbles inside my stomach, the terror of what it means to do what I'm doing. Jed stops beside me. He must feel my hesitancy. He knows my story, knows why this is hard. He understands the complexity.

"You don't have to do it, you know," he says. "You can wait. Maybe try some clip-ons first."

I meet his eyes, but quickly slide to the diamond studs in his ears. I want to be that brave. That free. The idea of falsehood rattles me.

"No."

I march to the glass counter in the center of the store, sweeping past the things that might distract me: Harry Potter backpacks, snowflake necklaces, Pokémon socks, and tattoo books. The girl at the counter smiles at me when I arrive in front of her. "How can I help you?"

Before I lose the courage, I say, perhaps a little brashly, "I need to pierce my ears."

"Of course." She sweeps some loose hair behind her left ear, simultaneously pulling forms from beneath the glass counter. "Where on your ear would you like to get pierced?"

I mark her assortment of earrings, now uncovered. It's as if she's giving me options, and I can count four. Two lobes, a daith, an industrial. "Just the lobes," I tell her. She nods and hands the forms to me.

I wonder if I'll want more than the lobes someday. I hear the others hurt more and take longer to heal than a simple hole in the earlobe. Breaking through cartilage is much more painful than simply carving away some skin.

"You still use needles, right?" Jed asks. "Not a gun?"

The girl laughs. "Yes, yes, we use hollow-point needles."

Hollow needles. I'd done the research on them. I'd heard rumors that piercing guns were more dangerous and ended up hurting more, so instinctively, I wanted the needle anyway. In addition, while guns punch through the ear, pushing the skin apart by sheer force, hollow needles are, in fact, hollow. Instead of pressing apart the skin, it fully cleaves away a fraction of the ear. This creates a space for the jewelry to exist. It crafts a clean hole, allowing room for the wound to drain and, someday, heal.

Needles have historically been the preferable approach to create a hole in the body. And perhaps what frightens me so much is the idea of not being able to go back—the permanency of the act. Jed tells me that if I don't like them, I can just remove them and let the hole heal over. I don't have to keep the space if I don't want to.

I know this is true because Matthew pulled his out at some point. I don't have any recollection of when he did it, but I know by the time I came out as gay to him, they were long gone. I sometimes wonder if I just imagined him having them—like I imagined his absence when I was ten. But I don't think so. If I were to take a closer look, I'm sure I'd see the white pinpricks of scarring where there had once been space. A part of him that's been closed off.

The night I came out to him, the same night I came out to my parents, I was much too distressed to care about pierced ears. Matthew was living with his partner in Salt Lake City at the time, and I was living at home with my parents—a twenty-minute drive away. He'd come for dinner, and I had just finished screaming at him because he told me not to join a multi-level marketing investment with my friends. At nineteen, I knew the foolishness of joining, and yet, Matthew's words of caution had left me lying on my bed, sobbing, screaming into my pillow.

My mother came into the room and held me for a long time before asking, "Andrew, what's really going on? This isn't about Matthew. This isn't about that pyramid scheme."

More weeping, more screaming, more utterances of *I can't say I can't say* before I finally broke enough to speak the words, "I think I'm gay."

Without a moment's hesitation, she pulled me close to her and held me with everything she had. She stroked my hair and let me weep into her arms, her sleeves drooping under the weight of my tears. "I love you, Andrew," she said to me. "I will always love you. That will never change."

When I was finally able to pull myself up and look at her, I found that she was crying with me. She asked if she could bring in Matthew and my dad. She'd later say that the coincidence of Matthew being there on that night wasn't a coincidence at all, that maybe things happen for a reason.

When I told Matthew, he didn't say anything at first. Like my mother, he wrapped his arms around me, hugging me tight. I wondered if he wanted to protect me from all the pain he'd gone through, all the horrors his life threw at him.

He whispered into my ear, "No wonder you've felt so alone."

When we parted, I stared into his eyes, also wet with tears. I felt his closeness, felt the way he loved me, and we saw each other in that moment, connecting in a way we never had before.

2.

I wasn't close by Matthew when he relapsed in 2019. I was working sixty-hour weeks at various theme parks in Orlando, Florida; he was an instructor at a university near Chicago. We hadn't talked in a few weeks, so I didn't know what to make of a text to my family's group chat where his partner stated that he had smashed Matthew's phone with a hammer, so no one knew where he was now. I thought it was a joke, that I had missed something, and when I asked what it meant, nobody answered. It took a half-hour for my brother Marcus to text me, to explain that Matthew had started using meth again, that he had used his phone to find drugs, so his partner broke it. Marcus told me to call our parents if I wanted to be filled in more.

When I did call them, they told me that Matthew relapsed again and had gone missing two weeks earlier. He'd come back, but he'd disappeared after his partner smashed his phone. I wondered if it was things like this that made me believe he had disappeared during my childhood.

"Why didn't you tell me he left?" I asked my parents.

"It wasn't our place to tell you, Andrew," my mom said.

"This is Matthew's thing," my dad added.

"But he would never tell me." My tears fell heavy. I'd heard all the stories—the ones where the brother relapses, where they find him, days later, overdosed in a bathtub in a stranger's apartment. I wanted to ask them, *what if he dies?* But I couldn't bring myself to do it. I don't know which I was more afraid of: their answer or their inability to answer at all.

I learned later that week that I'd been accepted into a graduate school in Utah. I'd wanted to call Matthew before anyone. I'd wanted to tell him that I'd made it; I'd made the decision to change my life for the better like he had when he'd gone to graduate school, but I was halfway through the ringing before I remembered there was no one left on the other end. My mom told me to call his partner. Matthew had come home.

I couldn't bring myself to do it.

I.

Two months after Matthew's relapse, Marcus joined me in my move from Florida to Utah. We stopped at Melissa and Steve's house in Indiana to stay the night, just a few hours away from Matthew's place in Illinois. After tucking in their daughter, Steve and Melissa joined Marcus and me at their kitchen table. Melissa pulled out some cookies she'd made the previous day, and the four of us munched as we talked late into the night—about everything. Jobs. Relationships. Politics. School. There was a beautiful peculiarity when religion came up, seeing as we'd all left it behind years ago. An upfront quality we'd never used before. An honesty in how we all felt. It was enough to convince me I had never been alone in my doubts and fears and frustrations.

Inevitably, we came to the discussion of Matthew. Marcus told me he'd set up a time to meet Matthew in Illinois the following afternoon as we made our way toward Utah. I mentioned it to Melissa and Steve, and I cried. And they asked me what was wrong, and I told them about how I hadn't talked to Matthew since he'd relapsed. How even though it wasn't the first time he'd relapsed, in the past I had always been able to talk to him afterward. I always wanted to talk to him any chance I had to do so. Even more, it meant everything to me to be someone he could turn to in pain. And he'd be the same for me. Before this, the relapsing hadn't stopped me from trying to reach out. And he'd always come back.

But that night, something between anger and fear swelled in me at the thought of seeing him. Of talking to him. I wondered if he'd recognize the pain in my eyes, the way I'd stayed up all night when I learned he'd gotten a new phone and my parents said he would try and call. I wondered whether he'd even remember that he hadn't. I wondered what I'd feel when I saw him. Guilt. Love. Pain. Sick. Joy. Relief. Fear. Anger.

"Why is it different this time?" I asked them, sobbing into my hands.

Melissa sat next to me and wrapped her arm around my shoulder, pulling me in for a hug, telling me, "I know it's hard. I know. I feel it too."

"Me too," Marcus said. "I've been trying so hard to keep talking to him, to be there for him, but I don't know how anymore."

I could hear pain in their voices, a longing so alike to mine. "He hasn't called me," I told them. "I thought he would call me."

"Have you tried calling him?" Melissa asked me.

"No," I said, looking into the dark backyard outside the window, feeling tears drip down my cheeks. "I don't want to be the one to reach out this time. Why do I always have to be the one to call first?"

"That's really fair," Marcus said. "I call him because I know he won't be the one to call me. I guess to me, being in contact, reaching out, is the best way I can help him."

It was the same thing I thought every time previously, but this time felt different. Perhaps it was because I couldn't reach out to him when I'd heard about getting into grad school. And maybe because I couldn't tell him about Jed leaving and my struggle to leave too. And then hearing about how he'd separated from his partner too. And I thought that maybe there was someone who could really understand the weight of what all this felt like, and then that person was gone. And I understood for the first time what it might be like if Matthew died. The pain was just too palpable, the anger at his selfishness too real, the memory of his selflessness too foreign.

"You have to decide what's right for you," Steve said, his voice soft. "No one can decide for you."

"I don't want to see him," I said, the pain of my own selfish thoughts piercing deeply, making me cry harder. "I know some part of him loves me, but this isn't it. This isn't love. He can't disregard his own life and love me at the same time."

No one spoke, and I sputtered out the words, "I want him to know what it's like to lose a brother."

I saw they were all crying too, all feeling my same pain, grasping the same loss, and we held each other in the stillness.

The following afternoon, Marcus and I met Matthew's partner—his ex-partner now—in a Costco parking lot. Matthew was running late. They weren't living together anymore. They'd separated after Matthew's relapse and after the smashing of his phone. I was sure there was more to the story; I just hadn't heard it yet.

When Matthew finally arrived, he wasn't alone. Another man had come to drop him off: his new boyfriend, I would later learn. The man stayed in the car while Matthew clambered out of the passenger seat of his rusty old green Toyota. Matthew walked around the car, dropping two large duffle bags on the asphalt, and embraced Marcus in reunion. His hair had grown longer. More wiry. It seemed redder than I remembered, but maybe there was simply more of it than before. His red beard had grown out too, covering up most of his face in a twisted tangle of hair.

When they parted, he turned to me. I didn't know what to do with the feeling that I didn't want him to walk toward me. It was utterly foreign and unrecognizable. There'd never been a moment in my life when I hadn't wanted to run to my brother and hug him. There'd never been a time I'd felt this kind of unease, this wanting to turn away. To go back. To hide. To disappear.

But he walked toward me, and I embraced him too. A scent of alcohol and smoke and something unrecognizable reached out to me. His beard scritched across my neck. His brown leather jacket somehow felt cold against the mid-July heat. And we parted. He looked into my eyes and said he missed me. I told him I missed him too. I stepped back, creating a bit more space between us.

o.

I can create space by crafting a hole—one that can be filled with an assortment of different materials. Silver and gold are the most common nowadays. Throughout history, different materials filling the gaps had different meanings. For instance, the Aztecs, Mayans, and Incas pierced their septums with jade and gold to symbolize the water and sun gods. In Italy, it was once believed that simple metal could keep demons from entering into the mind through the ears—that maybe space could protect them.

And when the girl behind the glass case asks me what kind of earrings I want in my own pierced lobes, I wonder whether it actually matters. There isn't much choice. Just two kinds of studs. One, a metal bar with a tiny ball at the end. The other, the same, but it has the faintest shine of a diamond inside the ball—a little light inside the metal. That one costs five dollars more.

I choose the regular ball, the one without a faux diamond. That's not the important part. What's important is the bar, the piece that will hold my skin apart, the one that will fill the hole.

After filling out the paperwork, they take me to the back room. It's small—a tight but comfortable space. A padded table, much like the ones in hospitals and massage spas, stands in the center of the room. A man sits by the head of the table, a small tray of silvery tools beside him. The girl has me sit on the table, facing her. With a small toothpick-like pointer, she pricks my ears with an inky material and tells me to look in the mirror.

"Make sure they're even and where you want on the earlobe."

I look into the glass at my own reflection. I reminisce on when I looked in a mirror, at a puffy-eyed boy who had just realized that he loved men instead of women, whispering the words, *You're gay*, at my own reflection. The moment had been one of release, of understanding, of freedom. I wonder what I'll feel after this piercing. This intentional wounding. I wonder what it can do for me.

Sushruta, a great Indian surgeon, advocates ear-piercing by saying that it prevents diseases like hernia and hydrocele. There are those who say it might prevent hysteria and other diseases. There are even some who say the flow of spirit in the human body is maintained by wearing earrings. That maybe we can find peace by opening ourselves up.

There are those who wonder if, before written communication, before words, letters, and pictures, maybe we pierced our bodies as a form of communication. That maybe I could tell you something by the way I crafted holes into my own being. That maybe you can understand me in the spaces of my body.

And when I can't find a way to call my brother on his birthday, my mother will tell him to call me. And when he does, he'll tell me that he's in a polyamorous relationship with people who have told him that he can have a healthy amount of meth. This will be the last time I talk to my brother before I pierce my ears. He won't reach out, and neither will I.

I'll think of this conversation when my new psychiatrist diagnoses me with ADHD and asks if I want to try Adderall to help manage my symptoms and I tell her I'm afraid. And when she asks me why I'm afraid, I'll tell her about Matthew and all he's gone through and how I'm terrified some kind of addiction could be lurking within me too. But she'll tell me this is different. That I'm different. That my life is my own, and all these choices are mine to make.

So each week, when my therapist asks me what we need to talk about, I will keep telling her that I'm trying to understand my own identity—that I've covered up my being in becoming an antonym of my brother. That I yearned to be the good gay son. That I can't tell my parents that I drink alcohol because I'm so afraid that they'll think I'm becoming my brother. That contracting HIV makes me feel like I might be half-way there. That, somehow, my being equates with his addiction. That I might become the absence.

And one day, when Melissa calls my parents while I'm in the room, she'll mention that Matthew isn't coming around for Thanksgiving because he's using again, and I'll think about how he also just lost his job at the university where he taught theater classes, but I'll stay silent. After she hangs up, my mom will hold her face in her hands, and I will hold back the response, *I'm not really surprised.*

And when I see him again, years later, when all the siblings gather for my mom's sixtieth birthday celebration, I still won't fully recognize him. But I'll ask him to sit with me on the bench in front of my parents' home, and he will. And we'll talk. And I'll tell him why I've been so distant. I'll tell him how much he's hurt me, and he'll apologize for it. He will always apologize for these things. And, maybe against my better judgment, I'll feel like we might be on a path to healing.

But the next time I'll see him is over a year later at my grandfather's funeral—the grandfather who shared my middle name. And on the night before Matthew leaves, I'll overhear a conversation about how his boyfriend won't come pick him up at the airport unless my parents pay for the gas to drive there. And this will trigger something in me, some distant recollection of being abandoned on the side of the road, and I'll tell Matthew that he deserves better than this, but this will only make him angry and defensive. So we'll fight. And we'll scream. And we won't patch things up before he leaves. I'll wonder if we ever will.

But when I think of earrings and piercings, I'll never be able to forget that he had them too and that he removed them at some point that I don't recall; and I'll think about how I created space and he closed himself up; and I'll remember, like how he transformed from a pierced brother to a scarred brother, he also became someone else after his partner smashed his phone.

And I'll think of the article disputing gay men using earrings to iden-tify themselves, and how there is a quote from a woman with a pierced tongue, saying, "You'll feel it all the time. You know that you've done it with every word you say."

So when my therapist asks me what I'm most afraid of, I'll tell her it's that my parents will someday call me to tell me my brother has died. And I'll tell her that my actual worst fear is that it won't hurt because the brother I recognize is gone. And I'll tell her how this feels like a betrayal. And I'll weep, and she'll tell me it's okay to feel this way, but I won't be sure if I believe her.

So, when I lie down on that table and the bearded, tattooed, black-capped man tells me to breathe in, I do. And I think of how, when I breathe in, I might be breathing in at the same time a child takes their first breath in the world. And when he tells me to breathe out, I hope my brother can breathe out with me.

And the hollow needle carves through my earlobe, removing enough skin to create the space I need. He fills the hole with metal so my ear can heal around the wound.

When he finishes with both ears, I look back into that mirror, and the girl asks me, "What do you think?" But I don't answer. I stare into my reflection. My eyes sweep from ear to ear; I try to take in the studs, the small metal balls without diamonds, and my eyes water.

And when Jed laughs lightly, saying, "I think he likes them," the girl laughs too. And I smile, nodding because my words cannot express the feelings inside. But I feel like they understand.

And, a year later, when I will learn I've contracted HIV, I won't call Matthew right away. My mom will have to push me to do so. And when I finally do tell him, our voices reaching out across invisible telephone wires, the conversation will feel jagged. He'll say thoughtful words just like he did when I came out to him all those years ago, but I won't be sure he means them. I won't be sure of anything.

I'll wonder again about the path I'm treading, whether it leads to the place I've always feared, whether I'll see Matthew's face in the mirror when I look at myself. But I will walk a leaf-strewn path in autumn on the day I've tested positive, and I will tell my friend I don't want to hide my diagnosis, that I want to tell the story, that I want to tell it loud. And she'll remind me of how much I've changed.

And when my parents pick me up from the Salt Lake City Airport two days after I'm pierced, they'll hug me and tell me they missed me, and I'll see them glance to my ears. I'll wonder if they have a flashback to a different gay son. But then I'll see them smile, and they'll compliment them, and I'll know that they see me.

But I am not there yet, and none of that matters now. Because when Jed and I leave JBP, I run to the bathroom. "You just want to see your earrings again," Jed says as he laughs, and I agree.

I stare at my reflection in the bathroom mirror of a mall in Tacoma, Washington, and I don't recognize myself. It's a different Andrew. An alternate Andrew. An Andrew unafraid of holes. And there's something like mourning in my eyes. Maybe more like liberation. Maybe more like joy. But I see it there: the space between selves, between my body, my spirit. I lean in closer, the stone counter pressing into my stomach. A little pressure. A little pain. I don't care. I just want to see a little better, to feel a little closer.

Searching for Spirits in Quarantine

I WANT TO WAIT FOR THE FULL MOON, but at the beginning of the COVID-19 outbreak, as snow falls on a cold spring night—the night of April Fool's Day no less—it seems as good as any time to cry. Though, I'm skeptical about whether the tears will fall. I wonder if they can. I wonder if I want them to. Legends are one thing. Pain is really quite another. But it's what I'm going to search for. In the dark. In the night. In a cold and snow-laden graveyard.

The Weeping Woman statue in Logan City Cemetery has every reason to cry, and I'm told she's supposed to. Crafted for Julia Emelia Cronquist in 1917, it stands for her grief. In the course of just twelve years, five of her eight children died, none of whom were older than six years old. And while those facts are easy to find, it's difficult to know where her legend originated—who first said her cemetery statue wept on certain specific nights. Who claimed the statue cried on the anniversaries of her children's deaths or said it only happened during the full moon? No one knows who crafted these varied lists of different circumstances needed in order to watch her weep, but the legend's claim is always the same: the Weeping Woman cries, and she cries for the deaths of her children.

In the confines of my graduate folklore course at Utah State University, we talked about the statue as one of our local legends. We also discussed legend tripping—a pilgrimage folklorists take to reenact a legend. In that classroom, we watched a video of the Folklore Club making a legend trip to the Weeping Woman, attempting to discover the reality of her pain, the wetness of her tears, the glistening of water against stone. They recorded the event, and as we all watched the footage, a few claimed to see streaks on her hard cheeks. I wasn't sure.

Ghost stories like this aren't strange to me. In my freshman year at Southern Utah University six years ago, we often discussed a different ghostly woman who was supposed to appear in the windows of the Old Main building on full moon nights. Her spirit would weep against the window, crying into the night. I never saw her either.

Tonight isn't a full moon, and I don't know if the Weeping Woman will weep. I still don't know if I want her to.

~

In the late fall of 2015, while sitting in a café on the Utah State University campus, my phone flashed with a message from a friend, Mason, who I hadn't talked to for over a year.

Have you seen this? he asked alongside an article from KUTV blazed on the screen: *LDS church to exclude children of same-sex couples from membership.* My eyes glazed over the title—no, I hadn't seen it. My thumb hovered over my phone screen. Mild panic clogged my throat as I prepared to open the link, as if I knew things wouldn't be the same once I did.

I met Mason in 2012, at my first USGA meeting after I came out— before Jed, before Walt Disney World, before Chris and the affair and my move back to Utah. Most of the queer people I knew at the time came from that group. I was trying to find a place for homosexuality and spirituality in my life, trying to prove to everyone that I could somehow have everything—and for a few years there, it felt like things were getting better between the Mormon Church and the queer community. I'd marched with Mormons Building Bridges at a pride parade. BYU stopped expelling students because of their sexuality (though students could still be kicked out if they were caught *acting* on that sexuality). And most importantly, the Church had finally accepted the fact that sexuality couldn't be changed, even if they still believed it could be overcome or ignored. They created a website to showcase this: mormonandgay.lds .com. The website, like so many other things, is gone now—one step forward, twenty steps back. But we'll get to that. Digression began in this article, with what came to be known more colloquially as *The Policy Change.*

~

On the night I venture out to see the Weeping Woman, I call my friend Sophia. Though we're in the early months of COVID-19 and we're all afraid of being too close to one another, I don't want to be alone tonight. Plus, Sophia had said she had always wanted to see the Weeping Woman too. In the end, we determine we'll keep a certain amount of social distance in order to be together on this legend-trip.

We meet at the graveyard. I had thought the night would be dark, but the mixture of a near-full moon and the freshly fallen snow gives us plenty of light. I'm grateful, though not because light will make it easier to see Julia Cronquist's tears. I don't really think there'll be anything to see. I'm grateful because walking through a graveyard in the middle of the night is spooky enough as it is.

The snow groans beneath my feet when I step from my car. A chill creeps across the back of my neck, and I pull my coat and scarf a little tighter across my body. I had already put away all my winter things before tonight, thinking I wouldn't need them again for another seven months. A vain hope. I suppose it's the universe's idea of an April Fool's joke.

Sophia climbs from her car in a similar fashion, bundling herself up as we move into the frozen air. She's told me about her genetically caused poor circulation. I have it too, so I know how hard it can be to deal with a cold night like tonight. It makes me even more grateful to have someone like Sophia in my life—someone to brave the cold and unknown with. Someone to discuss ideas with. School. Boys. Astrology and music and nature and prejudice. Someone with whom I can attempt to understand the steady decline of the world. As if understanding it could be enough to solve it . . . Still, it's nice to talk it out.

Spirituality is often brought up in our conversations. While I grew up Mormon, Sophia didn't. It offers both of us alternate perspectives on how we ended up with the beliefs we have, both preferring to not force a religious label on ourselves—I have no clue what I believe about spirituality anymore. Though I don't care for the label, I suppose I could be considered agnostic. I like to believe that there's some kind of power in the fabric of the universe that holds us together. I just don't like to think there's an all-powerful man in the galaxy trying to pull my strings. I gave up that idea many years ago.

"It's such a beautiful night," Sophia says as we begin our walk toward the moonlit graveyard.

"It really is," I say. "I thought it'd be creepier going into the cemetery at night like this. But this makes it all brighter." Sophia laughs and agrees.

The snowflakes fall heavy across the sidewalk. They seem larger than just about any I've ever seen, some as big as a quarter on my sleeve. I wonder if it's because they're falling out of season. Perhaps winter is giving it one last try before dissolving into spring.

⁓

On November 5, 2015, my coffee chilled against a hard table; my arms shivered against the edge; my eyes dried from the harsh light of my phone screen; my thumb hovered over Mason's link. I wanted to press, to understand what the words meant: *LDS church to exclude children of same-sex couples from membership.* I kept rereading the title, my mind lingering on certain words.

LDS church.

Same-sex couples.

To exclude.

To exclude.

To exclude.

Before my courage died, I tapped.

An article sprouted from my finger. I read quickly, my eyes sweeping from end to end, trying to digest the words, trying to understand what they meant. My stomach twisted tighter and tighter. A numbness moved through me. Two things were immediately apparent. As the title suggested, the children of same-sex couples were to be immediately illegitimized by the Mormon church. They would not be given blessings or names by the religion. They wouldn't be allowed into the religion until they were eighteen, until they lived outside their parents' home and denounced their parents' marriage. This is because the policy also placed anyone in a same-sex marriage under the category of apostates.

Apostates. It wasn't a common term I heard growing up in the church, but I had heard of it before. It was a name generally held for those who turned away from the principles of the gospel, who actively opposed the religion, who openly disagreed with its leaders. They were people who'd be "cursed" and "condemned" for their evil. People who'd end up in Outer Darkness for eternity.

Growing up, I had always imagined the term to mean people who picketed General Conference and Temple Square and other Mormon gathering places. Apparently, it would now include me. I hadn't fully turned away yet, but I was going to marry a man. I had in an instant become an apostate to my own religion.

As I stared at the article, I considered the previous four years of my life, four years I had dedicated to bridging the gap between Mormonism and the LGBTQ+ community. I thought of all the events I'd sponsored. All the panels I'd spoken on. My vice presidency in USGA. My march in the Salt Lake City Pride Parade with Mormons Building Bridges. I couldn't help but wonder if any of it had mattered.

Numbness was replaced by anger, by fear, by pain. I threw my phone into my pocket, snatched up my bag, and sped from the café, my coffee, bitter and cold, left abandoned on the table behind me.

~

My feet scrape against the asphalt of Logan Cemetery as Sophia and I move toward the Weeping Woman. We'd given in and discarded the COVID warnings, linking our arms to walk together through the cold night. I worry we've betrayed ourselves and all the efforts of social distancing, but it also feels nice to have her close, to feel another person beside me. It somehow makes me feel less abandoned in the chaos of the world.

I can't help but think about Julia Cronquist's children, specifically the four who died of scarlet fever between 1889 and 1901. The illness spreads so similarly to the COVID-19 pandemic the world battles now. Both are most commonly passed by coughing and sneezing. By touching infected objects. By touching each other. So, I wonder, if Julia could see me now, would she hate me? Would she see Sophia and I touch and feel rage at how cavalier we could be about a virus such as this—about a virus so similar to the one that killed her children? I wonder if that would make her weep.

I try not to think about it. Instead, I think about the days, years ago, in which I would traverse this graveyard. It sat on the edge of the Utah State University campus, between married student housing and the rest of the school. Jed and I used to live in the townhouses over there. We would often take our husky Kira on walks through the graveyard in the evening, soaking in the peaceful and emotional atmosphere it brought— though I did find it strange that I felt so much calm and serenity in an area so full of the dead.

Ironically enough, that time with Jed marked my initial introduction of the Weeping Woman statue, though I didn't know the legend back then. I was embarrassed to admit that the first time I'd heard the name of the statue was when the *Pokémon Go* game was released in the summer of 2016. The creators had asked fans to send in landmarks of their hometowns to use as parts of the game. One of the first I saw was the Weeping Woman, her statue pictured on the game. I recognized it as one I'd seen in passing, but never paid too much attention to. And I wondered why she was considered to be weeping. I figured she was probably just carved that way.

Jed and I, like much of the world, found an obsession in *Pokémon Go*, and we adjusted the path of our evening walks accordingly. We made sure we included pathways which could traverse the landmarks of the game. The Weeping Woman was perhaps the one we'd hit most often. She was the closest to our home. She came to mark the beginning and end of our walk.

We weren't the only ones who found the Weeping Woman at this time. The *Pokémon Go* obsession was widespread and fanatic, and the landmarks were a popular piece of the game. There were some, called "gyms," where different designated teams could battle for control. The Weeping Woman was one of these. As such, it became rare to walk through that graveyard and not see several cars parked beside the white, weeping statue, and I remember feeling a conflict when I saw them— and even more when I was a participant in it. It felt wrong to gather around someone's grave in order to play a Pokémon game. Yet, without it, I wonder if I would have lived those years never knowing of Julia's statue—the way her head hung in despair, the way she curled her body into a ball, the way her name gleamed from her pedestal. Maybe it brought her some kind of happiness to be surrounded by joy.

I wonder if she'll look different now, four years later, under this shining moon. I wonder if seeing her will feel differently now that my Jed and I have separated. I wonder if I'll see something more. Something new. I wonder if, because I know her name and the names of her children, her pain will feel more real. I wonder if mine will.

Tears press against my eyes, and I sniff. I persuade myself it's because of the cold, snowy night.

~

The policy change on November 5, 2015, didn't feel real at the time. After reading the article, I immediately received a call from Matthew. We talked at length about what such a decision meant. I told him how it felt like ten steps back from the progress we'd seen over the past few years. It felt like a betrayal of how much of my life I'd given to advocating a bridged life between these two pieces of myself.

"I don't know if I can forgive them this time," I told him, trying to keep my breath even in the cold autumn air, tears running down my cheeks.

He told me he understood. He felt the same way. Neither of us had answers. Neither of us knew what to say, but the moment would mark my exit from Mormonism. The last straw, so to speak. I turned away from religion, and along with it, my advocacy for holding such diverging identities.

I learned later that my dad, after teaching gospel doctrine for over twenty years, called his Bishop after hearing the news. He told the Bishop that he was unable to continue teaching, and he never went back. My mom had stopped attending over a year before because the general attitudes toward queer people made her too upset to take part anymore. Melissa and Steve disbanded from the religion too. Marcus had stopped attending after returning from his mission years before. Christopher and Jenn left within the next year or so too. For over a week after the policy change, both my mom and my dad called me every day to make sure I was okay.

I told them I was doing the best I could.

The weekend after the announcement, many of my friends joined a mass gathering in Salt Lake City to submit letters of official resignation from The Church of Jesus Christ of Latter-day Saints. I was invited to go along and join, but part of me feared doing something so drastic. My friends understood and supported me, but I had a hard time understanding my own hesitation, especially when I learned of an organizer of the mass exodus, Emily Vought, handing out pins reading *apostate*— as if it could be something to be proud of—that a person could pin the label over their heart like a badge of honor. In what felt like a lifetime ago, I'd done the same with a missionary name tag. And some months later, when I walked in the Salt Lake City Pride Parade, I'd placed a label of homosexuality on myself and found I could bear it proudly. But I didn't know how to do that with *apostate*.

Emily said in an interview, "If church officials are going to call me apostate, then I am . . . I will proudly be an apostate."

I dug inside my gut to find some sort of pride in the word, but I couldn't stop myself from feeling like I'd made a mistake when I believed god could love me.

～

The first thing I notice as Sophia and I turn the corner onto the street with the Weeping Woman is that the stone is not as white as I remember. While a tombstone beside the statue glows white as the snow resting atop its surface, the Weeping Woman stands darker. Like a shadow in the center of the cemetery. Perhaps a darkness surrounding her space. I find it especially strange because as we step across the snow-covered pavement, I notice there are no trees hanging over this area. The usual lines and clusters of tall evergreens are one of the main reasons I love this graveyard. So much life scattered across the holy earth made it seem like death was not strong enough to suspend it. It inspired me.

But there are no trees above us here. Nothing to block out the glistening moon. And when Sophia and I stop at the gray statue, we both look up in reverence. I think about all the times I've been here before, all the moments I stopped to play a game or to look at the statue's intricately carved lines. Tonight feels different, though I can't immediately put my finger on why. Maybe it just is.

She kneels on her right knee, her right hand resting limp across her leg. Her left elbow presses against her left kneecap, bracing her hand against her forehead. Her back is bent, she gazes at the ground. It's a position of grief. Of unending sorrow. Of a pain I doubt I'll ever understand.

"I thought she would be upright," Sophia points out, her gaze locked on the statue. She's never been here before. "She's so beautiful."

I nod. "She really is."

There are multiple small headstones pressed into the ground around the base of the statue. Her family. Her husband. Her children—all eight of them. It makes me sick to think that over half of them were buried before they were six years old. It seems so unfair they should get such a short life. Four died of scarlet fever. One was stillborn: Lilean. She didn't even take a breath before she was separated from her mother. I wonder if Julia even got to hold her.

I suppose it's moments like this that make me hope for some sort of god or heaven to exist. I want Julia to have some peace. Her children and husband too. I want Julia to have reunited with them in some kind of afterlife—that they may have all found happiness together there. Yet, if I want to believe in heaven for them, does it mean I must believe in hell for me? If angels exist, do demons haunt me too? Did I really spit on god's feet when I said I loved a man? Maybe it's simple selfishness to not believe in god. Maybe it's my own way to survive.

I look around the graveyard. Like Julia's statue, the evergreen trees that border the area are permanently bent by the wind sweeping down Logan Canyon. The trees don't break; they simply bow beneath the power, and I consider the fact that they're still standing. They're still big and strong and tall. They survive. Just like Julia did. All I've ever wanted is to do the same. I take a step onto the fresh, pristine snow, feeling it groan beneath my weight.

Perhaps the emptiness here is less about a lack of life and more about the need for a little space to breathe. A little space to be.

~

Three years before the 2015 policy change, my first boyfriend broke up with me. The following Sunday, I stayed home from church. A mixture of rage toward god and confusion of my own beliefs boiled inside me, and I determined my time would be better suited to a more meditative practice. A friend had told me that when he felt overwhelmed, he went somewhere peaceful to think. I wanted to do the same. There was a beautiful, short hike a mile from my parents' house that led to a serene waterfall. I figured it was as peaceful a place as I could come up with.

The hike up was uneventful, though peaceful. It brought back memories of when I used to hike trails like this with my family. I remembered back to high school, when my friends and I hiked up there. Dhane, Dallin, Jake, and I—we hiked even farther than the waterfall there, moved off the dedicated trail, edged across the side of a cliff. A pretty foolish idea, thinking back on it now, but at the time, it felt good to be dangerous. To take the risk.

At one point, I jumped from a ledge and landed on a hillside covered in fresh mud. My feet were swept from the ground, and I slid a short length of the mountain. Rocks tumbled down beside my head ripped from their resting place by my desperate hands. Afterward, when my friends ran down to make sure I was okay, I contemplated how lucky I was that I didn't get hurt. Dhane called it a miracle. We were both deep in the religion then, and I wondered why I'd used the word "luck" instead of something more spiritual. Maybe I'd already stopped believing in them. Maybe I just didn't think god would grant them to a sinner like me. Either way, I stopped believing in miracles long ago.

I sat on a rock near the waterfall because I liked to hear how the water slammed against the rocky stream below, echoing out from the slot-like cave. The stream rushed beside my feet, higher and wider than I remembered. We'd gotten a lot of rainfall that season; perhaps change could be that simple.

Not really knowing what to do, I sat for a while. Some hikers passed by, but I ignored them, hoping they'd give me the solitude I wanted. They moved on. And after about twenty minutes of mulling, I felt a tingle in the back of my head, something like a whisper, telling me to pray— maybe because I didn't know what else to do. But I didn't want to.

"No," I said aloud. But the feeling flared up inside. Burning. Boiling. Churning.

So I did, and words crashed from my clenched jaw: "Okay god, fuck you." And what followed was an indescribable amount of time in which I cursed god and all the universe. I howled about how unfair it was to finally grant me love after twenty years of being alone—only to have it stripped away by the words "I don't love you anymore." I told god that I hated him, that he didn't deserve his place in the universe, that he was a lousy father and I had a perfectly wonderful one down here, so I didn't need him. I told him I wished he would disappear. I screamed, "I hate you! I fucking hate you," over and over and over again until my voice grew hoarse.

When I finished, I wept into my hands, tears dropping into the stream, blending with the water. I wanted it to sweep me away too. Guilt and shame ravaged me, my stomach twisting and twisting and twisting. My breath came in harsh rasps each time I tried to inhale.

Then, my crying slowed. Anger bled from my body, and a coolness spread across my skin. Without really meaning to, I said, "I'm sorry."

I felt it immediately: a voice so clear it felt like it was beside me, like it had come bounding out from the forest.

It's okay, Andrew. I forgive you. I'm here.

～

Wet snow crunches beneath my shoes, immediately soaking into my socks. I don't care. I move toward the Cronquist statue. Sophia stays back on the drier concrete. Whether it's because her feet are already cold or because she can see more clearly than me, I'm unsure. All I know is that I need to feel a little closer to the stone.

Up close, I can see the anguish in Julia's complexion. Her husband had commissioned the statue to mark her grave three years after her death. The grief crafted here is supposed to mimic the grief Julia felt as she wept over her children's graves in this very same spot. I imagine her coming here day after day, crying for the children she lost. Fearing the loss of more. Cursing god. Pleading with him to take care of her children in heaven. I can't imagine the pain, but I can see the grief carved across the statue's face. I look closer, so desperate to understand her. I turn to Sophia. "I'm supposed to tell her to weep, I guess."

"Oh, really?" she says. In her voice, I can hear the aversion she has to the concept, and I feel it too. Julia has already felt so much grief—why would I command her to shed more tears over her children's graves? I'd rather believe that she's with them somewhere out in the universe.

"I also saw someone in a video climb up and see if there were tears being shed," I tell her. I glance up and down, attempting to imagine how in the world I'd even climb up the statue. My gaze lingers on the indented Cronquist name carved into the middle of the plinth. I suppose I could hook my foot into that space if I wanted to. I could reach up and feel her face, see if there's some warm tears dripping against the cold, snow-capped statue.

"I don't want to do that," I add after a moment's pause.

"I don't think you should," Sophia agrees. "This all just feels . . . reverent."

I nod and look from the statue to Sophia before dropping my eyes to the small tombstones scattering the snowy ground. Even among the white, I see Lilean's name glisten from beside my feet. The anniversary of her death is in five days. I think that might be the day of the actual full moon, but I can't quite remember. Still, I wonder if it would be enough to make Julia cry. I wonder how someone could ever stop crying after going through what she had.

"She must have had so much courage," I say, looking back at Sophia. She smiles back at me and dips her head as if in prayer.

~

The voice in the forest rang hard against my ear. I looked up from my feet, from the water that rushed beside them. I knew the voice was in my head, but I also felt it wasn't. It was as if a friend were speaking to me—someone who understood me so fully. Someone I had never actually spoken to.

"Is that you?" I said aloud.

Yes. The answer seemed to appear in my head, like flipping a light switch, like I wasn't in control of the words entering my mind—only the ones leaving my mouth. It didn't make any sense, but it felt real. And I spoke.

Some time later, as the sun began to set, I glanced at my watch. I was surprised to find I'd been up on the mountain for three hours. No interruptions of hikers walking past me. It was just me and the forest, the waterfall and the river, the wind. I had released my emotions and questions and doubts and fears, let them flow from me like the river sweeping the rocks beside my feet.

I started back down the trail, and as I did, I asked the questions I'd always been too afraid to ask: "Is it all right that I'm gay? Will I marry a man someday? Or am I wrong in all of this?"

There was a pause before I felt an overwhelming sense of love and compassion. *That choice is yours*, the voice pressed onto me. *You will find happiness either way. It will be hard, but it will also be beautiful. You deserve that story.*

I wept again, but not from rage or shame. I felt a release. An unburdening. A freedom I had never felt before. And I yearned to hold onto it, to never forget the feeling of those words. And as I stepped down that mountainside, waves of exhaustion and hunger washing over me, I determined I had two choices. I could believe it was all fake, that I just told myself what I wanted to hear—or I could believe it was some higher power guiding me. I thought I had to choose between them. I didn't understand there was a third choice to be made.

⁓

I wander around the base of the Cronquist statue, removing snow from each small grave I come across. I read the names of her children: Margaret, Olif, Oliver, Orson, Elam, Emilia, Inez, and Lilean. The dates on Lilean's tombstone still strike me the hardest. 1894–1894. Her life was so short. And in five days, her mother is supposed to cry. I look back to the Weeping Woman and feel my stomach clench.

I wonder if, in five days, I could come and find her crying. I wonder if that will be better for my research, for the legend trip, whether it could make whatever I'm trying to say more credible. But I still don't want to see her cry. I still want her to have moved on, whether or not it's heaven, no matter what it might mean for my own salvation.

There are accounts throughout the history of Logan depicting Julia's presence here. Some are as simple as tears appearing in the eyes of the weeping statue. Others have claimed to hear her howling wails from afar. Some say they saw the statue moving around the cemetery in search of her lost children. There have even been accounts of Julia's spirit kneeling before the Weeping Woman statue, over her children's graves, separate from the statue. I don't think I want any of it to be true.

Though the Cronquist name is inscribed on the statue, I know Julia's husband Olif didn't have it commissioned in her actual image. I could never find a solid reason as to why that was; I suppose he just had it crafted as a memorial to her. I wonder if he didn't want his wife's real grief depicted in stone forever. That makes sense to me.

So, if the statue isn't Julia—and Julia has a separate tombstone beside her husband—maybe the Weeping Woman is just a marker for their family. It has the Cronquist name, a name that symbolically tied Julia and Olif together. The same name that tied their children to them. Even with all the grief and death over their years together, the family all fit under this one umbrella, this one statue, this one space in which they could lie together. I find it to be a beautiful idea.

And then I notice something on the plinth, something aside from the Cronquist name—streaks of darker lines on the stone of the statue's base, as if water has dripped down the sides.

"Sophia," I call urgently. "Can you see this?"

"See what?"

"These lines on the statue. They're darker than the rest."

She pauses. She makes a little gasp. "They look like water," she says.

I pause too, grappling with my own thoughts. "Do they kind of look like streaks? The kind tears leave on your face."

My fingers press against the icy gray of the statue's surface. I sweep my hand across the lines of darker and lighter grays. But there's no liquid. Like water having already dried. Or, rather, like the water hadn't ever been tangible in the first place.

～

Seven months after my first breakup, seven months after I prayed in the forest to find god, seven months after I made the decision to believe the message I heard was from god, I found myself standing in the middle of a street in Salt Lake City. The mid-June sun beat down on the back of my neck, but I didn't care. My nerves twisted in anticipation. In mere moments, I was going to march with the front line of Mormons Building Bridges in Salt Lake City's Pride Parade. It was my first Pride celebration, my first insight into the world I'd hidden away from for so long.

Because Mormonism valued a sense of modest dress, we'd all been asked to wear church clothing. As you already know, this most commonly meant white button-ups, modest ties, and black slacks. I decided to take my own small twist on the clothing, wearing a blue, short-sleeved button-up and a black vest. And, upon arrival, my friend Madison snatched up a free small rainbow flag for each of us. I placed mine in the pocket of my vest.

It didn't take long for me to realize that even though we were a part of the parade, we looked different from most other groups. We stood right behind a giant orange float with a huge rainbow stripe stamped across the side where guys in tight, colorful speedos laughed and hugged each other. They blasted music from the sides of the float to pump themselves up. People all around us danced to the sound and invited us to join in. My foot tapped against the ground, something Madison noticed.

"Do you want to go over there?" she asked, nodding toward the men in speedos.

I laughed and felt my face burn. "No, no. I can't dance like that."

"Sure you can!" she said with a chuckle. "I've seen you do it before."

I laughed too, but still didn't move. "It's okay. I don't need to," I said, but I knew I was lying. I couldn't tear my eyes away from the ever-growing group of dancing people, their smiles as bright as I'd ever seen. I ached for the chance to be one of them.

~

I step away from the Weeping Woman, back out to the gravel where Sophia stands in wait. "Are you ready to go?" I ask her.

"Sure," she says. "But are you?"

I glance back to the statue: the gray stone that's turned dark under the moonlit night, the powder that lays atop her head and shoulders like snow-capped mountains, the name carved into the stone base, the streaks of darker color that run like tears down the bottom half of the statue.

Holding out my arm, I say, "Yeah, I'm ready to go."

As we walk, Sophia comments how there was a gravity there with Julia, a reverence she can't quite explain. I agree. Not a type of gravity that pulls us down, but rather one that grounds us in place, in her space, like maybe she's trying to grant us all some peace within our losses.

When we're about to turn the corner, we both glance back. The statue still looks gray against the white of other grave markers. It looks the same as when we arrived, no more streaks. All that's changed is the scattering of snow surrounding the base, evidence of the footprints I made around their graves. I hope they can forgive my disturbance.

And as Sophia and I exit the graveyard, walking back to our cars, holding each other close to keep warm, I wonder if the streaks we saw could be the tears they speak of in the legends. Maybe they are, or maybe they're just snow melting off the surface of a statue, dripping down to the consecrated earth below. Or perhaps we both just imagined them.

I'm beginning to think, maybe all that matters is what we can take away from seeing them.

~

I yearned to take part in the celebration on that float, to live like the boys in speedos did, to dance with them, to be as free as them. I ached to leap up and run, throw off the confinement of my modesty in order to live freely. Madison disagreed when I told her I couldn't dance like them, but she'd mistaken my meaning: I meant that I couldn't live like that, love like that, breathe like that. I couldn't allow myself to taste that freedom. Perhaps god would tolerate my homosexuality, but he would certainly never endorse it. And yet, against my better judgment, I popped open one more button on my shirt, showing the tiniest fraction more of my chest.

The parade moved slowly at first, stepping lightly from our backstage area into the streets of Salt Lake City, but its speed built fast. Within minutes we had moved from barren sidewalks to overcrowded streets where people hung outside parking garages and high-rise windows, waving down at us. I reached up my hand and tried to wave back, trying to meet every eye I could. My smile was so big it hurt my face, but I couldn't help it. Every bit of stress and invalidation I had been feeling had disappeared. Whether god marched with me or not, I knew I was standing up for myself.

About a quarter-way into the city, a middle-aged man sprinted from the crowd as we marched. He wore a simple pair of blue jeans and a red T-shirt that said PROUD DAD.

Stopping right in front of me, he asked, "May I hug you?"

A bit flustered but still smiling, I said, "Yeah, I guess so."

He wrapped his arms over my shoulders. He pulled me close, held tight, then parted. Tears painted his face, white streaks crafted from poorly applied sunscreen beneath his eyes. "Thank you," he said. "Thank you for what you're doing." And he ran off, disappearing back into the rainbow crowd.

He wasn't the only one to do something like this. All of us on the outside border of our group had multiple hug requests, multiple people wanting to shake our hands, endless crowds of human kindness that showed up to support. Tears dripped down my own cheeks as I waved. Each pair of eyes that locked with mine was a connection, even if just for a moment. Each one was a human worth considering, a person worth reaching.

I found it then, that third choice, a third belief. Not in god, not without god. Something more like energy, invisible wires of the universe surrounding me, connecting me to that Proud Dad and all those who gathered to celebrate love and queerness and joy. Perhaps gods are just energy, and heaven this place of pure, unadulterated, bare compassion. The voice I heard in the forest could have been someone out in the universe screaming, howling, begging me to love myself, to allow myself to be loved. Or maybe I simply chose to forgive myself, to love myself, to free myself, my own words ringing beside me: *You will find happiness either way. It will be hard, but it will also be beautiful.*

So I smiled. I lifted my hand and waved—to crowds on the sidewalk, to marchers in the street, flags waving from the rooftops above, screams echoing down from a parking garage full of people just trying to fill the air with a little more love. I waved because all I wanted was to do the same. To release. To dance. To be wild and loved and cherished and free for whatever time I would be allotted in this life. On this earth.

Maybe it's the story I deserve.

Scene: The Wolf and His Shadow

SETTING: WOLF's den at the base of a large mountain. The cave's facade is cracked and broken, but otherwise it is like any other den. The sun begins to set, and shadows move and dance across the stage.

AT RISE: WOLF exits his den. He stands for a moment at the entrance in fine spirits, taking in the beauty of the sunset. Then, he begins to run.

WOLF

(to himself)

My, what a hunger has come over me. I slept longer than I'd hoped to.
(The sun shifts just so, to cast the wolf's shadow long and large across the ground)

WOLF (cont.)

(surprised and proud)

Why, see how big I am! I must be a hundred times bigger than I was!
(He leaps a few times and watches how his shadow leaps with him.)

WOLF (cont.)

Truly magnificent! I feel so powerful and big and free! Fancy me running away from that puny lion now! I'll show him who is fit to be king.
(WOLF laughs and runs to LION's den higher up on the cliffside than his own. LION's den is much more beautiful and well-kept. The light hits the stone with brilliance. LION is nowhere to be found.)

186

WOLF (cont.)

Hah! I suppose the lion must have seen my grand shadow from afar and fled. I will now be king of the mountain.

(Quite suddenly and out of nowhere, an immense shadow blots out WOLF entirely. LION has appeared behind him. Before WOLF can turn around, LION mauls him in a single blow.)

Ghost Boys: A Bricolage

Club Guy Makes a Move

It was 2021, I was nearly thirty, and no one ever taught me I could say no at the counter when the half-naked man there couldn't find my coat. When Terrence pointed to it on the rack, but the half-naked man wasn't listening. When a stranger, tall and limber, cupped my ass with his thighs and squeezed me against the counter, dick pressing hard and wild. I would just call it a mistake, a misstep, a jumble of moving men down the aisle to a cramped and smoky dance floor. Maybe the stranger hadn't seen me. Hadn't noticed. Hadn't felt his dick cram itself between me and his pants and his underwear and his skin. And the club floor kept bouncing, the countertop vibrating to the beat, and the stranger reached around my head to grab his coat from the half-naked man because that's the coat the man could find. And while bodies swayed to the music, in and out of motion, in and out and up and down, the stranger vanished into the crowd: this mass of men caked in leather and sweat and alcohol, where a guy in assless chaps smashed his tongue into the armpit of another. And the coat check man finally found my coat and handed it to me and apologized for the wait, but I told him it was fine, I was fine, I was okay—I wasn't upset.

How could I be upset? I told him.

There are just too many coats.

My History Tries to Teach Me Something

Last month, I made a timeline—pages of charts marked by date, age, and event. I am a forgetful person, and previous attempts to match up these memories left me picking at my lips or chewing my nails to their nubs.

I needed something easy to reference, something to contain my history, a box of little moments I could pull out and press together to create a story that made sense.

You know how it goes: I grew up as a Mormon in Utah. I also grew up gay. I went on a mission to Germany and Switzerland when I was nineteen. That same year, I was diagnosed with bipolar, depression, anxiety, and ADHD. I also came out. I met Jed on the dating app Jack'd when I was twenty. I married him at twenty-three. We moved to Florida a year and a half later, and six months after that, I had an affair with Chris, and I fell in love with him. Jed and I separated. I moved in with Chris, but after six months, I left him too. I moved back to Utah, into a little one-bedroom apartment in a little college town, and at twenty-eight, I found myself living alone for the very first time. It would be in this apartment, the one with crumbling walls and too many spiders, that I'd ask Jed for a divorce; I'd contract HIV; I'd meet Terrence on Tinder; I'd fall in love with him there.

I list these things because they are facts, and sometimes they're the only truth I can hold onto, the only bits that don't slip away—puzzle pieces and fragments. When I feel this life ticking by—not existentially, but more like fearing the story and its lessons—I hold these moments to the ground and try to find some stability.

GAY APP HIERARCHIES

I should preface: gay app profile photos tend to come in three categories:

1. Serious-face Selfies
2. Naked, Headless Chests
3. Blank

> *Note: BlankNoPictureBoy will ask for a dick pic; he will promise to send his afterward; he will tell you he is on the DL (translation: closeted and most likely married); he will probably delete the app in the next two hours; he will be the easiest to ghost because he wasn't ever really there anyway.

The Lesson:

GRINDR: Grindr is the OG hookup app, the main one—nearly every guy in the gay dating world has been on Grindr at least once. But you should know—you don't get on Grindr to find love.

SCRUFF: For guys with beards and muscles and daddy-vibes—and for guys
who want them. It's for hookups and dating. But mainly hookups.

JACK'D: Geared toward BIPOC communities, Jack'd tries to be the
healthier, less-racist version of Grindr and Scruff.

OKCUPID: Honestly, you're probably not going to meet anyone on here,
but that's okay—OKCupid is just for the fun question-and-answer
section.

TINDER: Tinder is more serious, so if you're looking for dates, go to Tinder.
Only about 50 percent of the guys there are looking for a quickie in the
neighborhood Walmart bathroom. Go ahead. Shoot your shot. What've
you got to lose?

SCRUFF GUY INVITES ME OVER

Okay, listen, I know these apps are toxic. I've always known. Of course
they are. Cold and hard. Invisible people behind a screen. But look: how
else was I supposed to find someone? I was living in that little crumbling apartment in that little college town nestled in the mountains of
northern Utah where there were only two bars and neither felt welcoming—small and stocked with beer on tap and warm canned wine.
The nearest gay club was an hour-and-a-half away. And sure, the nicely
dressed boy at Starbucks set off some kind of gaydar, but I'd rather not
ask. I'd been wrong about boys like him before. At least the apps are
sure.

In 2019, nine months before I met Terrence, I met this guy Rob on
Scruff. He was broad-shouldered, stubble-bearded, with dark green eyes
and short cropped hair. He was visiting Utah from New York, which he
claimed to do often because his family lived here and his mother was
sick. He said he wasn't looking for anything more than a hookup. If I'd
been honest, I would have told him I craved something more, something deeper, some substantial something that might feel like connection, might feel like love. More than anything, I just didn't want to be
alone. But a hookup was better than nothing, so I just said, *Same.*

You clean? he asked.

Translation: *Are you HIV-negative?*
  See also: *Do I get to cum in your ass?*
  See also: *I don't even buy condoms anymore.*

I hadn't contracted it yet.

I told him I was clean.

We agreed to meet at his place, which was actually his parents' place, but he said he had the basement all to himself and there was no way his parents would hear us because they lived three floors up at the top of their mansion built on the side of the east mountain. As requested, I left my car a block away, and at 2 a.m., on a snowy November night, I hiked a trail to his back door.

He met me in the doorway, fully naked. He pulled me into the warmth, wrapped one arm around my waist, placed a hand against my cheek, and pressed his lips against my own. He shut the door and stripped the cold clothes from my skin. Fresh snow from my coat puddled onto the tiled floor, and he led me deeper into the basement living room. He fell onto the couch. I fell against him. His tongue slipped between my teeth. His skin slid against my own, body like fire, beard scritching against my cheek, fingernails pressing into my spine. I sank into him.

After, he walked me back down the trail toward my car. At the edge of the road, he told me he'd text me next time he was in town. I told him *that'd be great.* I never saw him again.

APP BOYS GIVE ME THEIR PREFERENCES

For your consideration:

I'm just here for the free cheese samples. **Clean and DDF.** LOOKING FOR NOW. Masc for masc. No fats, no fems. I'm just not interested in white guys. I'm just not interested in black guys. **[Smiling devil-horned emoji]** [purple eggplant emoji] **[three asscrack peach emojis].** All these guys be ghostin'.

Don't say hi or how I'm doing. We all know why you're here. **Not here for a hookup. Looking for now. Hi.** *Girl it's Grindr, get over it.* Y'all such flakes. Looking for big booties, no fatties tho. **Definitely a nerd here. Love music, video games, and enacting meaningful social change.** Grindr is shitty for mental health. *Stop objectifying each other.* 420 friendly, clean and DDF, ub2.

Face required before anything. **White guys are a plus. BE
FIT.** Not interested in men who don't take care of themselves.
Negative, on PrEP. *Safe only.* **No fats.** No fems. **No fats no fems.**
*Masc 4 Masc—I'm here cause I like men, go be a girl somewhere else
please.* Str8 hung. **Don't waste my time.**

Can't host, can't travel, come pick me up for car play.
Wanna be your sugar daddy. Rarely on here. Slow to
respond. Delete often. Don't take it personally. *DDF. BE
CLEAN.* **Not interested in playing with Poz guys.** I'ma top vers.
Fem too. **No uglies, olds, or weirdos.** *CANT HOST.*
Looking for friends, possibly more. **Have a pic.** Cuddles are
my weakness and if anyone needs a leg I got an
extra. *Not looking for hookups so please don't ask.* **Wow can anyone
actually hold a conversation?**

Trust me I get ghosted too so don't take it personally.
Listen, I'm not into old, fat, nasty ppl. This dick will rock your
world, your eyes gonna roll behind your head. Looking
for friends mostly. **I owe none of y'all nothing!** If I don't
respond, don't take it personally. *I got standards. You
should too.* Into mature guys with huge dicks. **Not into twinky
guys, only fit.** BBC or BWC only. Make sure you know your status.
Not into dirty folks. *HIV neg only please.* **Who wants it?** U=U,
GOOGLE IT! Stop telling me your life story, I just
don't care. **BE CLEAN BE CLEAN BE CLEAN.**

I'm so tired of this bullshit.

Grindr Guy Makes a Request

I met John in the fall of 2020, in a COVID-19 world that left me desperate for any physical connection. This meant that when he asked, I
agreed to buy thick blue curtains so he could slip in more easily—more
discreetly—at 2 am through the crack of my glass-paned back door. And
when he came, he came in gym shorts and black tank tops and beanies
so he could look like he'd been out running. He told me he worked for
the government and had married a woman and he just needed some ass

on the side. I knew nothing else about him, and he didn't ask anything about me. It was easier to disappear this way.

And when he came, he wanted me waiting with mint-fresh breath and poppers on the bedside table, with lights dimmed behind the curtains to be sure we couldn't be seen. And because this isn't that abnormal in the gay hookup scene, and because I had cheated before too, I agreed. I agreed because I loved the way he could press against the folds of my body and growl, would tell me how he liked a little extra meat on the bones of the boys he fucks, how the red ribbon stretch marks on my sides looked like licorice smiles. I agreed because I wanted to believe him.

I wanted to believe he was being honest when he said his affair was always going to be an eventuality because of this world we live in, but I wondered whether he kissed her goodbye or said he'd be home soon because I know how easy lying like this can be. His clothes trailed the ratty carpet and his skin was sticking to my leather couch and he was kissing my neck and all I ever wanted was to plant my body somewhere safe, and maybe I deserved it: that cool summer night, a ringing belt buckle, a gentle hand on the back of my neck pushing me down till I choked, the future that would inevitably come. But what if I wanted to feel a stranger's skin rubbing against my teeth like this? I had left the door open. I let him come inside.

When he left Utah for the summer, he told me how I better be waiting for him when he returned. I told him I would be. I didn't know then that I was lying.

My Astrological Chart Tells Me I'm a Lion

I'm a Leo, and I'm told that means I'm ruled by the sun, that I thrive on emotional connection and undivided attention—and I do know I'm aroused by these things—turned off by what feels robotic or cold. There's a heat I crave: on my skin, in the marrow of my bones, in the pulsing beat of my temples. I want my eyes and throat to burn. I want a man to hold me close, to whisper passion deep into the crevices of my body. My life has proven this to be true: one-night stands; letting strangers use me to get off; a sexless marriage leading to an affair with a boy who so lovingly wanted to fuck me: in a Disney World bathroom, in his storage unit, against the window of his apartment.

I've always been afraid of ending up alone.

TINDER BOY LIKES HORROR

In the summer of 2020, a month after John left, I sat on my living room couch with a different boy, Michael, a guy I met on Tinder. He was short, tattooed, and muscular; he liked horror movies and showing off his sleeve tattoos and going to the gym on weekends. And though these likes differed widely from my own, I didn't care. Our empty plates of orange chicken, brown rice, and potstickers lay abandoned on the coffee table while we cuddled close on the couch. We had just finished watching his favorite movie, *Hereditary*, a horror movie I'd never seen because I was too afraid to watch it alone. After, we turned on *Midsommer*, another horror movie, but we didn't really watch it. Instead, I traced Michael's sleeve of geometric tattoos with my finger. He leaned in closer and rested his hand on my thigh. He told me he wanted another sleeve of tattoos on his left arm. I told him I was afraid of doing something so drastic, so permanent. I showed him the simple statement of *I choose joy* tattooed on my forearm, and he told me he liked it.

He kissed me then, and I kissed him back. He pulled me onto his lap. Night pressed against the window and, piece by piece, our clothes struck the linoleum floor. We pulled each other closer. Our heat mixed; our limbs tangled; the taste of his skin stained my tongue and teeth and lips. The couch became the floor, the floor became a mattress, and in the night, we cracked our bodies open. In the morning, when I tried to hold him closer, he pulled away. When he left, he said he'd had fun.

We had another date a week later, though we didn't have sex. We made breakfast together in the morning, and when he kissed me goodbye, he said he'd see me soon. A week after that, he blocked my number.

THE FOOL HAS SOMETHING TO SAY

I sat beneath a patio umbrella with my friend Sophia, just days after Michael's ghosting. Lying sideways in my chair, I dangled my feet over the arm. She sat cross-legged in hers, her long tangle of wavy blonde hair falling over her shoulder. Together, we flipped Tarot cards on a shaded, glass-topped table, and with each reveal, we paused to admire the art, searching images as if panning for gold: some glimmer of meaning here, a spark of something mystical we hoped we could understand. And I needed to understand—to know why he would vanish like this. And while I knew I wouldn't get an answer here, sitting at a table, flipping card after card after card, I didn't know what else to do. Sophia told me it was okay to hurt, and I told her I was fine. I'd only known him for a few weeks, after all. It shouldn't hurt so much, so of course I was fine. I was okay. I had to be okay.

Why wouldn't I be okay? I said to her before flipping over The Fool. *Because you're human,* she told me. *And it's okay to hurt.*

And she was right, of course. I looked down at The Fool, a card that's supposed to signify something new coming, though we're rarely sure of what it might be. The Fool just tells us to prepare. To stretch ourselves out. To get ready to rise.

On my particular card, The Fool stood on the edge of an intricate pillar, birds fluttering around their head, orange hair whipped up by the wind, arms stretched out as if ready to fly. I considered their feet, how their heels had lifted from the platform, how their toes caressed the edge. They were going to jump. I knew this, I could sense it, or maybe I just felt like I was about to do the same.

There's an imprint here if you look: a sun tattooed on the foot of The Fool, or the piece of Michael left behind. I'd fallen in love with him, and I'd fallen fast. Somehow, in just a few weeks, he caused something inside me to burn, to come alive. And I wanted to come alive, even if it wasn't with him—and I'd be very glad it wasn't with him. If I could learn something from the experience, maybe it's that I wanted to be with someone who was awake and ignited and free.

Ex-Husband and I Make a Decision

At sunset, two weeks after Michael's disappearance, I walked to a nearby park. I lay down in the grass and felt the blades pricking the soft spots of my skin. Golden hour approached, and I pressed myself against the ground. I took a breath and pulled out my phone and called my husband. After a bit of delicate chatter, I told him about Michael, about Sophia, about these thoughts in my head, how I wanted to believe he and I were deserving of something beautiful, how we both needed the chance to find someone who could activate us like this.

He didn't answer at first. We sat in silence, together and apart, he in Seattle, me in Utah, eight hundred miles away but slammed back together by this phone call—invisible wires crammed between the earth and my cheekbone. I could hear him breathing in my ear, and I was just breathing back because I didn't know what else to say. I grasped my shirt over my stomach, tried to clutch my body tighter, tried not to let him hear the ache behind my ribs because if he heard the ache, he may not say the thing he needed to say, and I was waiting for him to say it because I knew it now and I needed him to know too. So I waited. I waited and I waited and I listened to him breathe, listened to him live, listened to our wires snapping, a kind of understanding, both of us so sick and tired of explaining this attempt at replicating a marriage that appeared to be anything more than a mirror of gross expectations—where he didn't touch me for a year so I fucked my coworker—and now I was just lying there in the grass fucking breathing and breathing and breathing and his voice was trembling from all those miles away, finally agreeing that it had to be over. It had to be over. And while this didn't make it any easier, I could finally let the stale air blow out from my body so I could tell him that I was sorry.

He hung up. And I remained. And the golden hour passed above me, but the grass was still prickling into my neck. The phone separated the world from my cheek. The waning sunlight slipped against my skin. The sky cracked open with all the galaxies and stars and lights burning millions of light years away. And I closed my eyes because it hurt to see, hurt to think, hurt to know how easy it could be to wink out of existence like this. I lay in the grass, pressing myself against the ground, waiting for the rain to wash my burning cells clean, for grass to blanket my eyes, for the marrow weight of my body to become just a little easier to bear. I could feel it coming. I could feel myself breathing. Wait, listen: can you hear it? I'm coming back to life.

NEW MAN EXCEEDS EXPECTATIONS

Watch closely:

It's nearing the end of August, just a week away from my twenty-eighth birthday. Two weeks after Michael's ghosting. A week since the divorce talk. A week since I determined a life lived fully alive was worth the possibility of ending up alone. I am sitting on my beat-up faux leather couch. My cat is asleep in my lap, five months old and snoring little snores. *Schitt's Creek* plays in the background while I sit swiping through boys on Tinder. At this point, I'm not really looking for anyone—hookup, friendship, relationship. It's just fun to see the possibilities.

This is when I see him, a beautiful boy smiling out from the screen. He looks strong and solid. Kind. Joyful. Brown-eyed and flirty. I swipe through his photos and read his bio. He's a fashion and tech designer. He loves cosplay and video games. He's goofy and nerdy. My heart beats a little faster. His name is Terrence, and he's about eighty miles away, which means he's probably in Salt Lake City where the nearest gay bar is located, an hour-and-a-half drive away. I use my single "Super Like" for the week on him, hoping he'll take notice.

You know where this is going. He messages me back. We talk. I ask if I can call him at some point, and when I do, I find myself telling him everything: I'm in the middle of a divorce; I'm also just getting over the ghosting of another boy; I'm a grad student and in therapy and just trying to do my best. He repays me with a similar truth: he lives across the country in Pennsylvania; he's in Utah to see another boy who has turned out to be awful and manipulative and cruel; he will be breaking things off with that boy; he's leaving Utah on Monday. And I'm infatuated with him, and we make plans to meet on Sunday before he leaves.

But we didn't meet then. On Saturday, I got sick. Some flu-like illness: a fever of 104.6, searing muscle aches across my body, a throbbing headache, exhaustion heavy enough to make a trip to the bathroom dizzying. So, Terrence flew back to Pennsylvania, and I stayed at home, quarantined because it was the summer of 2020 and I figured the sickness had to be COVID-19. Possibly the flu. I tested for both, just to be sure. And when both tests came back negative, I tested for COVID again. And when that test came back negative, I accepted I would likely never know what caused it. My birthday passed and Terrence was gone and I was stuck at home alone for the next week before I started to feel better.

Here's the interesting part: I didn't expect Terrence to want to keep in contact. It's pretty customary that after bailing on a meeting, most boys will disappear. But Terrence and I kept talking—on the phone, for hours at a time, talked and learned and questioned. We spoke of our histories, our likes and dislikes, our fears and dreams and those shadow lives we didn't live. I felt myself falling in love with him. Rapidly. Terrifyingly. I wanted to believe there was something brilliant out there for me, a person better than Michael, than my ex-husband, than the history of men flowing in and out of my life since I was nineteen. I wanted to believe it could be him.

So, we made a plan for him to come visit, and I made sure to prepare. Though I hadn't tested for STIs in six years, I knew if I really wanted this, if I really wanted him, I had to make sure we were safe.

If you think you know where this is going, I think I did too—like I knew something in my body had changed, that something inside me had turned dangerous. I couldn't know, of course. There was simply a lingering, a haunting, this phantom feeling inside me. Undefinable. Intangible. Acutely real.

Doc and I Do the Math

In a clean and sterile hospital room, my doctor had me make a list of men. After discussing the treatment process for my HIV diagnosis, we tried to trace the virus back to its source. *It's how we stop HIV from progressing,* she told me. *Just in case he doesn't know. If we can't cure it, we have to do everything we can to stop it from spreading.* It made sense, so I tracked the time with her, made a map: of my viral load, my CD4 cell count, the strange flu-like sickness I had, the boys I had sex with in the weeks beforehand. Like true crime podcasters, we gathered the names, the places, the clues; we pieced them together; we tried to make sense of them. We found a name: Michael. He was the only one who matched the profile.

When I told my doctor about him, she asked me if I'd feel comfortable reaching out to him, and I said I would try. And though he'd blocked my phone number and my profile on Tinder, I was able to find his Facebook page. I messaged him there. I told him about my diagnosis. I asked if he'd been tested recently. He messaged back to say he had. Last September. He said I was the first person he'd slept with since the pandemic started, but he said he'd test again. Just to be sure.

A few weeks later, he messaged again: *Negative,* he said with a smiling emoji. *Hope that helps you narrow down who it may be.*

It was the last thing he said to me. His answer was an answer that didn't make sense to me. It doesn't make sense to me. But I told him I was glad he was okay, and we never talked again.

So here we are at the gap—where I've mapped it out more times than I can count, where I've played out the scenarios, like some word problem I'm desperate to understand. I just want an answer because I don't know who it could have been if it wasn't him. If it wasn't him, it could have been anyone. John or Alex or Rob or Connor or any of the guys who never told me their names. I don't think I'll ever know.

So can you see the cavity in my story? There's this checkbox answer that remains empty. And while I tell myself it doesn't matter, I know that it does. I'm standing on the edge of something I'll never be able to scale.

These Needles Can Teach Me Something about Love

On the evening of the day I was diagnosed with HIV, I sat on the steps of my home, phone in my shaking hand, my thumb hovering over his name. *Terrence.* I had told him I would call, but then it was hours after my diagnosis, and I still hadn't found a way to do so. I kept thinking of the messages and bios I used to see on Grindr. On Scruff. On Tinder and Jack'd and all the other dating apps I ever used.

Be clean.

Be clean.

Be clean.

Be clean.

I wasn't. Not anymore. Some kind of mud in my bloodstream. Impurity. I knew the stories. I'd heard them all too often. Those *dirty* guys with HIV who were stigmatized and abandoned by the gay community because the gay community as a whole was far from pure-hearted. Racism. Sexism. Transphobia. Fatphobia. Homophobia. [Insert various judgments here]. I've seen them all. I've been struck by a few myself—too fat, too fem, not a big enough ass, too big of an ass—so here's another to add to the list of reasons men might disappear. Because when it comes to these days, I don't hear non-queer communities stigmatizing HIV. It comes from within.

But Terrence had been kind and wonderful and had spent money on a plane ticket to come visit the next week. I wanted to believe he was different, but how could I know what he'd say? After all, we had yet to meet in person. It would be so easy for him to disconnect, so easy to do what so many had before, what I had done to others before. He could become a ghost, some guy I remembered forever, someone I'd never hear from again.

Eventually, I tapped his name. I lifted the phone to my ear. It rang once before he answered, and I told him about my diagnosis. He was silent for a moment, and when he spoke, his deep voice was steady. *Would you like me to tell you my thoughts? Or would you rather me just be here with you?*

I felt rattled by the question. I told him I'd love to hear his thoughts.

Well, the first thing I want to say is that this doesn't change anything for me. You're just as attractive and beautiful as you've ever been. And I'm still coming to Utah—if you'll have me.

And if I'm honest, I don't know what came after this. I don't know what I said or what he said or whether I cried again. I figure I probably did. I just know that he was in Utah a week later, all brilliant and bold and beautiful. I know when I picked him up at the airport, he ran to me. He hugged me. He held my hand as we walked to my car. And later, as we stood in my living room feeling gushy and staring into each other's eyes, he kissed me. He wrapped his arms around me. He held me tight. I felt his heart beating beneath his skin, his warmth mixing with my own, his body moving with mine. And when our lips parted, we both let out a light breath, we both smiled, both laughed. We hugged again. We kissed again. We moved to the bed and I felt myself melt against him.

Here is the lesson. I'm begging you to understand. This is what it feels like to wake up. In his arms, I felt big and grand and light. Tangled up in his body, knowing I was alive in my own, I was ready to overflow.

The Fool Has Something to Say

I used to spend hours every day swiping on Tinder, scrolling through naked, headless chests on Grindr, replying to the *What's up* messages on Scruff. I once believed this to be the way of dating—to fuck enough men that I'd eventually find the one I was meant to be with. But this has turned cyclical, and I'm tired of going in circles. What remains is a ghost, some spirit remnant clinging to my body, my memory, my blood. I don't think there's an exorcism for this.

Here's the thing: I once tried to make a list of all the boys I've had sex with, as if I could bleed them from my body if I could place their names on paper. And now, as I read through it again, I can't remember most of their faces. I can't hear their voices. What sticks with me is random and fragmented. A stretch of dark hair. The sound of *Gilmore Girls* in the background. A tongue against the crevices of my skin. His shower beating down on my back. The mountain smell of his deodorant. The tungsten ring I once bought him. The cold edges of a bed. The lock that clicked as I sent him on his way.

These things don't leave me. I don't need them to. I am sitting here on this couch, in this room, in this home I have made my own. My cat purrs beside me. Terrence traces the length of my fingers with his. He places his arm around my shoulders. I snuggle in a little closer. He kisses me on my cheek.

Here: ask me what it feels like to come alive; my body is telling the story. Shh, shh—come here and listen—this is more than I could have imagined.

END ACT III

WOLF BOY CODA

Of course I wanted to see the world, to experience its fullness. I wanted to be a real part of it, rather than the passing shadow I so often felt like. I wanted to devour the world.

—Saeed Jones, *How We Fight for Our Lives*

I once heard falling in love is supposed to feel like falling out of our own life and into someone else's, and after Jed and I signed our divorce papers on the hood of his Malibu outside a January-frozen Starbucks, I realized the reason our relationship fell apart was because I had done exactly that. After signing, when he drove out of the mud-and-snow-crusted parking lot, I remained, shivering against the door of my crimson SUV.

I had thought the moment would feel deeper, more painful, more unreal. But we'd separated nearly two years before, and I had checked out long ago. What I understood then as I stood outside the Starbucks, feeling the cold creep up the crisp sleeves of my coat, was that I didn't know myself anymore. I'd spent six years fitting myself into his life, but that wasn't his fault; I'd never learned how I fit into my own.

A week after my thirty-first birthday, I sat on a park bench with Terrence in a small town in Ohio. I felt jittery, tapping my heel against the ground in time with my rapid heartbeat. I was surprised to find myself so anxious; I was there to live out a dream—finally, after all the years of being told I couldn't, I was going to meet a wolf. An actual wolf. I was going to be able to pet its fur, feel its warmth, look into its eyes. It was a part of an ambassador program from the Ohio Canid Center—an organization dedicated to educating people on conservation efforts and a better understanding of wildlife. These ambassador wolves are representatives of their wild counterparts, specifically trained and socialized to be able to interact with the public.

They weren't fully wild. Not entirely tame. Just somewhere perfectly in between.

My stomach bubbled in uncertainty, and my foot tapped ever faster. I'd spent so many years craving this exact moment, but I had never stopped to think about what I actually wanted out of it; I'd run out of time to figure it out. Rachel, creator of the program, would be arriving with the wolf any minute.

Terrence and I stood to cross the park. We were to meet Rachel at the opposite edge, near the parking lot. We made our way there. Followed the path. Rounded a corner. Down a small hill. Around a slight curve. And there Rachel was, at a picnic table—and waiting beside her, regal and mythical and grand, was Eowyn—a wolf—a real and actual wolf.

I made an audible gasp. Moved my hand to my mouth. Tried to quiet my trembling fingers. Terrence smiled. He took my hand. We moved forward.

On the day I turned twenty-five, years before my divorce, I journeyed across the Idaho border with my dad and Marcus in order to view a solar eclipse in its totality. Deep within the great Idaho desert, we leaned against the burning hood of our car, slipping eclipse glasses over our eyes. To stare into a sun, even a sun 99 percent blocked out by the moon, can burn the retina, cause irreversible damage. Still, it upset me to think that such an astronomical beauty must be dimmed.

The sun hid behind the moon, became nothing more than a crescent of light, and the world turned over. It dimmed. Darkened: the mountains that surrounded us, the flat stretch of land between, the sky. As we reached totality, we found something like golden hour come early, a red glow of sunset, and we could remove the protective lenses.

The crescent light disappeared. The moon eclipsed the sun. We removed our glasses and found bands of waving light seeping around the dark moon like mist—the sun's corona, the outer layer of our star, nearly always hidden by the glaring blaze of its center. But on a day like that, we could see it. I could bask in its glimmer—a beauty so exquisite I shivered in awe. I could have screamed in joy and reverence and exaltation. I could have howled. Instead, I just watched.

I know of a wolf who is destined to devour the sun.

And just know, if I knew how to end this story, I would have already done so.

Once, when I was ten, I was too sick to attend a sleepover I'd been looking forward to all week. All my friends were there, but my parents said
I couldn't go—I might make everyone else sick too. I screamed at them
and screamed at them and found myself bent over a toilet, vomiting—
just another time I felt my body betraying me.

And I was so upset, so sad, my dad bought the new Disney movie
Atlantis: The Last Empire. I watched it in my parents' bed. My dad made
soup and cheese sandwiches and I studied my mom's fingers as she
cross-stitched a wondrous pattern of Noah's Ark. I watched her lace the
thread up and down, up and down, crafting each pair of animals. I
leaned on her warm shoulder; she raised a hand to my cheek and pulled
me closer.

The summer before Terrence and I moved to Ohio, my siblings and I
all came together to celebrate my mom's sixtieth birthday. With Melissa
and Steve in Indiana, Matthew in Illinois, and me being a little all over
the place, it wasn't always easy for us all to get together—but it was a
landmark birthday for her, and being together was all she wanted.

One night, the siblings all gathered at Christopher and Jenn's house
for a pizza and game night. We played our favorite tabletop strategy
games: *Shadow Hunters,* where humans, shadow creatures, and neutral
beings struggle to survive each other; and *Werewolf,* where someone is
a werewolf who comes at night to kill off the other players, and in the
day, you gather together and debate about who you think is the wolf. I
think we liked these games because they gave us an opportunity to talk
and argue and laugh with each other.

And while this wasn't the first game night we'd ever had with each
other, it was the first one when we'd ever shared drinks with each other,
by which I mean, alcoholic ones. One of the Great and Terrible Taboos.
And it felt so strange, sitting there with them, chatting and laughing,
bringing a glass of wine to my lips. Vulnerably. Proudly. Almost as if it
could be normal to do so.

I think someday it could be.

So, there's a contradiction here: it lives inside me—a knowledge that
Mormonism, for all the pain and anger it's caused, also caused this, our
family being so close. The five of us. Our partners. Our parents. We love
each other, but there's more too—some indefinable something. They're

the family I have. They're also the family I choose. And they've chosen me. And I know this closeness exists in part because of our upbringing in the religion, though whether that closeness comes because the church taught us that family was the most important thing or because we came together in leaving it behind—the result is the same. We were there—Marcus, Matthew, Melissa and Steve, Christopher and Jenn, Terrence and me—at that table, in that room, together because of what we'd gone through.

And how could I ever regret that?

There's a story, one of Cheyenne the Healing Wolf who lived at a sanctuary in the Rocky Mountains—the same mountains which surrounded my childhood home—and it is said that Cheyenne could sense wounds, both physical and emotional. If physical, she would lick and nibble and bite at the damage, and it would finally begin to heal—the catalyst to jumpstart change. It is said she even detected cancer in twenty-five people over the length of her life.

The movements she made to heal the mind and soul were more subtle, like she could sense pain within. She would walk to a person, lay her head in their lap, and breathe. As she nuzzled and pressed herself against a person's body, the person would relax. Their faces would collapse in relief. They'd find a way to start healing.

Maybe all I've ever wanted is to find healing.

When I was young, my family would visit the Utah Hogle Zoo in Salt Lake City. I would seek out the wolves on every trip, sprint up the hill to their enclosure. There were only two: one silver and tan, one pure white. I felt connected to them somehow, like they could understand what it meant to be me: in a cage, others watching, never seeing. I would stay with them for as long as I could, just hoping they'd meet my eyes.

In 2021, just a few months before I moved to Ohio, I brought Terrence to this same zoo. It was my first time going in nearly three years and, of course, I wanted to show him the wolves, but when we arrived, the wolves were gone. A red fox enclosure had taken their place. When I asked a worker where the wolves had gone, she told me that one of them had died.

Terrence reached over and wrapped his arm around my shoulders, holding me close.

When did that happen? I asked.

Just last year, the worker said sadly. *When she died, our other wolf needed a new pack, so now he's at a reserve. We hope he's happy.*

Tears burned in my eyes.

I hope he's happy too.

A few weeks later, Terrence and I attended a drag show. As it started, I pulled folded dollar bills from my pocket. On the stage, there was a man costumed in drag, Gia Bianca Stevens, more beautiful than any person I'd ever seen. She moved from the stage into the crowd, dancing to a song I didn't recognize. She pulled green from the fingers of adoring fans as she moved, and when she neared me, I reached out my fist with two folded bills. Her hand touched mine, she grasped my offer, and I met her eyes—shrouded in long lashes and dark red eyeshadow, intricate and balanced. She had rosy cheeks, blushed out simply. Each line was perfect, each contour meticulously implemented. Her lips, painted in deep red, curved up. She met my eyes, gave me a wink, and grasped my hands tight in hers, money nearly dropping from our fingertips. I feared she would pull me up to the floor, but she didn't. She simply held me, my hands cupped in hers. I could see her mouth moving to the lyrics, but I couldn't hear the words. I just saw her. I like to believe she could see me too.

Halfway through the following September, in the dying heat of summer, Terrence and I attended the wedding of his closest friend and cousin. Outside a richly dressed barn in middle-of-nowhere North Carolina, Miesa and Katie promised to love each other for as long as they could. Beneath a pink and scarlet silk-lined archway, they poured different colored sands into a box, a metaphor for how they would join their two lives. As they did so, my eyes lingered on Terrence up on the platform beside Miesa. Dressed in a bright scarlet suit and clean white Converse, he stood poised, hands crossed over one another. When Miesa and Katie jumped the broom as an homage to Miesa's African heritage, Terrence smiled, and my eyes crackled. It felt like such a cliché: to become so wistful at a wedding.

As Miesa and Katie started back down the aisle, moving between log benches and toward the decorated barn in which we'd have our dinner, they broke out in dance. Music boomed from the speakers as they twirled around each other, smiling and kissing and tripping over each other's untied white Converse laces. Katie's flowing white, brilliantly beaded dress brushed like waves against Miesa's white tuxedo, matching raindrop-shaped diamonds trickling through each bride's hair. I laughed and clapped with the crowd as each member of the wedding party danced their own way down the aisle after the newlyweds. It was different from the self-composed and reserved exit march of the Mormon weddings I was used to, and I happily joined in on the raucous hollering and applause of the crowd around me.

When Terrence strutted down the aisle, snapping his arms and legs to the beat of the music in all the ways he'd learned during his days of every-weekend clubbing, the cheers of those around me grew louder. Dirt from the pathway lifted from the ground and caked onto his white shoes, but he didn't seem to care. Didn't seem to even notice. His unbuttoned jacket and vest slapped his hips, and he bent over, twerking down the aisle. And as I watched him move his body so effortlessly, so freely, so vibrantly, a flutter ran beneath my skin. My own muscles tensed, my stomach rapidly expanding and contracting, something in me yearning to break free.

When Terrence passed from view, I dropped my gaze to the ground, to my own white shoes, pristine and clean. I twisted my foot into the dirt, tapped my heel, tried to match the beat of the song. It only took a few seconds for me to miss a step. I glanced around in fear that someone had seen. But no one watched me. All eyes were attached to the wedding party still dancing down the aisle. Feeling foolish, I flushed and shook my head. I returned to clapping with everyone else while, ever so slowly, my heel began to bounce.

Look: I just want to be alive, for that to be enough to satisfy a reason to exist. And still, as I place myself beside my story, the one with memories like boxes unpacked from a closet of my history, I can see it—the reason why: why my life began with a whimper, why Little Red left the path, why Aesop's wolf refused to come back down the hill. I think I understand why I nibble at these crossroads, why I lick and bite at these wounds I've crafted.

I understand now why wolves might seek to devour stars.

Maybe it's the end I've been searching for.

I stood at the entrance of a Sephora just days after the drag show and watched my friend Sophia march into aisles of makeup. Into rows upon rows of colors and shines and mattes and lashes. From within them, she held up a tube of something I didn't recognize, yelling that she thought the liner would look great on me. A blush rose in my cheeks. At first, I thought it was embarrassment. As I reached her, I realized it was excitement, a wave of renewed bravery, a crashing sense of place.

When the girl at the checkout counter—the one with the effortlessly sculpted mascara and flawless foundation—asked me if that would be everything, I looked into her startlingly green eyes and responded that I had no idea.

As we left the store, Sophia held my hand and said, *This is only the beginning.*

And on the night of Miesa and Katie's wedding, the dance floor thudded with beats of the music. Standing in a tight circle, I watched as their family and friends jumped into the center and danced their own dances. The crowd cheered and hollered and screamed their excitement. Their approval. Joy in seeing each other let loose.

And when Terrence jumped in, he held out a hand to me. Asking me to join him. To join in.

And I did.

And on New Year's Eve, when Terrence and I raised glasses of champagne, we toasted a year we hoped would be better than the last. We wrote down words to symbolize what the last had meant to us—beyond just good or bad. He wrote BREAK; I wrote OPEN. We both just meant that we had learned to be free.

In the end, we were weaving similar tales. Maybe good or bad, better or worse—they're just excuses. Maybe all I want is to continue. And if I can believe the last minute of a year is the same as a life beginning, I might wonder if my end appeared the moment I knew I was a wolf. But maybe the metaphors here are clichés, just a narrative that has already been lived. I know the tension isn't new. Someone has already lived through this climax, and perhaps my craving isn't any different from anyone else's.

These are just the things I think of when I attempt to claim my story, when I attempt to place ink on paper and form words that might explain to you how it felt to be a little boy eating sugar in secret when he should have been eating Cheerios. When I try to claim that transformation starts in this kind of rebellion—affairs and divorces, religious exodus and the longing for something sweeter than what you've been told is right, what's been expected. Even if it was unhealthy, and I knew it was unhealthy. But still, I ate it—perhaps—for a mere moment of joy.

Can you blame me?

And if I refuse to end the story, will you still listen? I have told you tales of which I am a part, stories that talk of change and alteration and hiding and transcendence. If I were a fairytale, I could tell you why it matters, what lesson you could take with you. But I'm not. And I don't have those answers. Only stories: Little Red, her grandmother, hunter, shepherd, sun, moon, lion, wolf, wolf, wolf, wolf, me. There's a metaphor here. Would you tell me which part I fit? I still have something at stake in the story: something to give, something to take. I'm done waiting.

And when a super blood moon rose over the winter sky to begin the year I would cleave myself from my marriage, the year I would contract HIV, the year I would find myself writing OPEN on a little blue sticky note, counting down the moments to the next one, I found myself standing beneath it, bathing in red light pulsing like a heartbeat against my skin. I raised my body and let my blood reach toward that bright sky like crashing waves.

And on the edge of a mountain, in a forest, under a speckled sky of stars and nebulas and galaxies, a wolf ran to the pace of his shadow in search of danger. But this time, I want to tell the story differently. I want to say he was right to feel that big and great and powerful. That he can survive the lion's maw.

So when I'm standing at the edge of a park with Terrence's hand in mine and I'm walking toward a wolf that I'll finally get to meet, I can take a breath. In and out. In and out. My heart can slow just a little, and I can take in the moment for what it is—for whatever it is. And we go sit in the grass, under the shade of a giant tree, because openness and space is what Eowyn the Wolf appreciates most.

I sit, and she circles. Wary. Attentive. Protective. She walks to me. She pauses. She stops. She looks at me, and in her eyes, I can see something majestic, some ancient kind of knowing. There's something mystical in her presence—as if she knows this is only a moment in passing—as if she knows what it means to me. And I reach out, brushing my fingers into her silver fur, a warmth that is immediate, her heartbeat strong, reverberating a rhythm against my skin, into my blood and body and bones.

She blinks.

I breathe out.

A car horn sounds in the distance, and her ears perk up. She moves away, circling. Curious maybe—or protective. She walks around us several times before coming back to me. She stops. Allows me to brush her fur again. She sees me, and I can see her now—a wolf who's just a wolf. An ambassador, yes, but she doesn't have to be anything else. For a moment, just a moment, she is there with me. And I am there with her. Meeting. Existing. Listening. Breathing. In and out. In and out. In and out.

Here: ask me again—what it feels like to be alive. The lesson beats beneath my skin. Come here and listen. A change is coming, or maybe something like healing, a reverberation in my body, in the air, like shadow bands shimmering beneath an eclipse—undefinable and real—where I'll reach out and grasp the heavens, rip open the sky, shatter the space between us because I refuse to believe we were meant to travel this ruthless world alone.

The finale comes. And it passes. Another year closes. The moon passes across the sun—perhaps a reset, or maybe I've discovered a way to keep going. If I found my mouth here, a howl like the music on this stage, I think this may be the key—my path out of the story. Stop. Listen. I'm here on the stage. I've found my way through. I'm ready to lean in close to the heart of the world and speak.

Acknowledgments

I was once taught that writing is a contradictory process, that the act of writing itself is a singular one, done alone. I've also learned that it is impossible to do alone. It has been a long, joyous, painful road to get here, and there have been people at every turn who have kept me going. My gratitude extends far beyond this short list.

First, a huge thank you to the Greater Columbus Arts Council and The Ohio State University, for giving me financial support through such generous grants and fellowships during the writing of this book.

To the magazines and journals that published earlier versions of these essays: *Black Warrior Review*, "Ghost Boys: A Bricolage"; *Great River Review*, "Piercing: A Schematic"; *South 85 Literary Journal*, "Gracious Ruin"; and *Sink Hollow Creative Writing Contest*, "The Becoming" and "A Re-established Poetic Dictionary of the Voiceless." Additionally, a big thank you to Nicole Walker for selecting an earlier version of this manuscript as the winner of the Utah Original Writing Competition, starting me on the path toward its publication.

To the faculty and staff at both Utah State University and The Ohio State University, for supporting and guiding me through the grand expanse of writing, academia, and literature. I am especially grateful to Jennifer Sinor, my first writing mentor, who showed me the power of the essay and taught me to be brave; to Lee Martin, who's confidence and quiet voice kept me going when I thought of quitting; and to Elissa Washuta—confidant, mentor, and fellow gamer—thank you for your open door, for teaching me so much about myself, for showing me that writing about joy is just as important as writing about pain.

To all those at the University of Wisconsin Press, for bringing this book to the world with such incredible care: Dennis Lloyd, Lisa Learish, Pahnia Lee, Anne McKenna, Tristian Lee, Casey LaVela, Julia Knecht, Adam Mehring, Jennifer Conn, Sheila McMahon, and Jessica Smith; to Alison Shay, for guiding me through so many parts of this process; to Jeremy Parker, for creating such a striking, enchanting cover; and to Nathan MacBrien, for believing in this book even before I did.

To Sophia Thimmes, for your gracious magic, adventurous spirit, thoughtful insights, and all our hikes; Shaun Anderson and Joshua Hortin, for opening your home when I needed one; Kylie Smith, for your steady heart, your unending support, and for holding my hand on the day of my diagnosis—I cannot thank you enough; and Megan Jones, who read and reread this manuscript in its various stages. Thank you for all the writing sessions, long walks, thoughtful insights, and generous friendship.

To my fellow writers who workshopped essays within this book: Alyssa Alexander, Brittney Allen, Nikki Barnhart, Cameron Gorman, Dani Green, Sophia Huneycutt, Tyler Hurst, Mia Jones, Macy Keith, Julie Kim, Arah Ko, Lizzie Lawson, Heather McCabe, Gabriella Navas, Danielle Ola, Claudia Owusu, Jay Paine, Kelsie Peterson, Macey Phillips, Kate Pyontek, Sam Risak, Anne Schill, Camille Sleight, Mark Smeltzer, Nellie Smith, Hannah Smith, Elle Smith, Amber Taylor, and Clancy Tripp. Thank you for telling me what I needed to hear.

To Christine Cooper-Rompato, for your guidance, wisdom, and unwavering kindness.

To Sara Boghosian and Meghan Kunz, for teaching me how to save myself.

To Rachel Robertson and the Ohio Canid Center, for making a lifelong wish come true.

To Helicon West of Cache Valley, for giving me the space to speak.

To USGA and all those I met in my time there—Bridey, Adam, Nathan, Sabina, JD, Robert, Samy, and so many others. You taught me to be proud.

To all my Walt Disney World and Universal Studios Orlando coworkers and friends, for helping me live out my fairy-tale dreams.

To my Logan community, for welcoming me back with open hearts; and to those in Columbus, for greeting me with the same.

To the army of friends and family who have carried me. Thank you for all your support, time, texts, letters, phone calls, friendship, and advice over the years.

To everyone whose lives are in these pages.

To my siblings, Marcus, Melissa and Steve, Christopher and Jenn, and Matthew, for your unwavering love, for cheering me on, for all the movie nights, game nights, and book discussions, for always making me laugh, for being my best friends, especially in the times when I felt I had none.

To my parents, my first fans and guiding stars, for never letting me believe I would be anything other than exceptional, for championing my every step, and for giving me everything you had to help me get to where I am today. Thank you for believing in this crazy dream. Thank you for everything.

Finally, to Terrence, my partner, my creative co-conspirator, my singing bard, my greatest love story. If I could choose, I'd go through it all again. It led me to you, and this is a pretty wonderful place to be.

LIVING OUT

Gay and Lesbian Autobiographies

DAVID BERGMAN, JOAN LARKIN, and RAPHAEL KADUSHIN,
Founding Editors

Midlife Queer: Autobiography of a Decade, 1971–1981
MARTIN DUBERMAN

Self-Made Woman: A Memoir
DENISE CHANTERELLE DUBOIS

The Black Penguin
ANDREW EVANS

*The Man Who Would Marry Susan Sontag: And Other Intimate
Literary Portraits of the Bohemian Era*
EDWARD FIELD

Body, Remember: A Memoir
KENNY FRIES

In the Province of the Gods
KENNY FRIES

Travels in a Gay Nation: Portraits of LGBTQ Americans
PHILIP GAMBONE

Abuela in Shadow, Abuela in Light
RIGOBERTO GONZÁLEZ

Autobiography of My Hungers
RIGOBERTO GONZÁLEZ

What Drowns the Flowers in Your Mouth: A Memoir of Brotherhood
RIGOBERTO GONZÁLEZ

Widescreen Dreams: Growing Up Gay at the Movies
PATRICK E. HORRIGAN

Plain: A Memoir of Mennonite Girlhood
MARY ALICE HOSTETTER

The End of Being Known: A Memoir
MICHAEL KLEIN

Through the Door of Life: A Jewish Journey between Genders
JOY LADIN